Public
and
Private
Lives
of
Psychotherapists

William E. Henry

John H. Sims

S. Lee Spray

Public
and
Private
Lives
of
Psychotherapists

 Jossey-Bass Publishers
San Francisco • Washington • London • 1973

PUBLIC AND PRIVATE LIVES OF PSYCHOTHERAPISTS
by William E. Henry, John H. Sims, and S. Lee Spray

Copyright © 1973 by: Jossey-Bass, Inc., Publishers
615 Montgomery Street
San Francisco, California 94111

and

Jossey-Bass Limited
3 Henrietta Street
London WC2E 8LU

Library of Congress Catalogue Card Number LC 73-49

International Standard Book Number ISBN 0-87589-168-3

Manufactured in the United States of America

JACKET DESIGN BY WILLI BAUM

FIRST EDITION

Code 7311

The Jossey-Bass
Behavioral Science Series

General Editors

WILLIAM E. HENRY, *University of Chicago*

NEVITT SANFORD, *Wright Institute, Berkeley*

Preface

Public and Private Lives of Psychotherapists is a continuation of the examination of the lives of psychotherapists that we began in *The Fifth Profession: Becoming a Psychotherapist* (Henry, Sims, and Spray, 1971). In that volume we presented an account of the ways in which some men and women become psychotherapists. They start in three broad training systems, those of medicine, psychology, and social work, and subsequently move selectively into the specialities of psychiatry, psychoanalysis, clinical psychology, and psychiatric social work. Some from each of these routes, the subjects of our study, later emerge as psychotherapists.

In studying these psychotherapists, we were impressed with two factors that are not at all apparent from the presence of these separate training systems—factors, indeed, that tend specifically to be denied by these training systems. The first is that those who in their varying ways go through these quite different systems and emerge as psychotherapists turn out to have come from highly similar cultural and social backgrounds. They come, in effect, from a narrowly circumscribed sector of the social world, representing a special combination of social marginality in ethnic, religious, and political terms. The second factor is that, during their progress through their separate training routes, they have in fact made individual choices of learning experiences that appear to parallel the choices made by their colleagues in the other systems. Members of any one

ix

training route do in effect select from that route experiences that serve in time to make them more and more like their colleague psychotherapists in other programs.

In *Public and Private Lives of Psychotherapists,* we continue the study of this group of psychotherapists but ask questions related to the ways in which they conduct their current professional practice—their public lives—and questions related to their early development and family experiences—their private lives. In the early chapters, we attempt to show how the personal and social characteristics of these therapists interact in their therapeutic practice and in their professional life. In the later chapters, on private lives, we attempt to show how the growth and development of therapists appear to parallel the typical experiences of most educated persons. In examining their early social, sexual, and intellectual development and in inquiring about their relations and emotional experiences with their early families, we found no factors that appear to distinguish therapists from persons in other professional groups.

Combining our findings from the two volumes, we find increasingly that the life ways of psychotherapists constitute a homogeneous and integrated system of belief and behavior that most often begins in family-situated early religiocultural experiences and that progresses selectively toward a common concept of a psychodynamic paradigm for the explanation of all behaviors—a paradigm that guides their choices and behaviors as they emerge from the training years into the practice of psychotherapy. The final chapter examines the implications of this homegeneity for adaptation to new roles in community mental health.

Again in this volume, we express our indebtedness to the many persons who contributed their time and talent to our study: to the National Institute of Mental Health, United States Public Health Service, which, through Grant MH-09192, provided financial support; to the experienced professionals who served as initial informants, as distinct from subjects, about persons and processes in the mental health areas from which we gathered our main data: Theodora Abel, Francesca Alexander, Jules Barron, Virginia Bellsmith, Hedda Bolgar, Arthur Carr, Catherine Cullinan, Mary Dunkel, David Fanshel, Hyman Forstenzer, Eugene Gendlin, Ernest Greenwood, Robert Holt, Oliver J. B. Kerner, Henry Maas, Robert McFarland, Mortimer Meyer, Helen Perlman, Nathaniel Raskin, Melvin Sabshin, Harold Sampson, Jackson Smith, Fred Spaner, Anselm Strauss, William Thetford, Harold Visotsky, Ruth Weichelbaum, Joseph Wepman; to the colleagues and students who assisted in the collection and analysis of data: Robert Beck, Bernice Bild, Byron Boyd, Richard Ford, Richard Gilman, Harold Kooden, Marylou Lionells, Marc Lubin, John Marx, Harvey Molotch, Joan Neff, Jean Prebis, Elliot Simon,

Josh Yeidel; to Estelle Buccino, Alice Chandler, and Hildegarde Sletteland for their splendid administrative support; and, most importantly, to the more than 4000 mental health professionals who contributed mightily of their time and understanding to help us to understand some portion of the origins and lives of those who devote themselves to the problems of others.

Chicago   WILLIAM E. HENRY
January 1973   JOHN H. SIMS
                                                      S. LEE SPRAY

Contents

Public
and
Private
Lives
of
Psychotherapists

1

Careers in Psychotherapy

The mental health field is a specific case of a general group of professions that has recently undergone rapid increase in both size and social significance. As such, it shares many characteristics with other professional fields, such as adult education and social welfare. In each of these fields, there has been a proliferation of practitioners from diverse professional specialities claiming a right to perform core functions. There has been a rise in new ideologies, which frequently become the basis of competing factions, and there have been innovations in the settings in which these professions are practiced. Although these changes have been under way in the mental health field for some time, there have been few corresponding changes in the models used to study the impact of these trends on professional career structures. In particular, progress in increasing our understanding of psychotherapists has been handicapped by the lack of a general framework that delineates the relevant factors implicated in career development and that, at the same time, provides a context for interpreting the wealth of evidence that has been accumulated on professional choice. In the main, this limitation does not stem from the quantity or quality of research done on the mental health professions, but rather from the scope of such research. Indeed, there have been a number of excellent studies of various facets of the mental health professions, including, for example, research on psychiatric institutions, therapeutic ideologies, and professional socialization. In terms of focus, however, there has been a heavy emphasis on vocational choice and on the social psychological dynamics of professional practice. But the full potential of these studies cannot be realized until we have a deeper understanding of the whole life of the professional and the ways in which his personal and public roles are related.

The ability to assess accurately the impact of various changes occurring in the mental health field, such as those associated with the advent of community mental health programs, is directly dependent upon the availability of baseline data against which these innovations can be compared. Our objective here is to contribute to the development of a more balanced view of professional careers in the mental health field by identifying some of the important social dimensions of career lines, by indicating some of the relationships among such dimensions, and by locating the individual mental health practitioner, as a professional and as a private person, within such a framework.

In an attempt to obtain data on both the professional and personal lines of therapists, we adopted the following strategies, reported in detail in the Appendix.

First, we included all four of the core professional groups—psychoanalysis, psychiatry, clinical psychology, and social work—that are now active in the mental health field. The assumption underlying this strategy was simply that career structures must be examined from a comparative perspective and that confining the focus to any one of these professions would have unduly restricted the scope and power of the study. This strategy was also based on the assumption that, in spite of the recent extensive and varied alterations in models of mental health care, these four professions still provide the most significant portion of treatment and serve as models for training in formal institutions. The individual professional associations that represent these several professions also serve as guides to the accreditation of professionals for practice and take over from training institutions significant aspects of the setting and maintenance of standards.

The second strategy we adopted was to use the metropolitan community as the sample unit. The metropolitan community was selected as the sample unit because it most closely approximates an autonomously functioning "service area" possessing the full range of personnel and facilities utilized in treating mental illness. The metropolitan community, therefore, provides a microscopic representation of the mental health field as a whole. This allows us to examine relations between, as well as within, the professions. To insure that the widest range of activities would be represented, the three largest metropolitan communities in the nation—New York City, Los Angeles, and Chicago—were selected for study. Finally, to guarantee comprehensive coverage, the total population of professionals working in the three metropolitan communities was surveyed.

As a third strategy for insuring that both structural and social psychological data would be produced by the investigation, we utilized two distinct, but related, methods of data collection. Specifically, in addition to surveying by mailed questionnaires the total universe of professionals in these cities, we selected a subsample of 100 in each of the three cities for intensive interviewing.

Finally, as a guide to data analysis, we adopted the following conceptual perspective. We assumed that career structures provide developmental continuity to professional behavior by organizing it into a professional career; that is, a general course of professional behavior over time that, within a given area of activity, has a discoverable continuity and direction and that, while itself changing, guides roles and orientations of persons in it.

This, then, was our approach to the study of professional careers. The findings that emerged from the study enabled us to examine in some detail various dimensions of professional careers, many aspects of which are reported in an earlier volume, *The Fifth Profession: Becoming a Psychotherapist* (Henry, Sims, and Spray, 1971).

Career Structure and Composition

As a first step in examining career structures in the mental health professions, we previously classified respondents according to their predominant professional activity and the setting of their professional practice at various points in time. Considerable stability was noted in career patterns with the majority of changes, in both functions and types of settings, occurring during the first five years of practice. Considerable homogeneity in social attributes is pronounced in those career patterns that have led ultimately to the private practice of psychotherapy. Careers terminating in the private practice of psychotherapy are populated, to a very great extent, by practitioners of highly similar cultural and social backgrounds. They come from a highly circumscribed sector of the social world, representing a special combination of social marginality in ethnic, religious, political, and social-class terms. There is variation in careers according to the emphasis placed upon administrative, therapeutic, or research and teaching roles. However, the greater the career involvement in psychotherapy—as opposed to these other roles—the more prominent are these social attributes of marginality. While this relationship holds for mental health professionals in general, interprofessional differences do exist with regard to vocational timing and social-class origins. Specifically, clinical psychologists and psychiatric social workers tend to have lower socioeconomic origins and to make their choice of a professional field later than either group of medical practitioners. Thus, social-class differences and differences in vocational timing create distinctions among careers that otherwise possess similar social profiles and long-term vocational commitments. Practitioners sharing these social characteristics constitute a substantial majority of the therapists in our three urban areas. Their division into separate professions seems more the result of events in the developmental history of the professions in question than of precareer disposition or the ultimate career commitments of individuals. Persons who select medicine as a career during their adolescence are able, when subsequent interest in psychotherapy is aroused, to become psychiatrists or psychoanalysts. Other individuals with similar social attributes and later interests who did not select medicine during adolescence pursue other routes to a career in psychotherapy. Thus, there are basic similarities in one important dimension of careers, that of recruitment, which professional distinctions have tended to mask. It may be that part of the professional divisiveness among psychotherapists is a historical accident, not produced by the content of the various disciplines, but by factors surrounding occupational choice.

Professional Socialization Systems

Like other professions, the socialization systems in the mental health professions have a dual focus. On the one hand, they are designed to produce graduates who have acquired technical expertise in a limited sphere of activity. On the other hand, they are designed to insure that the graduates develop the appropriate professional values, attitudes, and self-conceptions. While it is widely recognized that a diversity of factors contributes to the achievement of these desired outcomes, each profession attempts to organize its training program so that it incorporates the significant transformation experiences. Training systems thus contain within them an image of the fully formed professional and a model of the process of transformation required to realize that image. In the mental health professions, the professional image revolves around the specialized social interaction skills of the psychotherapist. The process of transformation consists of a series of developmental stages, with the early levels placing primary emphasis on intellectual preparation and the latter stages stressing practical experience.

Our findings concerning professional development in the four mental health professions clearly indicate, however, that the ways in which recruits become accredited professionals are only loosely organized by the formal training programs. Graduates of each of the professional training programs evaluated clinical experience as being much more important than course work. Since each of the professions has an elaborate structure of formal course work, the practitioners were, in effect, criticizing a large segment of the training system. In fact, the professionals who received the most exposure to formal course work, clinical psychologists, were the ones who were most critical of their training program. Similarly, in all professions the clinical work that was considered to be the most important in transforming recruits into professionals was that which occurred near the end of training and, consequently, was most "practical" in its content. While these clinical experiences were important sites for the acquisition of professional skills, they also contributed importantly to the development of professional values, attitudes, and self-images. Perhaps of equal importance in this regard was personal psychotherapy—an experience formally incorporated into the training program of but one of the four professions: psychoanalysis. In fact, although a majority of each professional group had undergone psychotherapy, the place of this experience in the various programs of professional preparation was so vague that many professionals considered its primary influence to be on their personal, rather than their professional, life. This is true in spite of the fact that it is, it seems, safe to assume that no mental health professional would deny that personal psychotherapy affects the way he relates to patients in a therapeutic relationship. In sum, the process of becoming a psychotherapist is loosely organized by the professional training programs in at least two respects. First, many of the experiences that are strongly emphasized in the formal training programs are seen to be of only minor importance by graduates of the systems. Second, at least one socialization experience considered to be highly important by a majority of the members of each group of professionals is not formally incorporated into the training programs of three of the four professions.

While there are important differences among the four mental health professions with regard to specific aspects of professional training, our general conclusions apply uniformly to all the professional groups. In part, this uniformity reflects the fact that the looseness in the training programs produces among practitioners important distinctions that do not flow along the lines of professional boundaries. Since the skill system revolves around competence in a particular kind of social interaction and since such socialization is, by necessity, highly personal, perhaps the sharpest distinction that emerges is one that revolves around the degree of commitment to the performance of psychotherapy. In only one profession, psychoanalysis, is psychotherapy uniformly accepted as the core act of the profession. In the other three professions, variation exists among the membership as to the importance of individual psychotherapy in the total constellation of professional functions. This has important consequences for the way graduates of professional training programs evaluate their training experiences. In particular, one might expect those committed to psychotherapy to evaluate negatively those aspects of training that do not contribute to the acquisition of psychotherapeutic skills. Since there is considerable uniformity in the types of training experiences evaluated negatively and positively, these considerations raise the possibility that the process of becoming a psychotherapist might be more effectively organized into one program stressing the positive and most relevant experiences rather than, as now, be found as subparts of four different training systems.

The proposition that mental health institutions are not simply places where members of various professions gather to perform standard professional roles but rather settings in which roles are adopted and distributed according to situational demands has been confirmed by a series of studies over the past two decades. However, the primary focus of research in the past has been on institutions organized primarily for the provision of inpatient psychiatric services. These studies have provided valuable descriptive data as well as hypotheses about the small number of specific institutions. However, the main movement in the treatment of mental illness is away from hospitalization toward treatment in a wide range of outpatient facilities and other institutions. Exactly how far this movement has gone is revealed by the distribution of our sample of mental health professionals across a wide range of institutions: 16 percent of our sample were employed in educational institutions, including medical schools and counseling centers; 14 percent were employed in psychiatric clinics; 12 percent were working in general hospitals; 10 percent held positions in various social service organizations; 8 percent were employed in health- and/or mental-health-related homes and foundations; and 3 percent were employed in mental hospitals. While mental health professionals are widely dispersed among various kinds of institutions, much less variability exists in the types of careers they are pursuing in these organizations. Specifically, when professionals are classified according to their major job activities, we find that administration is the single largest functional category for practitioners in all types of organizations, except educational institutions. Careers that have the performance of psychotherapy as the primary role are still confined to the one-third of our sample who are in private practice. In fact, of all professionals giving psychotherapy as their major job activity, the number in private practice is more than twice as large as the number working in all types of institutions combined. Even when individual and group therapy are combined with psychological counseling and psychiatric casework, the highest proportion of professionals engaged in treatment in any type of setting is only slightly more than one-half. This suggests that a large proportion of treatment occurring in mental health institutions is done by professionals on a part-time basis. Thus, it seems clear that one of the direct influences of institutional settings on the distribution of labor in the mental health field is to draw professionals away from treatment careers into careers in mental health organizational administration.

Estimates of the extent to which professional care of the mentally ill has moved from the private office to the institutional setting have, in the past, been based on findings from case studies of psychiatric institutions. In light of the findings presented here, it would appear that the general tendency has been to overestimate the amount of change actually produced by this trend. To a certain extent, this is one specific instance of the general tendency to overestimate the extent to which members of the core mental health professions have become involved in new organizational arrangements for treating the mentally ill. Community mental health centers represent the prime case in point. Thus, for example, only 15 percent of our sample of over 4000 mental health professionals claimed that they spent any time engaged in what they would consider to be "community mental health" activities. Further, of those who were engaged in community mental health programs, fewer than one in every ten identified such involvement as their primary job.

Some of the reasons why large numbers of mental health professionals have not, as yet, moved into the community mental health field are undoubtedly related to the characteristics of mental health centers as career sites. Most salient in this regard is the fact that, compared to other mental health institutions, the community mental health center represents not only a new organizational form, but also a new organizational purpose. The new form, essentially a collation of formally discrete care and treatment units into a single entity, is designed to provide easier entry into and easier exit from institutional care for the patient. The major requirement is that the professional enters into active collaboration with other professionals and nonprofessionals with whom he has had limited contact in the past, and then only in highly role-structured situations in which lines of authority were clearly drawn. The new organizational purpose is nothing less than that of determining how to discover the needs of people and how to adapt schedules, techniques, and procedures so as to anticipate and meet those needs. There are two major requirements here: (1) to provide services to all segments of the population, thereby extending treatment to groupings (racial, economic, ecological) heretofore inadequately served; and (2) to develop programs of prevention, involving entry into the community and utilization of community resources. Careers containing these requirements represent courses that, in terms of orientation, training, and experience, currently practicing mental health professionals are ill-prepared to pursue.

Some of the background for this suggestion was found in *The Fifth Profession* (Henry, Sims, and Spray, 1971), as we there observed the highly similar cultural backgrounds of therapists and as we noted the manner in which they become more alike in the process of selecting particular clinical experiences, from whichever system they are in, as they progress through training.

The ways in which these factors might be reflected in the realities of their current lives and professional activities are examined in the present volume. In particular, we will here show how the presence of three distinct routes into the field has resulted not only in a diversity of skilled persons but also in a diversity of professional images. The images and views that inhabitants of the mental health field hold of each other have been contaminated by three decades of dispute over the allocation of treatment functions. The atmosphere in the field, among persons who practice, with minor variations, the same skills to the same ends, is clearly conducive to professional misunderstanding and interprofessional disputes.

But if diversity exists within the professional community, it certainly does not within the patient population. With an unerring eye, therapists of various schools and training backgrounds select for treatment patients of highly similar properties. The homogeneity among patients, more marked for private-practice treatment than for institutional treatment, seems to relate to the degree of autonomy the therapist has to select his patients. In effect, the more choice he has, the more alike his patients will be.

Two implications of this patient homogeneity are immediately apparent. The one is the extent to which, in a verbal field dealing mainly with affects and individual interpretations of events, therapists choose patients who manifest much the same values and views and who can talk about them in psychodynamically relevant ways. And the second is the extraordinary constraint upon the experiential background of the therapist that such patient limitation implies. These two factors will emerge as crucial in examining the question of training for new concepts in mental health care.

Crucial to this issue as well is the extent to which institution-based mental health work, as seen in our sample of practitioners, tends to dilute the intensity of involvement in psychotherapeutic work, but also in the ways in which it shifts the focus from therapeutic activities to administrative activities. The institution setting, as opposed to the private practice setting, does indeed make a difference, largely in selecting those therapists for whom psychotherapy is not a crucial activity, thus leaving for the field of private practice those therapists for whom it is crucial.

Training programs, as well as professional discussions, have many and highly varied theoretical positions in the psychodynamic area. We will here examine the ways in which these appear to influence the thought and ideology of the practicing graduate of these programs. The belief systems portrayed in training programs do not find systematic reflection in practicing graduates. Beliefs and ideologies relevant to mental health do not, in fact, vary by profession, nor do techniques and therapeutic behaviors. The reality of therapeutic practice seems to suggest a kind of synthesis of ideologies and techniques derived idiosyncratically from the past experience of the therapists. There are similarities, of course, particularly in the overwhelming dominance of an essentially psychoanalytic view, but these appear to be segments of common ways of synthesizing therapeutic events that are not organized by profession or by theoretic school.

We observed earlier that we see careers as having a general course of development over time, a course that has a discoverable continuity and direction and that, while itself changing, guides roles and orientations of persons within it. In *The Fifth Profession* (Henry, Sims, and Spray, 1971), we outlined some of the broad social sources that help to give mental health careers their particular character, and we will in the early chapters of this book show how the realities of professional life and therapeutic practice both illustrate work continuities and serve as constraints on change. We have so far ignored the premise that mental health professionals are not only psychodynamic practitioners but are themselves the living result of certain of the early dynamic principles they find active in their patients. We do, of course, see some strong determinants of individual behavior residing in those early events that surround the religious and ethnic family lives we have already portrayed. These cultural views, acted out in family living, have undoubtedly been vital in forming certain of the emotional orientations, ways of living, and ways of believing about which our therapists, seen in later adult life, seem in considerable accord.

Much theory suggests that determinants more specifically related to intimate interpersonal relations in early childhood set courses of choice that tend to structure events of later life. For the eventual choice of mental health work, the temptation is great to search for some earlier determinant in emotional stress, some early examples of caring and helping, or some trauma partially abstracted and lived out in subsequent years. In the later chapters of this book, we will examine several areas of private lives in the search for such early determinants. We will report on our therapists' views of their own early childhoods, their parents, and their relations with siblings and peers. We will also examine development in sexual, social, and intellectual spheres in earlier family life and in contemporary living. In so doing, we will find little to support the premise that one mental health profession differs from another in these factors and equally little to suggest that mental health professionals as a group differ in significant areas of early life or emotional adjustment from their educated colleagues in other, non-mental-health professions. In fact, the mystique of the psychotherapist as a tortured soul who, from this inner light, helps others seems to us entirely unfounded. At the same time, the mystique that comes from highly special points of view, communicated in the private tongue of psychodynamic language, does seem a significant reality. This language, and the broader psychodynamic paradigm that it represents, is a very strong force, guiding the choice of roles that the therapist will enact, the patients he will choose, and the character of his adult social and professional life.

2

The Professional Community

The necessity for autonomy and individual discretion in the performance of central professional functions is a principal organizing theme in all professions. In the mental health professions, this theme is reflected in the high prestige accorded the most visible model of autonomy—one-to-one psychotherapy. While differing markedly in the degree to which they have achieved autonomy at work, the model of individual, one-to-one therapy is strongly emphasized in the training programs of all four core mental health professions. To the extent that the principles of individual psychotherapy are most readily realized in the private office, graduates of these systems of professionalization have all been encouraged to hold the private practice of psychotherapy in high esteem.

The ethos of individual discretion in therapeutic practice is most clearly expressed in the training programs of psychoanalysts and psychiatrists. Medical schools, medical internships, and psychiatric residencies are all designed to convey the notion that the private office is the ideal setting for professional practice. Thus, in lecturing to resident doctors, members of hospital staffs frequently place the greatest emphasis on factors associated with the performance of one-to-one psychotherapy (Muncie and Billings, 1951; Blain, 1953). Similarly, individual psychotherapy is openly acknowledged by many to be the most prestigeful topic in informal conversations among hospital staff members (Strauss and others, 1964; Kennard, 1957). Even the residency program for psychiatrists is designed as a continuum of discretion, with the resident first working with chronically ill and acutely disturbed patients in a highly controlled situation and then moving on to work with progressively less severely ill patients in less controlled situations until he reaches the point at which he begins to work with mildly disturbed patients in a highly autonomous one-to-one relationship (Blum and Rosenberg, 1968; Kartus and Schlesinger, 1957). Under these circumstances, it is understandable that even psychiatrists who are not themselves in private practice still consider individual, long-term psychotherapeutic techniques to be the preferred form of treatment.

Although clinical psychology has a much smaller proportion of members engaged in the private practice of psychotherapy than is the case for psychiatry, developments in the mental health field make it clear that psychologists have found the role of individual psychotherapist highly attractive. Most notable in this regard is the vigorous manner in which clinical psychologists have pressed the demand for the right to perform psychotherapy in all types of settings. The fact that clinical psychologists are deeply committed to individual psychotherapy is further indicated by the proliferation of professional associations explicitly designed to promote the performance of therapy by psychologists. Finally, with regard to individual discretion, the professional socialization of clinical psychologists is designed to inculcate many of the same expectations regarding the unfettered application of professional expertise that psychiatrists and psychoanalysts acquire in medical training programs organized around the doctor-patient relationship. Specifically, the early academic training of clinical psychologists emphasizes autonomy in the performance of teaching and research activities. Later in the clinical phase of professionalization, the theme of individual discretion is extended to the application of professional treatment and diagnostic skills. At no time in this process of professionalization is the clinical psychologist encouraged to define his role as ancillary to other professionals. To the contrary, the objective of the clinical psychology training program is to transform neophytes into professionals who are fully competent to function autonomously as teachers, researchers, and therapists. (Henry, Sims, and Spray, 1971; Rushing, 1964.)

Psychiatric social workers, like clinical psychologists, have increasingly shown an interest in expanding their formally recognized sphere of competence to include psychotherapy. To be sure, the job title of caseworker has been retained, but the professional perspective on the etiology of human problems has shifted from one that emphasized social factors to one that stresses personality characteristics. The salient dimensions of this historical shift in professional orientation has been succinctly summarized by Wilensky and Lebeaux (1958): "From viewing the case as a product of impersonal forces in the social and economic environment, social work came to the image of the case as a product of unconscious impulse needing restoration to an unchanged environment by self-mastery. This shift in theory is intimately related to a major shift in practice: from preoccupation with reform to preoccupation with technical professionalism" (pp. 325–326).

The shift in social work from a social to an individual perspective on aberrant behavior began when psychiatrists started working in child guidance clinics and other institutions that employ social workers. Through their contact with psychiatrists, social workers were exposed for the first time to a systematic theoretical framework that they could use to establish guidelines for their encounters with clients. As a result, social workers were quick to embrace the psychodynamic orientation espoused by psychiatrists. The most popular psychodynamic approach at this time was, of course, psychoanalytic theory. Later, the development of psychiatric training programs for social workers during World War II, combined with the continuing demand for their services in psychiatric institutions, served to solidify the commitment of social work to psychoanalytic theory and methods. The adoption of psychodynamic theory not only changed the character of casework activities but also led psychiatric social workers into the field of individual psychotherapy. Although the bulk of individual therapy performed by psychiatric social workers still occurs in an institutional context, a small but increasing number of psychiatric social workers are entering private practice. In sum, it is clear that psychiatric social workers are trained to expect and are effectively demanding autonomy in the performance of diagnostic, counseling, and psychotherapeutic functions in the mental health field.

When these observations are summarized, they lead to the conclusion that the professional image, which is both reflected and reinforced in all four professional training programs, puts individual psychotherapy at the core of the profession. Since aspirants to each of the professions are required to undergo a prolonged and intensive period of professional socialization, it is understandable that graduates emerge from these training programs with a strong emotional attachment to the role of psychotherapist. Undoubtedly this is one reason why the overwhelming majority of the members of each of the four professions have gone through psychotherapy as a patient. Psychoanalysts must, of course, undergo a personal analysis as part of their formal training. Although personal psychotherapy is not a formal training requirement for members of the other three professional groups, it is clearly a highly valued experience, as attested to by the fact that approximately two-thirds of the psychiatrists and psychiatric social workers and fully three-fourths of the clinical psychologists in our sample have voluntarily sought out and received individual psychotherapy. Moreover, this commitment to individual psychotherapy not only affects the course of professional preparation but also influences subsequent professional practice. Specifically, several detailed findings will be presented later in this volume that, when summarized, conclusively demonstrate that the overwhelming majority of our sample of practitioners confine their therapeutic activities to one-to-one psychotherapy.

In sum, the accumulated evidence strongly suggests that individual psychotherapy not only serves as the focal point for professional training programs but also functions as the symbolic core of professional identity in the mental health field. If individual psychotherapy does indeed symbolize the essence of professional identity in the mental health field, then the attributes associated with this performance should constitute an important basis of professional evaluation. Thus, an examination of the role of the practitioner of individual psychotherapy provides a convenient point of departure for attempting to understand the basis of individual and collective professional images currently extant in the mental health field.

Individual psychotherapy holds a unique position in the repertoire of skills possessed by mental health professionals; it clearly constitutes the core act performed by the practitioner, yet it is the least understood and least objectively documented of all the professional services performed. That is, to date it has been virtually impossible to achieve an objective evaluation of therapeutic results or to make valid comparisons among psychotherapists utilizing different approaches. The lack of objective criteria for evaluating psychotherapeutic performance stems, in large part, from the highly private nature of the individual therapeutic transaction. The privacy theme in psychotherapy has been described by Allen Wheelis (1956), using psychoanalysis as a model: "The therapeutic transaction is not open for inspection. The analyst and analysand can report what happens, but as both are involved neither can be disinterested. Except for rare tape-recorded sessions, the most direct view that any third person gains of the analytic process occurs during the course of training; the student analyst reports to the training analyst what happens, hour by hour. But even here the margin of distortion is wide. Not everything can be reported, and what is left out may be more important than what is transmitted" (p. 156).

The fact that objective evaluation is precluded by the very nature of the therapeutic encounter means that training programs can only pass on to trainees general guidelines for the performance of psychotherapy.

Individual variation in therapeutic style is both acknowledged and expected. The concealed nature of the therapeutic relationship also means that professional evaluation cannot be based on assessment of actual therapeutic performance but must focus, instead, on personal attributes of individual psychotherapists. Specifically, since the guardians of professional standards are unable to observe the actual application of therapeutic skills by practitioners, they are forced to resort to scrutinizing social attributes and personality characteristics of psychotherapists. Of course, focusing on the individual attributes of the therapists ensures wide variability in the process of professional evaluation. Given the fact that there is available little systematic evidence that clearly links any particular set of personal attributes of therapists to therapeutic behavior, professional evaluators are forced to rely on their own experience in determining the criteria used in assessing competence. Since members of the four mental health professions differ in terms of their experiential background, it is inevitable that they will also differ in terms of the criteria they use to make distinctions among professionals in the field. Thus, the image the professional develops of his fellow practitioners will directly reflect the criteria he uses to differentiate among mental health professionals. To the extent that the way a psychotherapist relates to his fellow practitioners is influenced by his image of them, the bases of interprofessional conflict in the field can be assumed to reside in the differentiating criteria utilized by mental health professionals to order their occupational work. Therefore, the way in which practitioners classify their colleagues provides a major clue to the focus around which information about other professions, and, by inference, about themselves, is organized. With this assumption in mind, mental health professionals in our sample were asked to respond to the following questionnaire item: "What is the most significant criterion for differentiating and/or categorizing professionals in the mental health field?" The frequency with which members of the four professional groups utilized each of the five response categories is contained in Table 1.

The fact there are three separate, distinct routes into the professional mental health field clearly has a divisive effect on the way professionals view their fellow-practitioners. Professionals who enter the mental health field through psychology are much more likely than other professionals to use the functions and activities performed as the basis for differentiating among practitioners. For clinical psychologists, the dominant view is one in which practitioners from diverse professional backgrounds are grouped according to primary function, that is, therapy, research, teaching, or administration. In short, relative to other professions, clinical psychologists deemphasize the importance of professional affiliation. This is, of course, a fitting perspective for members of the

Table 1. DIFFERENTIATING CRITERIA BY PROFESSION

Differentiating Criterion	PROFESSION			
	Psycho-analyst	Psychia-trist	Clinical Psycho-logist	Psychiatric Social Worker
	Percent and (Base Number)			
Professional Designation	36.7 (165)	33.8 (179)	17.7 (205)	34.4 (329)
Functions and Activities	20.0 (90)	24.7 (131)	49.8 (576)	38.2 (366)
Therapeutic Orientation	36.4 (164)	26.2 (139)	17.2 (199)	15.6 (149)
Setting of Practice	2.0 (9)	3.4 (18)	2.7 (31)	3.6 (34)
Amount of Experience in Therapeutic Work	4.9 (22)	11.9 (63)	12.6 (146)	8.3 (79)
Total	100 (450)	100 (530)	100 (1157)	100 (957)

profession that first challenged organized medicine's monopoly over the treatment of mental illness, thereby initiating the continuing debate over the therapeutic rights of various occupational groups to perform psychotherapy. Psychiatric social work has also been implicated in the debate over the therapeutic rights of various professional groups, but to a much lesser extent than is true of clinical psychology. In particular, the models of practice implicit in social work training programs as well as the careers available to psychiatric social workers upon completion of training are still, by and large, confined to institutional settings. Since the organizational positions available to social workers are frequently defined in terms of professional emphasis (for example, caseworker, community worker, supervisor, and the like), it is understandable that they would place greater reliance on professional designation than do clinical psychologists. However, despite these countervailing pressures, functions are still the differentiating criterion most freqently used by psychiatric social workers. Thus, members of both nonmedical professions are much more likely to be interested in knowing *what* functions are being performed by fellow-practitioners than they are in knowing *where* they practice or detailed information concerning either their *experience* or their *therapeutic orientation*.

Practitioners who take the medical route into the mental health field are likely to base their evaluations more on either the practitioners' professional affiliation or his therapeutic orientation than on the functions he performs. Psychiatrists and psychoanalysts who rely on professional affiliation as the major differentiating criterion are, of course, adopting a perspective that is consistent with the official statement, issued in 1954 by the three concerned medical associations (American Medical Association, American Psychiatric Association, and American Psychoanalytic Association), to the effect that "psychotherapy is a form of medical treatment and does not form the basis for a separate profession" (p. 385). For psychiatrists and psychoanalysts, the basic implication contained in this statement is that psychiatric programs provide better clinical training than is true of either psychology or social work programs. By subscribing to this view, psychiatrists and psychoanalysts can use professional affiliation as a rough index of clinical preparation. This perspective is particularly useful to psychoanalysts, since it provides them with a basis for distinguishing themselves from psychiatrists, as well as from nonmedical professionals. The primary difference between psychiatrists and psychoanalysts resides in the much greater amount of highly specialized clinical training received by analysts. Since this clinical training is exclusively Freudian in orientation, professional identity and therapeutic orientation come to mean the same things to psychoanalysts. Hence, it is understandable that in differentiating among psychotherapists, psychoanalysts use professional designation and therapeutic orientation with equal frequency.

It should also be noted that a second implication can be drawn from the official medical statement on psychotherapy; namely, that the training received in medical school constitutes the basic foundation for the treatment of mental illness. This is, of course, an issue that has produced a great deal of controversy within psychiatry. Since psychiatrists who agree with the statement differ radically from those who do not and since there are distinct therapeutic orientations associated with both groups of practitioners, it is not surprising that members of the psychiatric profession frequently use orientation as the basis of their evaluation of colleagues.

Finally, these findings take on added significance when it is realized that the professional differences in images of the field are based, by and large, on informed conviction rather than vague opinions. That is, if the professional differences in the classification of fellow practitioners were due simply to judgments made on the basis of insufficient information, stemming from infrequent contact among some members of each of the four professional groups, then the problem could be easily solved by an informational program. Unfortunately, the evidence indicates that, with but one exception, the rate of interaction with other professionals does not alter the distributions contained in Table 1. Specifically, when rates of professional interaction are dichotomized at the mean for each professional group, there are no significant differences in the differentiating criterion used by the resulting "high" and "low" groups in three of the four professions. The only exception is found among psychiatric social workers, where those who have a low rate of interaction with other professionals are less likely to rely on professional designation and more likely to rely on either the practitioner's experience or his therapeutic orientation.

In sum, the evidence contained in Table 1 clearly indicates that the image of the mental health field held by professional practitioners has been contaminated by the residue of three decades of dispute over the allocation of treatment functions. The advent of multiple, distinct routes into the mental health field has resulted not only in a diversity of skilled personnel but also in a diversity of professional images. Thus, while there may well be considerable overlapping in the functions performed by members of the four core mental health professions, the way practitioners categorize their colleagues is still distinctly related to professional affiliation. Since the use of incongruent criteria for evaluating colleagues can only result in incongruent assessments of them, the perceptual atmosphere in the mental health field is certainly conducive to professional misunderstandings and interprofessional disputes. Having established the existence of the conditions necessary for interprofessional conflict, the problem remaining is to determine the location of its occurrence. To explore this issue it is necessary to determine the climate of opinion prevailing among the specific professions.

Images of Specific Professions

To initiate our investigation of professional images, respondents in the interview sample were asked to consider the differences between the four mental health professions with respect to the problems they treat, the patients they serve, and the kinds of therapeutic techniques they use. Although these are discrete issues that have been separated for the purpose of reporting the findings, respondents typically considered the issues simultaneously, touching on all of them in one general statement that implied that they are seen as overlapping and interrelated characteristics. The interview excerpts below are typical of the kinds of comments made by respondents.

A psychiatric social worker expressed these evaluations:

> I think social workers try not to treat psychotic patients or those who may have homicidal or suicidal tendencies. Psychiatrists, of course, take all

kinds of cases. The psychiatrists have the broadest perspective of all the mental health professionals. Nonmedical people in private practice are cautious about the kinds of patients they treat, and currently they tend to treat very few hospitalized patients. Psychiatrists can use chemical, physical, and institutional treatments. Otherwise, I believe that analysts, both medical and nonmedical, in private practice use much the same techniques. Social workers usually work in agencies or in clinic settings and tend to be less often found in private practice. This is important because it means a difference in the amount of personal responsibility social workers assume. It also means that social workers don't use methods like a couch. Analysts of all kinds tend to use techniques aimed at bringing about the longest, deepest, and most intensive personality changes. Also, social workers rarely see patients more than one time per week. On the other hand, analysts in private practice rarely see a patient only one time a week and usually much more often.

One clinical psychologist saw the situation as follows:

I think psychiatric social workers tend to deal in social interaction more than with the individual. Their major focus is not on the individual's inner problems. Psychiatrists, on the other hand, often hospitalize patients and use drug therapy and shock treatment. Even in psychotherapy, psychiatrists tend to be more oriented to treatment of the individual's inner processes. Clinical psychologists are somewhere in between these two approaches in that they are oriented to the treatment of the individual's inner processes, but they are also stepping out more into group therapy, community psychiatry, and similar approaches.

According to another clinical psychologist:

Whatever the person's training was, what he does overlaps . . . [with what members of the other professions do] . . . and we all treat or are capable of treating a wide range of types of patients and problems; the only exception is those purely medical matters. The professional training of a mental health worker doesn't mean nearly as much as his personality. I refer people to social workers as readily as I do to psychiatrists.

A psychiatrist made the following comments:

Medical mental health people deal more with persons who are in active trouble in society. Social workers deal with those who suffer most. Psychiatrists deal with those who are functionally sick. Psychologists tend to deal more with problems of living, rather than with the more overt behavior aberrations. Often the practitioners who are least well prepared see the sickest people. That is, the most experienced practitioners see the better integrated people who can, for instance, tolerate psychoanalysis. Regarding social class, the social worker is the only one who sees the vast multitude of people and then only in casework. The other mental health personnel see mainly middle- and upper-middle-class people. The current situation is that psychiatrists tend to treat hospitalized people and middle-class neurotic people. This determines some of the techniques used. Social workers are more suitable for and aware of community mental health needs and in many ways better equipped to work with the lowest socio-economic status people than are psychiatrists. In private practice, psychologists see some of the same types of people as psychiatrists. Regarding specific techniques, the psychologists and the psychiatrists use more one-to-one therapy, stressing intrapsychic aspects, whereas social workers do more therapy with groups, stressing interpersonal and reality-oriented approaches.

Another psychiatrist saw a blurring of distinctions among the professions:

Only people who can afford to pay out a considerable amount of money for a long time can afford psychoanalysis. Analysis is only available to the white-collar class and above. It is not the mode of therapy for the population as a whole. At the community level, psychiatrists function best as leaders of teams of psychologists who can play important roles in administration, research, or therapy if properly trained. Social workers used to examine families seen by therapists and often got into important therapeutic relationships with family members. Professional images are getting fuzzy. This is unfortunate because with a division of labor you can usually get people to work together as a team. It is obvious that some social workers have a better feel for patients than some psychiatrists. Some people have a better feel for others than other people and this doesn't necessarily follow professional lines. But there still have to be lines of responsibility which require some professional differentiation.

On the basis of responses such as these, categories were established to classify practitioners' views about the kinds of patients served, therapeutic techniques, and training and experience that differentiate the various mental health professions. Respondents were most explicit in describing the differences in the characteristics of patients served by the various professions. Table 2 presents those categories mentioned by at least 5 percent of the interview sample.

Table 2 reveals remarkable uniformity among the four groups of psychotherapists in the way in which they characterize the types of patients treated by the various professions. That is, only two of the ten responses were given with significantly different frequency in the four professional groups—the view that psychiatric social workers treat patients who are of lower socioeconomic status than the patients of other professionals and the view that psychiatrists see a wider range of patients. Psychiatric social workers are disproportionately likely to feel that members of

Table 2. PROFESSIONAL DIFFERENCES IN THE PATIENTS SERVED

Categories Specified	Percent of Respondents
Psychiatrists treat hospitalized, very ill patients	30.5
Analysts treat the less ill	26.0
Analysts treat wealthier patients	19.0
Depends on setting more than the profession	15.5
Social workers treat patients of lower socioeconomic status	15.0
Psychiatrists see a wide range of patients	14.5
Social workers treat the very ill	14.0
Less difference than in the past	11.5
Psychologists do not treat hospitalized very ill patients	9.0
Psychologists see a wide range of patients	7.0

NOTE: $N = 200$—45 psychoanalysts, 47 psychiatrists, 50 clinical psychologists, and 58 psychiatric social workers. The percentages total more than 100 because each respondent could mention more than one factor.

their own profession treat lower-class patients much more than do other professionals—24 percent of them took this position while the corresponding figure for clinical psychologists was 16 percent. The opinion that psychiatrists see an unusually wide range of patients compared with other professional groups is most prevalent among psychiatrists—23 percent characterized their profession in this manner. Psychiatric social workers virtually rejected this view of psychiatry (only 3 percent agreed that psychiatrists have the most diverse clients), while psychoanalysts were only slightly impressed with the view (13 percent agreed). Surprisingly, clinical psychologists are most likely to endorse the view presented by psychiatrists; fully one-fifth of the psychologists believe that psychiatrists treat the widest range of patients; thus, both psychiatrists and psychiatric social workers hold self-images that are only partially validated by fellow practitioners. The claims made by psychiatrists are apparently not convincing to either psychiatric social workers or psychoanalysts. Psychiatric social workers, in turn, receive little support for their self-views from either group of medical professionals.

The existence of these contradictory views of psychiatry and psychiatric social work might be a reflection of the fact that psychiatrists and psychiatric social workers are making false claims for their professions or it could indicate that the nature of these two professions is misunderstood by other mental health professionals. For psychiatric social work, considerable misperception exists at each level. Specifically, in the questionnaire survey we asked respondents to report the family income of the patients they were currently treating in private practice and in institutions.* The results, contained in Table 3, reveal that psychiatric social workers are more likely than other professionals to treat patients from the lower income brackets in institutions. It should be noted, however, that psychiatric social workers are not only more likely to treat lower-income patients but also more likely than other professionals to know the income of their institutional patients. Since social agencies frequently use family income as one criterion for screening potential clients, it is not surprising that psychiatric social workers are, in general, more likely to be aware of the financial standing of their institutional patients than is true of other mental health professionals. However, it is indeed unexpected to find that the distinction between psychiatric social workers and other professionals may be due as much to differential knowledge of patients' incomes as to actual differences in the income levels of patients treated in institutions. Thus, economic characteristics of patients seen in institutions is, at best, a rather crude and unreliable criterion for distinguishing among psychotherapists.

The distribution by income level of patients treated in institutions by the four professional groups undoubtedly reflects the operation of organizational constraints on patient selection much more than it reflects the preferences of individual psychotherapists. That is, patients receiving psychotherapy in institutions characteristically go through an organizational screening process that is designed to assess compatibility between the patients' needs and abilities and the institutional resources. As a rule, this screening process includes an initial intake interview conducted by someone other than the therapist who eventually ends up treating the patient. Consequently, the psychotherapist has relatively little freedom in the choice of patients he treats in institutions.

However, in private practice the therapist usually conducts the initial interview with the potential patient and decides, on the basis of information gained personally, whether or not to accept the individual into psychotherapy. Consequently, private-practice psychotherapists are

* Specifically, the respondents were asked to reply to the following question: "How many of the patients you see regularly per week are from homes which have a total income of: under $5000, $5,000–$10,000, $10,000–$20,000, $20,000–$50,000, over $50,000, Don't know."

relatively free to choose the types of patients they wish to treat. Thus, if members of the four professional groups differ in their preference for patients from various socioeconomic backgrounds, it should be revealed in the distribution of patients treated in private practice. In particular, if the self-image of psychiatric social workers is based on a preference for treating patients from lower socioeconomic backgrounds, then it should be revealed in their private-practice clientele. However, the evidence contained in Table 3 indicates that, in private practice, there is no significant difference among psychiatric social workers, clinical psychologists, and psychiatrists in the proportion of patients having family incomes of less than $10,000. In fact, the tendency for psychoanalysts to treat wealthier patients represents the only clear-cut professional difference among private-practicing psychotherapists. This professional difference undoubtedly reflects an income differential between patients undergoing psychoanalysis and those receiving other forms of psychotherapy.

The conclusion that emerges from summarizing the findings contained in Table 3 is that psychiatric social workers do not exhibit a pronounced tendency to treat proportionately more patients of lower socioeconomic status than do other psychotherapists. This is true, despite the fact that the data indicate that psychiatric social workers specialize to a greater extent than do other mental health professionals in the treatment of institutional patients and that, on the whole, the income levels of patients receiving treatment in institutions is lower than that of patients receiving private office treatment. With regard to socioeconomic status of patients treated, it would appear that the professionals who were most accurate in their perception of the situation were those who stated that the types of patients seen depend more on the setting of practice than on professional affiliation.

Whereas psychiatric social workers encounter difficulty in securing social validation of their self-image as specialists in the treatment of patients, psychiatrists fail to gain professional approval for their view of themselves as therapeutic generalists. That is, while none of the professional groups deny that psychiatrists treat very ill, hospitalized patients, psychoanalysts and psychiatric social workers are not convinced that psychiatrists see a wider range of patients than is true for other psychotherapists. As it turns out, the skepticism of the psychoanalysts and social workers is well founded. That is, results from the survey indicate that when members of the four professional groups classify their patients according to standard diagnostic categories, psychiatrists do not emerge as unique in terms of the range of patients treated, although they do treat more patients suffering from psychosis than is true for other psychotherapists. Table 4 reveals that, in institutions, severely disturbed patients con-

Table 3. Distribution by Income of Patients seen by Each Profession

Family Income of Patients	PROFESSION				
	Psychoanalyst	Psychiatrist	Clinical Psychologist	Psychiatric Social Worker	Total
			Percent and (Base Number)[a]		
			In Institutions		
Under $10,000	70.8 (1672)	69.7 (5228)	61.4 (7112)	78.1 (10,589)	70.3 (24,601)
$10,000–$20,000	5.0 (119)	5.1 (384)	9.7 (1130)	8.6 (1165)	8.0 (2798)
$20,000–$50,000	2.8 (67)	1.4 (102)	1.7 (192)	1.9 (262)	1.8 (623)
Over $50,000	0.5 (12)	0.3 (23)	0.3 (31)	0.8 (110)	0.5 (176)
Income Unknown	20.8 (490)	23.5 (1760)	26.9 (3115)	10.5 (1427)	19.4 (6792)
Total Percentage	100	100	100	100	100
Total Patients	(2360)	(7497)	(11,580)	(13,553)	(34,990)
Total Number of Professionals	220	335	731	735	2021

[a] The numbers in parenthesis refer to number of patients.

Under $10,000	25.3 (2554)	38.7 (4702)	41.0 (5182)	41.4 (1350)	36.1 (13,788)
$10,000–$20,000	33.2 (3355)	32.8 (3982)	32.8 (4155)	39.1 (1275)	33.5 (12,767)
$20,000–$50,000	25.1 (2533)	12.7 (1549)	11.2 (1414)	12.0 (392)	15.4 (5888)
Over $50,000	7.4 (748)	2.8 (338)	2.8 (361)	1.8 (58)	3.9 (1505)
Income Unknown	8.9 (901)	13.0 (1575)	12.1 (1539)	5.7 (185)	11.0 (4200)
Total Percentage	100	100	100	100	100
Total Patients	(10,091)	(12,146)	(12,651)	(3260)	(38,148)
Total Number of Professionals	536	512	817	269	2134

Table 4. Distribution by Diagnostic Categories of Patients seen by Each Profession

Diagnostic Categories	PROFESSION				
	Psychoanalyst	Psychiatrist	Clinical Psychologist	Psychiatric Social Worker	Total
			Percent and (Base Number)ᵃ		
			In Institutions		
Relatively Healthy	7.6 (148)	5.9 (445)	23.3 (2626)	17.7 (2097)	16.3 (5316)
Psychoneurotic	15.5 (303)	16.7 (1252)	27.5 (3094)	26.7 (3172)	24.0 (7821)
Character Disorder	28.5 (559)	19.2 (1442)	20.8 (2338)	25.5 (3022)	22.6 (7361)
Psychosomatic Illness	4.2 (82)	6.4 (480)	4.0 (448)	5.3 (642)	5.0 (1642)
Functional and Organic Psychoses	35.9 (703)	44.9 (3365)	20.2 (2269)	20.5 (2434)	26.9 (8771)
Addicts and Alcoholics	8.3 (163)	6.8 (511)	4.3 (480)	4.2 (502)	5.1 (1656)
Total Percentage	100	100	100	100	100
Total Patients	(1958)	(7495)	(11,255)	(11,859)	(32,567)
Total Number of Professionals	192	297	693	700	1882

ᵃ The numbers in parenthesis refer to number of patients.

Relatively Healthy	5.1 (530)	6.2 (764)	12.8 (1577)	10.2 (321)	8.4 (3192)
Psychoneurotic	42.5 (4416)	41.2 (5039)	44.2 (5424)	42.9 (1355)	42.7 (16,234)
Character Disorder	33.2 (3444)	21.3 (2600)	26.9 (3305)	34.0 (1074)	27.4 (10,423)
Psychosomatic Illness	5.5 (570)	9.2 (1122)	5.8 (710)	4.3 (136)	6.7 (2538)
Functional and Organic Psychoses	11.8 (1224)	19.6 (2394)	8.3 (1016)	7.3 (230)	12.8 (4834)
Addicts and Alcoholics	1.9 (196)	2.5 (309)	1.9 (238)	1.4 (45)	2.1 (788)
Total Percentage	100	100	100	100	100
Total Patients	(10,380)	(12,228)	(12,270)	(3161)	(38,039)
Total Number of Professionals	542	514	815	366	2137

stitute a larger proportion of the patients seen by psychiatrists than by any other professional group. However, both clinical psychologists and psychiatric social workers see proportionally more relatively healthy and psychoneurotic patients than is true for psychiatrists. More importantly, both psychologists and social workers have a more uniform distribution of patients among the various diagnostic categories than is true for psychiatrists.

In fact, the major distinction in types of patients treated is between the medically and nonmedically trained psychotherapists, rather than between psychiatrists and the other three professional groups. However, apparently, rather than the presence or absence of medical training per se, the differences between the medical-organic and the psychological approaches to the treatment of mental illness produce the professional division of labor. That is, in discussing therapeutic techniques, 46 percent of the entire interview sample noted that the therapeutic approach of psychiatrists emphasizes the fact that they are physicians; hence they can and do use techniques such as medication and electroshock therapy to treat severely disturbed patients. Psychoanalysts were not mentioned in this respect because they place greater reliance on psychologically oriented therapeutic techniques. The professional differences in the frequency with which interview respondents held this view provides additional support for this interpretation. Approximately one-half of the psychiatrists, clinical psychologists, and psychiatric social workers singled out the medically based techniques as characteristic of psychiatrists whereas only one-quarter of the psychoanalysts mentioned these techniques as associated with psychiatry. This difference undoubtedly reflects the fact that analyst-psychiatrists, unlike general psychiatrists, tend to eschew medical-organic techniques. Thus, the reliance by psychiatrists on their medical background as a basis for treating mental illness serves not only to distinguish them from nonmedical therapists but also to set them apart from psychoanalysts who treat patients in institutions.

In private practice, the difference between psychological and medical approaches to the treatment of mental illness tends to produce the same cleavages between physicians and nonphysicians and between psychiatrists and psychoanalysts, although the relationships are much weaker. This is readily understandable, since both severely ill patients and psychiatrists relying on a medical treatment perspective are most likely to be found in institutions.

When the interview and survey findings are summarized, the general conclusion that emerges is that psychotherapists' interest in patient characteristics is primarily an integrative rather than a divisive influence in the mental health professions. That is, when professional groups are typed according to the characteristics of the patients treated, there is remarkable interprofessional consensus in the resulting professional images. Similarly, at the level of actual practice, there is a high level of uniformity in the types of patients treated. In fact, the interprofessional differences in images and practices are not actually reflections of differences in professional preferences for types of patients but, rather, reflections of differences in the distribution of practitioners by setting of practice and/or therapeutic orientation. As a result, professional differences in types of patients treated are, by and large, confined to institutional practice. Uniformity in patient preferences among psychotherapists in private practice tends to blur professional boundaries. In sum, homogeneity in clientele seems to be directly related to the degree of professional autonomy in the selection of patients.

Professional Personalities

In addition to characterizing their fellow practitioners in terms of the types of patients they treat, psychotherapists are also keenly interested in the attitudes, values, motives—in short, personalities—of other practicing therapists. Of course, psychotherapists recognize that personality characteristics of practitioners represent a very indirect measure of therapeutic behavior but, since the concealed nature of the therapeutic transaction precludes direct observation of professional performance, personal assessment of the individual therapist is generally conceded to be the best available basis for evaluation.

In order to investigate the extent to which psychotherapists anchor their personal stereotypes of colleagues in the various professional groups, the interview respondents were asked to consider whether there were personalities that they felt were characteristic of each of the four professions. As illustrated by the interview excerpts presented below, there was wide diversity in the response given to the question.

As a psychiatric social worker put it:

> Clinical psychologists tend to be more interested in research; they are more experimentally oriented people. The types of personalities coming into social work are those people who are flexible, have a certain amount of warmth, a certain amount of acceptance, and a desire to be helpful.

According to a clinical psychologist:

> I don't think it's so much a matter of personality as of training and ability. I think there are all sorts of personality types in psychiatry as there are in clinical psychology and psychiatric social work.

A psychiatrist said:

Psychologists tend to be individuals who value analytical and intellectual approaches. The psychologist is more interested in theory than the social worker. The social worker is motivated by impulses that are maternal and nurturing in character and are more concerned with the welfare of others than in an experience of an intellectual type.

Another psychiatrist evaluated professional personalities as follows:

In a general way, the psychiatrist has more of a clinical orientation, dealing more with the totality of the patient. He tends to be more effective in his work. Psychologists tend to be more intellectual, more cerebral about their work; they are less clinical. Social workers still carry a bit of the old social work image of "lady bountiful." They either tend to be slightly overpermissive or bend over backward to be the opposite. In their personalities, social workers tend to be more giving and sometimes more easily exploited by patients because of this.

A third psychiatrist expressed the following opinions:

I think that a lot of men who end up as clinical psychologists or psychiatric social workers are people who, because of their own problems, might not be able to become physicians. Also, it takes a certain type of person to be able to deal with the low income attached to being a clinical psychologist or a psychiatric social worker and the rather marginal or fringe position they hold if they go into private practice. I think this is especially true of men who enter psychiatric social work or clinical psychology.

For purposes of analysis, the specific personality characteristics attributed to typical members of the various mental health professions that bore some similarity to each other were combined into a single category and those categories representing at least 5 percent of the responses were enumerated. Using the resulting nine categories, Table 5 presents respondents' descriptions of the personalities that they believe are characteristic of the various professions.

The relationship between personality characteristics and professional affiliation is clearly most pronounced for clinical psychology. The personality characteristics most frequently used to describe clinical psychologists were "theoretical," "intellectual," and "able to conceptualize." In fact, the most frequent discrete response used to characterize any of the professions was "clinical psychologists are interested in theoretical matters and intellectual approaches." Even disparaging remarks about clinical psychologists stress their intellectual or theoretical characteristics: 11 percent of the sample claimed that members of this profession characteristically "overintellectualize" and "overtheorize."

Table 5. PROFESSIONAL DIFFERENCES IN TERMS OF PERSONALITY

Descriptions of Personalities	Percent of Respondents
Psychiatrists are authoritarian; have a godlike complex	12.5
Psychiatrists want to heal the sick; they are patient-oriented	9.0
Clinical psychologists are interested in theory; intellectual approach	21.5
Clinical psychologists are intelligent; able to conceptualize	11.5
Clinical psychologists compete with psychiatrists	10.5
Clinical psychologists overintellectualize	10.5
Clinical psychologists are aggressive	6.5
Psychiatric social workers are people-oriented, concerned with helping others, dedicated, maternal, nursing	21.0
Psychiatric social workers are passive	18.0

NOTE: N = 200—45 psychoanalysts, 47 psychiatrists, 50 clinical psychologists, and 58 psychiatric social workers. The percentages total more than 100 because each respondent could mention more than one characteristic.

Table 5 also reveals two other closely related characteristics that respondents attribute to the personalities of clinical psychologists; these professionals are seen as competitive—particularly with psychiatrists—and aggressive. Seventeen percent of the sample mentioned one or the other characteristic in describing clinical psychologists. There were, moreover, no significant differences in the frequency with which the various professions attributed these specific responses to clinical psychologists. The interpretation of these findings will be deferred until the data are reclassified in terms of total positive and negative personality characteristics attributed to each professional ground and presented in Table 6. That table will provide support for the assertion that the dominant conception of clinical psychologists is overwhelmingly negative. In the context of the findings in Table 5, this suggests that the most prevalent image among other psychotherapists is that clinical psychologists are characteristically intellectually aggressive and competitive as well as impractically overintellectual.

The only response category in Table 5 containing significantly different proportions of respondents from the various professional groups referred to psychiatrists who were characterized as "authoritarian," "rigid," and having a "godlike complex." Almost a quarter of the clinical psychologists mentioned one of the qualities as characteristic of psychiatrists' personalities as did a sixth of the psychiatric social workers. In contrast, less than 5 percent of members of either group of medical professionals mentioned any of these characteristics. The large proportion of clinical psychologists who attributed these strongly negative personality characteristics to psychiatrists lends considerable credence to those who claimed that clinical psychologists compete with psychiatrists. Another 9 percent of the sample described psychiatrists as wanting to heal the sick and as the "most patient-oriented" professional group. However, there were no significant interprofessional differences in the frequency with which these relatively neutral qualities were seen as characteristic of the personalities of psychiatrists.

The personality characteristics that respondents used to describe psychiatric social workers clearly reflect the traditional cultural image of the profession as a female vocation. Consequently, descriptions of social workers were heavily weighted with terms commonly thought to be feminine qualities. For example, 21 percent of the entire sample described social workers as characteristically "people-oriented," "concerned with helping others," "dedicated," "maternal," or "nursing." Another 18 percent of the sample described these professionals as characteristically "passive." There were no significant interprofessional differences in the prevalence of these views of the personalities characteristic of psychiatric social workers.

These nine categories represent the only responses that were made by more than 5 percent of the entire interview sample. In order to include those discrete responses representing less than ten members of the sample in the analysis as well as to obtain a more general view of the relative frequency with which favorable and unfavorable personality characteristics were attributed to the various professions, the data were reclassified. Responses pertaining to each profession were classified as either positive, neutral, or negative. Very few of the neutral responses referred to personality characteristics. Almost all these responses were descriptive statements about the profession such as "psychiatrists want to heal the sick, they are patient-oriented." For this reason, the proportion of neutral characteristics attributed to each profession is not included in Table 6, which presents the relative frequency with which favorable (positive) and unfavorable (negative) personality traits were used to characterize each professional group.

Superficial inspection of Table 6 immediately reveals the advantages of classifying the personality characteristics attributed to each professional group in terms of whether they are positive or negative attributes. For example, no specific attributes were held to characterize the person-

Table 6. POSITIVE AND NEGATIVE PERSONALITY CHARACTERISTICS OF THE DIFFERENT MENTAL HEALTH PROFESSIONS

Attributed Personality Characteristics	Percent of Respondents
Analysts	
Positive Characteristics	8.0
Negative Characteristics	1.0
Psychiatrists	
Positive Characteristics	0.0
Negative Characteristics	12.5
Psychologists	
Positive Characteristics	14.0
Negative Characteristics	28.5
Social Workers	
Positive Characteristics	27.0
Negative Characteristics	23.5

NOTE: N = 200—45 psychoanalysts, 47 psychiatrists, 50 clinical psychologists, and 58 psychiatric social workers. The percentages total more than 100 because each respondent could mention more than one characteristic.

alities of psychoanalysts by at least 5 percent of the sample; hence, no statements about the personality patterns of analysts were included in the previous table. Nevertheless, Table 6 suggests that in terms of the ratio of positive to negative personality descriptions, analysts are most favorably viewed in the sample as a whole. Eight percent of the sample made unequivocally positive statements about the personality characteristics of psychoanalysts, but only 1 percent had any unfavorable characteristics with which to describe the typical personalities of analysts. This finding suggests that the placement of psychoanalysts at the top of the professional prestige hierarchy by other psychotherapists rests on a firm foundation of overwhelmingly positive views of the "character" of individual analysts.

The next most favorable ratio of positive to negative personality characteristics is the virtually 50:50 split for psychiatric social workers. This ratio takes on added significance when note is taken of the fact that the total number of positive and negative personality traits attributed to psychiatric social workers is considerably larger than the total for any other professional group. That is, the proportion ascribing favorable personality traits to psychiatric social workers is almost twice that for clinical psychologists and more than three times that for psychoanalysts. However, these professionals are also second only to psychologists in the proportion of the sample attributing unfavorable personality characteristics to them. This finding must be interpreted in the context of the fact that psychiatric social work holds a distinctly subordinate position in the hierarchy of mental health professions. The subordinate position of psychiatric social work has both subjective and objective determinants. Subjectively, in the eyes of other professionals, psychiatric social work is the least prestigious of the four mental health professions. The lesser training of social workers is the reason most frequently cited by practitioners for placing psychiatric social work at the bottom of the professional prestige ladder in the mental health field. Objectively, when psychiatric social workers work in institutions that employ members of the other three professions, they characteristically hold subordinate positions and rarely are in positions that permit them to exercise formal authority over physicians or clinical psychologists. Thus, for other mental health professionals, psychiatric social workers constitute a highly visible but relatively nonthreatening professional group. Consequently, members of the other three professional groups are relatively uninhibited in their search for personality traits with which to characterize the "typical" psychiatric social worker. The equanimity with which the other three professional groups view psychiatric social workers is also reflected in the fact that there are no significant interprofessional differences in the relative frequency with which respondents attributed either positive or negative personality traits to psychiatric social workers.

Finally, we can now examine the two professional groups that are most interesting in terms of the personality characteristics ascribed to them: psychiatrists and clinical psychologists. Of the interview respondents, 12.5 percent mentioned unfavorable personality characteristics in connection with psychiatrists whereas not one respondent described the personalities of psychiatrists in favorable terms. This suggests that respondents reserved any favorable attributes they saw in physicians for their characterization of psychoanlysts and relegated all the unfavorable traits of medical psychotherapists to psychiatrists. As a result, analysts have the highest ratio of positive to negative personality characteristics attributed to them while psychiatrists have the largest ratio of negative to positive characteristics of the four professional groups. As was the case in Table 5, clinical psychologists are most likely to view psychiatrists in terms of negative personality characteristics; psychiatric social workers follow psychologists in this respect, but there is a distinct difference in the prevalence with which these two groups assign negative traits to psychiatrists

—24 percent of the responses of psychologists were negative while the corresponding figure for social workers was 16 percent. Psychoanalysts and psychiatrists are equally likely to attribute negative personality characteristics—4 percent of the responses of each group were unfavorable. On the basis of these findings, it appears that nonmedical psychotherapists as well as general psychiatrists make a clear-cut distinction between psychoanalysts and psychiatrists whereas analysts, who are also psychiatrists, do not. That is, respondents in each group were least prone to ascribe unfavorable personality characteristics to members of their own profession. Since psychoanalysts see themselves as psychiatrists, it is natural that they were no more likely than psychiatrists to assign disparaging characteristics to psychiatrists.

In many respects, clinical psychology represents the strategic case. Table 5 revealed that the cluster of personality traits of clinical psychologists that were most salient to members of all professions included "theoretical," "intellectual," "conceptual," and aggressively "competitive." Table 6 reveals that the dominant evaluation of these characteristics, when applied to clinical psychologists, is overwhelmingly negative. Clinical psychologists received a larger proportion of unfavorable descriptions than any other professional group. Although psychiatric social workers also received a large number of negative attributes, they also received the largest proportion of positive descriptions; the proportion of favorable remarks about the characteristic personalities in social work is almost twice that of clinical psychology. Moreover, every positive characterization of the personalities of psychologists was offset by two negative descriptions.

In view of the fact that clinical psychologists are most critical of the characteristic personality of psychiatrists and were accued of competing with psychiatrists by more than 10 percent of the sample (Table 5), it would be reasonable to expect the brunt of the negative characteristics attributed to psychologists to come from psychiatrists. Surprisingly, this is not the case. Psychoanalysts, not psychiatrists, are most likely to ascribe unfavorable personality characteristics to clinical psychologists. Moreover, psychologists were not more likely than other professionals to describe psychoanalysts in negative terms—and no professional group had many unfavorable remarks to make about analysts. Fully 44 percent of the psychoanalysts, compared with 30 percent of the psychiatrists, made unfavorable assessments of the personality types they saw as characteristic of clinical psychologists. This reveals a fundamental asymmetry in interprofessional relationships among the mental health groups: psychologists are unfavorably disposed toward psychiatrists—in terms of the personality characteristics they attribute to psychiatrists—but not toward psychoanalysts; whereas analysts, much more than psychiatrists, are most critical of the personality characteristics of psychologists. This finding merits further consideration.

The fact that clinical psychologists are the primary source of unfavorable descriptions of psychiatrists is not difficult to explain, if we take into account the social location of the four professional groups in the mental health field. That is, in our sample of practicing psychotherapists there was general agreement that, when the four professionals were ranked in terms of prestige, psychoanalysts were at the top, followed by psychiatrists, clinical psychologists, and finally psychiatric social workers. As a relative newcomer to the mental health field, clinical psychology has been challenging the prestige, authority, and, in many cases, prerogatives (such as private practice) of the more established professions engaged in the treatment of mental illness. There are several reasons why this challenge is most focally directed at psychiatrists. Psychiatric social workers pose little threat; this profession, by virtue of its limited training program, sex composition, and traditional orientation, has considerably lower status than clinical psychology. It also has no important functions or prerogatives that clinical psychologists want—such as private practice. Psychoanalysts have the greatest prestige among the mental health professionals; but, for a variety of reasons, psychologists are reluctant to make unfavorable remarks about these practitioners. Psychoanalysts are, of course, the high priests of psychoanalytic theory and as such they are inappropriate targets for psychologists' attacks on medical-organic and pharmacologic approaches to the treatment of personality disorders. Another factor restraining clinical psychologists from criticizing psychoanalysts is that analysts are almost exclusively in private practice. Most clinical psychologists are primarily engaged in organizational practice settings directed by psychiatrists. As a consequence, clinical psychologists have less contact with psychoanalysts than with psychiatrists and, at the same time, are frequently subordinate to psychiatrists in institutional settings. Thus, to the extent that an upwardly mobile profession strives to dislodge the particular group that is directly above it in status and privileges and with which it comes into frequent contact and conflict, we would expect clinical psychologists to be much more critical of psychiatrists than of psychoanalysts.

Assuming that the foregoing is a plausible explanation for the descriptions clinical psychologists gave of the personality characteristics of psychiatrists, why are psychoanalysts, rather than psychiatrists, most critical of clinical psychologists? That is, each of the factors discussed above can be used to suggest that, of all the professional groups, psychiatrists should be most negative in their descriptions of the personality characteristics of clinical psychologists. Specifically, psychiatry, not psychoanalysis, is most directly threatened (and actually attacked) by clinical psychology; psychiatrists, not psychoanalysts, actually interact with psychologists in various types of mental health institutions; psychiatrists, far more than analysts, base their prestige and authority on their medical status and tend to find the psychosocial orientation to which psychologists are limited, by their training and by law, somewhat alien. Yet, in spite of all these factors, the greatest volume of antagonistic comment with respect to clinical psychologists comes from psychoanalysts rather than psychiatrists. What factors underlie this paradox?

The only explanation that can be offered is clearly speculative; we have no data that either support or contradict these views. Nevertheless, several factors seem to be operative: the greater salience of the medical-nonmedical distinction to psychiatrists than to psychoanalysts; the greater importance to psychoanalysts of "theoretical," "intellectual," "conceptual" considerations; and the similarity between the possessions of analysts and the aspirations of clinical psychologists. Specifically, we have repeatedly argued that the medical-nonmedical distinction is more salient to psychiatrists than to psychoanalysts, in spite of the fact that analysts themselves are psychiatrists. To the extent that this is true, psychiatrists feel more secure and isolated from the encroachment of clinical psychologists than do psychoanalysts—who view themselves as "doctors of the psyche," that is, as the specialists in psychopathology. Clinical psychologists are challenging the medical basis of this "psychopathological" expertise; they are not, however, challenging the psychosomatic or biological jurisdiction of the more organically and psychopharmacologically oriented general psychiatrists. Thus, the very psychological orientation that distinguishes psychoanalysts from psychiatrists makes the former group more threatened by the entrance and growth of clinical psychology in the mental health field. Another related factor is that psychoanalysts were accorded undisputed acclaim as the "theoreticians" and "antimechanistic" practitioners in the mental health field—until the post-World War II immigration of clinical psychologists into the professional arena. Lacking medical training, and concomitant status, but relatively sophisticated in psychological theory, clinical psychologists were the first professionals to challenge the intellectual prominence of psychoanaylsts. These developments provided a firm basis for psychoanalysts to develop antagonistic views of clinical psychologists—manifested here in their unfavorable descriptions of the personality types that characteristically enter psychology. These developments also laid the foundation for the development of asymmetrical interprofessional relationships among the mental health professions. Specifically, clinical psychologists view psychoanalysts as theoretically similar allies, in contrast to their views of psychiatrists, whereas analysts perceive clinical psychologists as a threat to their intellectual prominence in the mental health field. By extending the challenge beyond intellectual concerns to practical issues, clinical psychologists provided psychoanalysts with another reason for being antagonistic toward psychology. That is, clinical psychologists have openly acknowledged the desire to participate in the rewards (both material and immaterial) that accrue to private psychotherapeutic practice. The professional literature is replete with references to the desire on the part of many clinical psychologists to become "junior psychoanalysts," that is, private practitioners. In this respect, psychologists represent a greater threat to psychoanalysts than to psychiatrists.

We have suggested at least some of the factors that appear to be responsible for psychoanalysts' unfavorable descriptions of the personalities characteristic of clinical psychologists. All these speculations represent an a posteriori attempt to account for a totally unanticipated finding; taken together, however, they make the asymmetrical interprofessional relationships revealed in Table 6 more comprehensible.

The data in Table 6 suggest that psychiatric social workers are much less antagonistic to psychologists and much more critical of psychiatrists than the extant literature on interprofessional role relations indicates. (Rushing, 1964; Zander, Cohen, and Stotland, 1957). That is, social workers mention almost as few unfavorable personality characteristics of clinical psychologists as do the psychologists themselves. In contrast, they attribute considerably more unfavorable characteristics to the personalities in psychiatry than do either psychiatrists or psychoanalysts. If the proportions of favorable and unfavorable personality traits seen as characteristic of a professional group are a reflection of more general positive and negative attitudes toward that group, as we have assumed throughout this discussion, then psychiatric social workers are more unfavorably disposed toward psychiatrists than toward psychologists—relative to the rest of the sample. This contradicts the prevailing conceptions, based on earlier studies by Zander and colleagues (1957) and Rushing (1964), that psychiatric social workers resent the intrusion of the more highly trained clinical psychologists into their field and are threatened by competition with this group; these studies also reported that psychiatric social workers were extremely positive toward psychiatrists.

The most obvious reason for the disparity between our data and the findings of other studies on the attitudes of psychiatric social workers toward both psychologists and psychiatrists, is that these previous investigations did not distinguish between psychoanalysts and general psychiatrists. There are sound reasons for believing that psychiatric social workers have extremely favorable opinions of psychoanalysts. Thus, when psychoanalysts and psychiatrists are both subsumed under the label "psychiatrists" as in other studies, the high regard for psychoanalysts overshadowed and obscured the unfavorable opinions psychiatric social workers held about psychiatrists. Consequently, these studies found social workers to express more favorable views about "psychiatrists" (analysts and psychiatrists) than about clinical psychologists. By differentiating these two groups, the data in this study suggest that psychiatric social workers hold relatively unfavorable views about psychiatrists and, compared with the rest of the sample, are surprisingly uncritical of the personality characteristics of clinical psychologists. This finding may reflect two considerations: first, that psychiatric social work is no longer actively competing with clinical psychology for status, prestige, or positions in the mental health field and, second, that psychiatric social workers tend to be a subordinate to psychiatrists, rather than clinical psychologists, in multiprofessional organizational settings in the mental health field.

Conclusion

In view of the extensive literature describing interprofessional conflict and competition in the mental health field, it is not surprising that the evidence we have presented indicates that existing relationships among the core psychotherapeutic professions are somewhat less than ideally harmonious. It should be noted, however, that our examination of professional relations among mental health practitioners also produced several findings that tend to corroborate some of the generalizations emerging from previous studies that were designed to document sources of professional cohesiveness and consensus. It is not difficult to explain the paradoxical position of the present study. The primary focus of previous studies was either on structural uniformity and value homogeneity or on structural diversity and value diversity. Up to the present, little consideration has been given to identifying forces operating simultaneously to produce professional consensus and cleavage in the psychotherapeutic professions. The identification of these forces sets the present study apart from a sizable portion of the extant literature on the mental health field.

In assessing interprofessional relations in the mental health field, the paradox of increasing heterogeneity and increasing homogeneity emerges as a critical factor. The proliferation of practitioners from diverse professional backgrounds claiming the right to perform therapy, the rise of new treatment ideologies, and innovations in treatment settings have combined to markedly increase the degree of intraprofessional diversity. At the same time, older sources of diversity, based on functional specialization by profession, have receded in the face of the combined influences of public opinion and governmental policies that have made mental health professionals accountable for an increasing range of human problems. As a consequence of this trend, professional specialization in the mental health field is being reduced by increased functional similarity.

While these innovations in the modalities of professional practice in the mental health field have been under way for some time, there have been few corresponding changes in the social organization of the separate psychotherapeutic professions. Each of the professions has maintained its own distinct program of professional training. Similarly, each profession has its own entrance requirements, certification procedures, occupational subculture, and formal association. Each professional group also pays homage, in its own way, to the principles of colleague control, limited sphere of competence, and individual professional responsibility. Finally, and perhaps most importantly, each occupational group has developed its own elaborate system of professional socialization. This process of professional socialization is designed to produce a high level of identification of self with professional role and involves the systematic manipulation of the attitudes, values, and motivations of future practitioners. Although the actual mechanisms of professional socialization differ in the four professions, each occupational group is pursuing the same general objective; namely, inculcating a strong emotional commitment to a specific professional identity. We earlier suggested that the skills associated with the performance of individual, one-to-one therapy represent the core of professional identity in each of the mental health professions. Since the individual therapeutic transaction is not accessible to outside observers, inference and conjecture become, by necessity, the principles by which practitioners assess the professional identity of their colleagues. Since the therapist's own personality constitutes the basic professional tool in the therapeutic encounter, it is natural for colleagues to base their conjectures on their understanding of the individual practitioner's attitudes, values, and motivations. Thus, configurations of personality attributes become intertwined with dimensions of professional identity to such an extent that interest in the attitudes and values of fellow practitioners leads to a preoccupation with the social status and prestige of the professional groups with which they are affiliated. Undoubtedly, this is one major reason why we found the relative prestige of the various professional groups to be a powerful determinant of the interprofessional views of mental health practitioners. Specifically, the distinct prestige differences among psychoanalysts, psychiatrists, clinical psychologists, and psychiatric social workers resulted in all but analysts being characterized primarily in terms of negative personality attributes. The high degree of interprofessional consensus with regard to the clientele served and treatment techniques utilized stands in direct contrast to the pervasive conflict at the level of professional personalities. In sum, psychotherapists apparently understand fairly well what their colleagues in other professions are doing but this does not alter their generally negative stereotypes of the kinds of persons working in the other professions. To the extent that the way a professional relates to his colleagues is influenced by his image of them, reduction in the current level of interprofessional conflict can be brought about only by reducing the prestige differentials currently existing among the four mental health professions.

3

The Organization of Professional Practice

Although interrelated in many respects, practicing psychoanalysts, psychiatrists, clinical psychologists, and psychiatric social workers represent the end product of separate, distinct training programs, which vary not only in the amount and types of specialized training but also in the intensity of professional socialization that aspirants are required to undergo in order to obtain certification as qualified practitioners. These differences in training programs should not, however, obscure the fact that professional specialization in the mental health field has been markedly reduced by recent social and political movements that have tended to make psychotherapists accountable for an ever-increasing range of human problems. As a consequence of these developments, not only do analysts, psychiatrists, clinical psychologists, and psychiatric social workers share a societal mandate to care for the mentally ill but, to the extent that the role-allocating processes in the mental health field are no longer under the exclusive control of the separate professions, they also share a common set of skills and techniques for implementing the mandate.

The blurring of professional boundaries in the distribution of roles within mental health facilities has important implications for patterns of interprofessional relations in the mental health field. The blurring of professional distinctions has even more important implications for the social organization of the established professions in the field. That is, to the extent that the maintenance of professional authority is contingent upon the ability of a group of practitioners to maintain exclusive jurisdiction over a specialized body of knowledge and associated activities and to demonstrate the linkages among skills, doctrine, and existing training programs, the phenomenon of role-blurring suggests that the traditional bases of professional authority are being undermined in the mental health field.

In one sense, of course, the existence of a threat to the authority of established professions in the mental health field is not problematic. That is, there is a sizable body of literature documenting the extent to which bureaucratic features of psychiatric institutions stifle professional claims to exclusive spheres of competence and foster the desegregation of professional roles (Rushing, 1964; Greenblatt, Levinson, and Williams, 1957). Such studies have clearly demonstrated that mental health organizations are not simply places where individuals from various professions come together to enact standard occupational roles but rather places where professional roles are constantly being developed, often in a climate of interoccupational competition and conflict. To the extent that organizational practitioners hold different views on such basic issues as the etiology of mental illness, the nature of personality, and the nature of therapy, it is not surprising that conflict seems to be endemic to mental health institutions. Although these issues obviously affect many spheres of professional life, they all reflect change and variability at the level of professional practice. The institutional setting of professional practice has become increasingly more dynamic in recent years, but there have been few corresponding changes in the social organization of the separate mental health professions. Each profession has maintained its own standardized training program, designed to insure that the individual acquires the appropriate professional norms, as well as technical and theoretical skills necessary for the achievement of basic service goals. However, formal training is not the only mechanism by which the professional groups attempt to control individual members; the four therapeutic professions also attempt to control professional practice by molding selected aspects of the individual's character in order to produce a strong emotional commitment to a specific professional identity by creating a high level of identification of self with professional role. Since we have little systematic evidence on the ways in which professonal identity affects the lives of practitioners variously situated in the mental health field, the existence of threats to this latter dimension of professional control is distinctly problematic. Specifically, we have neither baseline data from which to measure changes in professional identities nor any systematic knowledge of the extent to which professional identity influences professional behavior. Consequently, it is not clear whether the discontinuity between specialized training and diversified practice indicates that the residue of professional socialization is becoming less salient in the lives of practitioners or simply reflects the proliferation of specialized training programs within each of the professions. At issue then is the question of how mental health practitioners become attached to various patterns of action such that their activities conform to institutionalized modes of professional conduct. This issue is problematic because the extant literature dealing with the mental health professions has tended to discuss career commitments without specifying "the conditions under which commitments actually come into being" (Becker, 1960, p. 35). The nature of committed action is not difficult to specify in sociological terms. For example, Goffman (1961) uses the term to refer to a type of orientation to a social role that is based on "impersonally enforced structural arrangements" and describes the nature of commitment in the following manner: "An individual becomes committed to something when, because of the fixed and interdependent character of many institutional arrangements, his doing or being this something irrevocably conditions other important possibilities in his life, forcing him to take courses of action, causing other persons to build up their activity on the basis of his continuing in his current undertakings, and rendering him vulnerable to unanticipated consequences of these undertakings. He, thus, becomes locked into a position and coerced into living up to the promises and sacrifices built into it" (pp. 88–89).

Since we are interested in the bases of commitment, our major concern is with the conditions under which professional groups or organizations succeed in placing a "social claim" on various patterns of professional action such that practitioners become obliged to engage in their performance. Thus, we are primarily concerned with the social relationships and organizational arrangements involved in eliciting action patterns rather than the attitude of the individual toward his professional role. In particular, we are interested in the relative salience of organizational claims and professional claims in determining how mental health practitioners become committed to various professional roles.

Professional schools are designed to produce graduates who have developed a commitment to professional roles and not organizational roles. In the mental health professions, the training systems have a dual focus. On the one hand, they are designed to produce graduates who have acquired technical expertise in a limited sphere of activity. On the other hand, they are designed to insure that the graduate develops the appropriate professional values, attitudes, and self-conceptions. While it is widely recognized that a diversity of factors contributes to the achievement of these desired outcomes, each profession attempts to organize its training program so that it incorporates the significant transformation experiences. Training systems thus contain within them an image of the fully formed professional and a model of the process of transformation required to realize that image. In the mental health field, the professional image revolves around the specialized social interaction skills of the psychotherapists. The process of transformation consists of a series of developmental stages, with the early levels placing primary emphasis on intellectual preparation and the later stages stressing practical experiences. Obviously, the extent to which the practitioner is bound to institutionalized patterns of action by social ties originating in these training systems depends on the nature of available professional roles.

Cluster Analysis of Roles

In an attempt to determine the roles performed by mental health professionals, we asked the respondents to indicate the average number of hours per week spent in nineteen different activities. The responses were used to calculate the proportion of each individual's time accounted for by each of the activities. The intercorrelations of all possible pairs of items were then computed and a cluster analysis performed to determine the sets of activities that were sufficiently highly related as to constitute a role "cluster" (Tryon, 1939). The results of that analysis are presented in Table 7.

Before turning to a discussion of the substantive findings contained in Table 7, a few technical details should be mentioned. First, within each box in the table the average relationship of each activity with the other activities in the cluster is presented. To meet the requirements of cluster analysis, two patterns should be revealed in the table. First, each activity should show its highest relationship with items in its own cluster. By looking at each row in the table we see that this requirement is met. Second, for each column in the table, the relationships within the box should be higher than all the relationships outside the box. This is true for each column. We can conclude that each activity within a given cluster is highly related to each other activity and that each activity has a lesser relationship with other clusters and with unclustered activities. This means that the roles, as defined by the clusters of related activities, are mutually exclusive.

Turning to the specific clusters, we find the following content represented in each set.

Cluster A—Group Therapist. This cluster, composed of group therapy and family or marriage therapy, strongly emphasizes the role of

Table 7. CLUSTER ANALYSIS: PERCENT OF TIME SPENT IN VARIOUS ACTIVITIES

Cluster	Activities	Cluster A	Cluster B	Cluster C	Cluster D	Cluster E
A	Group Therapy	**.097**	−.065	−.022	−.079	−.050
	Family and/or Marriage Therapy	**.097**	−.088	.022	−.092	−.077
B	Psychoanalysis	−.118	**.075**	−.125	−.128	−.037
	Professional Associations	−.037	**.075**	−.038	−.017	.046
C	Diagnosis and Referral	−.011	−.099	**.116**	−.093	−.091
	Case write-up	.028	−.132	**.179**	−.117	−.108
	Clerical	−.011	0	**.052**	−.056	−.020
	Testing and Interpretation	−.017	−.094	**.043**	−.077	−.039
D	Administration	−.105	−.088	−.100	**.044**	−.059
	Training and Supervising Trainees	−.065	−.041	−.072	**.044**	−.049
E	Teaching	−.058	0	−.072	−.038	**.099**
	Research	−.076	−.064	−.071	−.061	**.070**
	Writing	−.048	−.026	−.072	−.039	**.119**
	Reading Professional Literature	−.072	.063	−.047	−.078	**.074**
	Somatic Therapy	−.031	−.047	−.045	−.072	−.041
	Individual Therapy	.019	−.122	−.080	−.280	−.168
	Community Mental Health	−.030	−.039	−.049	−.031	−.039
	Consulting	−.059	−.065	−.030	−.036	−.031
	Education	−.007	−.005	.001	−.075	−.003

social and interpersonal factors in the treatment of mental illness. The emphasis on family therapy apparently reflects the view that family interaction is an important agent in the etiology of mental illness. However, this cluster reflects little concern for broad social and environmental factors that extend beyond the boundaries of small-group interaction. That is, the activities in this cluster are not related to other items such as consulting or community mental health.

Cluster B—Psychoanalyst. The activities contained in this cluster provide a clear behavioral portrait of the highly specialized world of the practicing psychoanalyst. That is, the professional association referred to here is undoubtedly a psychoanalytic association affiliated with a psychoanalytic institute. Similarly, the performance of psychoanalysis is negatively correlated with the performance of other types of individual or group psychotherapy. In brief, the role of the psychoanalyst is both unique and uniform.

Cluster C—Diagnostician. The activities contained in this cluster (diagnosis and referral, case write-up, clerical duties, and testing and interpretation) provide a comprehensive description of the process of screening and labeling patients performed by mental health professionals. The role of the diagnostician requires him to classify patients and allocate them to various mental health facilities, rather than to assume personal responsibility for their treatment.

Cluster D—Administrator. This cluster, composed of administration and supervision of trainees, indicates that these two activities tend to be combined in organizations that employ mental health professionals. This cluster is unique in that it involves service to other professionals, rather than to patients, and, hence, it is a role that we might expect to be performed by the elite in each profession.

Cluster E—Academician. This cluster, composed of classroom teaching, research activities, writing, and reading professional literature, is straightforward and needs no extended discussion.

In addition to the five clusters it should be noted that five activities showed no strong relationship to any of the other activities and, hence, are listed as isolates in the table. Two of these activities, individual psychotherapy and education (that is, attending classes and participating in professional study groups) are isolates because they are highly specialized functions performed by professionals who do not engage extensively in other activities. The other three activities, somatic therapy, community mental health, and consulting, are isolates because they account for a small proportion of the time of all professionals. Thus, the five role clusters plus the isolated activities of individual psychotherapy and education make up the dominant professional roles in the mental health field. Given the content of these roles, it is clear that, if professional training experiences provide the "social cement" that binds the practitioner to his professional role, then psychoanalysts, psychiatrists, clinical psychologists, and psychiatric social workers should be differentially distributed among the available roles. Moreover, differences among members of the four professional groups should directly correspond to variations in the degree of fit between training experiences and the content of the various roles.

Roles and Professional Ideologies

We have already documented the fact that the dominant ethos of the training programs of both psychoanalysts and clinical psychologists revolves around the belief that the ability to modify human behavior is primarily dependent upon the ability to explain it in terms of cause and effect relationships (Henry, Sims, and Spray, 1971). This is achieved by analysts through the constantly evolving body of psychoanalytic theory and by psychologists through the constant application of the scientific method. These professional ideologies contrast sharply with those of psychiatry and social work. For the latter two groups, systems of causation are not of such overwhelming importance; they are not as inextricably tied to what is done. Both professions are more pragmatically oriented, concerned more with the how rather than the why. Psychiatry is focused on treatment per se, on the alleviation of the symptom; social work is focused on caring for the socially handicapped and on creating social reform. The intellectual goals of understanding per se and of contributing to professional knowledge are less salient for both psychiatry and psychiatric social work. To the extent, then, that these training systems instill in their students a particular orientation toward professional work, we would expect graduates of various programs to gravitate toward roles that provide support for their work orientation. To examine this possibility, we assigned each professional to the particular cluster of activities that accounted for the largest proportion of his or her time. Table 8 presents the results of this procedure. Somatic therapy, community mental health, and consulting do not appear in the table because the small number of professionals classified under each heading precluded meaningful comparison.*

* Specifically, when psychoanalysts were classified according to the activities that accounted for the largest proportion of their time, only 7 fell into the category somatic therapy, 7 in the category community mental health, and 1 in the category consulting. For psychiatrists, the comparable figures were 34 in the somatic therapy category, 16 community mental health, and 8 consulting. Similarly, 4 clinical psychologists were classified in the somatic therapy category, 8 in the community mental health category, and 49 in the category labeled consulting. Finally, for psychiatric social workers the figures were somatic therapy, 11; community mental health, 20; and consulting, 24.

Table 8. Distribution of Roles by Profession

PROFESSION

Percent and (Base Number)

Professional Roles	Psychoanalyst	Psychiatrist	Clinical Psychologist	Psychiatric Social Worker	Total
Group Therapist	1.8 (11)	2.2 (15)	3.3 (46)	6.8 (75)	3.9 (147)
Psychoanalyst	47.0 (293)	6.1 (41)	7.1 (100)	1.2 (13)	11.8 (447)
Diagnostician	0.6 (4)	4.7 (32)	16.0 (224)	14.2 (156)	10.9 (416)
Administrator	6.4 (40)	12.4 (84)	13.9 (195)	34.1 (374)	18.2 (693)
Academician	8.3 (52)	9.6 (65)	21.0 (296)	6.9 (76)	12.9 (489)
Individual Psychotherapist	24.6 (153)	48.8 (330)	27.7 (389)	27.1 (298)	30.8 (1170)
Professional Educator	11.2 (70)	16.1 (109)	11.0 (154)	9.7 (106)	11.5 (439)
Total	99.9 (623)	99.9 (676)	100 (1404)	100 (1098)	100 (3801)

To a certain extent the role the practitioner becomes committed to is related to the type of program in which he received his training. The pragmatic treatment concerns of psychiatrists are reflected in their pronounced preference for the role of individual psychotherapist. The preoccupation of psychiatric social workers with social reform and caring for social-system casualties pushes them in the direction of becoming either administrators or individual psychotherapists. The intellectual and profession-oriented concerns of psychoanalysts are, of course, reflected in the heavy concentration in the role of psychoanalyst. That is, psychoanalysts are trained not only to develop causal explanations of human behavior but also to do so within the confines of the Freudian psychoanalytic framework. The profession is defined in terms of a single theoretical framework, and a major responsibility of all psychoanalysts is to contribute to the continual elaboration of that particular model. As a result, the role of psychoanalyst simultaneously serves the dual purpose of treatment and research for practicing analysts.

Unlike psychoanalysts, clinical psychologists acquire occupational skills that do not revolve around the application of a single theoretical framework but, instead, focus on the ability to develop explanatory statements by relying on the scientific method. Clinical psychologists acquire these skills by being trained in academic institutions where the requirements include courses in research methods and the successful completion of a dissertation. In addition, many practitioners enter the clinical program only after receiving some training in other branches of psychology. The clinical psychologist's flair for conceptualization and scientific methodology is reflected in the fact that psychologists constitute more than one-half of all the professionals performing the role of academician. The fact that the training of clinical psychologists focuses on a general *perspective* rather than a particular technique or set of problems probably also accounts for the fact that, as a group, psychologists are the most uniformly distributed among the seven professional roles. This distinctive feature of clinical psychology should not be allowed to obscure the fact that the training program for psychologists is similar to that of the other mental health professions, in that the professional socialization processes have, as a major objective, the acquisition of basic psychotherapeutic skills. Consequently, clinical psychology is like the other three professions in having a sizable proportion of practitioners committed to the role of individual psychotherapist.

The findings contained in Table 8 support, in general, the proposition that there is an affinity between the content of the professional training program and the type of role the practitioner will become committed to upon graduation. The findings contained in the table also suggest that variations in the *structure* of the training programs of the four professions may also serve to sort out practitioners into various roles. Specifically, the literature contains some evidence to the effect that the lack of a clearly defined body of professional knowledge and technical skills facilitates the maintenance of a general "lay" conception of an occupation throughout the socialization process while training organized around a clearly delineated body of knowledge and set of tasks leads to the rejection of the layman's conception and the substitution of a technical orientation toward the profession (Becker and Carper, 1956; Henry, Sims, and Spray, 1971). Since the training of psychiatrists and psychoanalysts is, in this sense, clearly more highly structured than that of either clinical psychologists or psychiatric social workers, this could account for the fact that the two medical groups are much more narrowly specialized in the range of roles they perform than is true of either of the nonmedical groups. This is evidenced by the fact that psychoanalysts are heavily concentrated in one role cluster and psychiatrists in one isolated activity, while clinical psychologists and social workers are much more uniformly distributed among the seven roles. Not surprisingly, the differential participation in the performance of one-to-one psychotherapy, in one form or another, distinguishes the medical from the nonmedical practitioners. Specifically, when the roles of psychoanalyst and individual psychotherapist are combined they account for an absolute majority of both psychiatrists and psychoanalysts. The corresponding figure for the two nonmedical professions is approximately one-third of the membership of each group. In fact, slightly less than four out of every ten clinical psychologists and only 35 percent of all psychiatric social workers devote the largest proportion of their time to any form of therapy, individual or group. To the extent that psychotherapy constitutes the core professional function in the mental health field, the inescapable conclusion emerging from these findings is that the vast majority of clinical psychologists and psychiatric social workers are still performing roles that are undeniably ancillary to those performed by physicians. The roles performed by clinical psychologists and psychiatric social workers are ancillary in the sense that they are composed of tasks that are not central to the primary commitment of psychiatrists and psychoanalysts and/or involve the provision to physicians of information that is not directly available to them through the performance of their therapeutic roles. The major ancillary roles performed by the nonmedical professionals are, of course, organizational roles requiring active collaboration with other institutional personnel for their successful performance. To the extent that the performance of the organizational role brings the practitioner into close contact with other mental health professionals, the problem of exclusive competence becomes critical, since the ambiguity of the function of the clinical psychologist or the psychiatric social worker is highlighted when it is viewed in the context of the roles performed by other professionals with whom they are closely linked in terms of theory and technique. Thus, the stronger the identification with treatment functions, the greater the likelihood that clinical psychologists and psychiatric social workers will come to feel that the team approach to the care of the mentally ill requires the prostitution of their professional skills. From the standpoint of those who perform organizational roles, this issue of professional identity is markedly decreased, if they do not legitimate their role performance with the same theoretical rationale that therapists use to justify their practices or if the various roles are segregated so that interprofessional contact is infrequent. Thus, the segregation of professional roles and the segregation of theoretical ideologies are two possible mechanisms by which mental health professionals may become committed to nontherapeutic roles. We will examine the second possibility first.

In his training for a profession, a student is subjected to a series of prolonged experiences designed to prepare him for his role in the professional community. The effects of these experiences may be classified into three distinct types: those that socialize aspects of the individual's personality, cognition, attitudes, and values; those that provide him with the norms, expectations, and appropriate behaviors for his assumption of professional roles; and those that allow him to acquire the specific information and the technical and theoretical skills necessary for the achievement of the service goals of the profession. In the present context, the goal is alleviation of mental distress through therapeutic practice. Given the present state of the mental health field, this latter process is, in a very real sense, training the neophyte professional to cope with uncertainty. That is, the causes, treatment, and consequences of mental illness remain, as yet, only partially understood and continue to be the subject of much public and professional controversy. In this context, both individual practitioners and professional groups have been forced to deal with mental health problems in the absence of certainty as to the most appropriate and effective preventive and therapeutic approaches or even of the consequence of various approaches. Moreover, these therapeutic actions touch upon fundamental moral issues that have not yet been resolved in the larger society.* As a result, there has been a proliferation of belief

---

* For example, the nature of many mental health treatment approaches has raised questions concerning the limits of privacy and professional confidentiality; the selective clientele of mental health professionals has broached questions about elitist tendencies among practitioners; and the introduction of professional opinions as legal evidence has generated debate over issues of personal responsibility and accountability. These are morally charged issues directly related to personal convictions.

systems that, when adhered to, permit the individual to "understand" a segment of the social world within which he must act but for which he has no scientifically tested knowledge on which to base his action. When these coherent systems of beliefs become shared and consensually validated, we may refer to them as ideologies. Specifically, mental health ideologies are generated by the difficult necessity of assuming professional responsibility for providing professional service in the face of uncertainty concerning the nature of mental illness and are maintained by the consensual validation of groups of practitioners. Since the performance of psychotherapy provides the focal point in the training of all four professional groups in the mental health field, it is understandable that the various ideologies are composed of beliefs that touch on the process of treatment. However, there is a wealth of existing evidence documenting the fact that treatment ideologies have a profound influence on all aspects of professional practice in the mental health field. Specifically, research on therapeutic ideologies has described the impressive differences between various ideological groups in the mental health field—in their formal and informal education and training; in their theories of behavior, personality, and psychopathology; in their dominant treatment approaches and techniques; in the patient population they serve; in their organizational settings, affiliations, and communication media; in their professional motivations, gratifications, and dissatisfactions; and in their personalities and personal biographies (Ehrlich and Sabshin, 1963, 1964; Gilbert and Levinson, 1956; Hollingshead and Redlich, 1958; Janowitz, 1954; Kissinger and Toler, 1964; Sundland and Barker, 1962; Sharaf and Levinson, 1957; Strauss and others, 1964; Wootton, 1963). Thus, the authors of one major investigation of psychiatric ideologies concluded: "Ideology makes a difference in the organization of treatment: in what is done to and for the patients and in the accompanying divisions of labor" (Strauss and others, 1964, p. 361.) This strongly suggests that the particular ideological position adhered to by the practitioner may determine the type of professional role to which he becomes committed.

Measurement of Therapeutic Ideologies

In order to obtain information on the treatment ideologies of mental health professionals, the following question was included on the survey questionnaire: "Considering that there are many therapeutic orientations, approaches, or schools of thought in the mental health field —such as Freudian, Jungian, Adlerian, Rankian, Rogerian, Existential, Social Psychiatric, Community, Somatic, Pharmacologic, etc.,—would you please specify, as accurately as such labels permit, what therapeutic orientation(s), school(s) of thought, or approach(es) best characterize your work? (If eclectic, please specify the components of your orientation)." The respondent was then asked to consider the following related question: "If you have listed more than one orientation, approach, or school of thought, please underline the *one* which you judge to be the *most* important in characterizing your current work." Each respondent's most important "therapeutic orientation" and up to three additional orientations he specified were classified into one of nine categories: psychoanalytic, neo-Freudian–ego psychological, Sullivanian, Rogerian, existential, eclectic, social psychiatric–community mental health, somatic–organic–pharmacologic, and unclassifiable. When the responses to the first questionnaire item were classified into these categories, fully 57 percent of all the respondents designated their major therapeutic orientation as being psychoanalytic. Since no other ideological position secured allegiance from more than 14 percent of the sample, the psychoanalytic orientation clearly holds a position of unparalleled popularity in the mental health professions. This ideological position was also unique in another important respect: When the data on respondents' major and additional therapeutic orientations were examined simultaneously, fully 53 percent of the 2013 practitioners who listed psychoanalytic as their major orientation claimed they had no additional orientation. Since the vast majority of respondents who claimed that their most important orientation was something other than psychoanalytic also listed at least one additional orientation that differed sufficiently from their primary orientation as to require classification in a different category, the psychoanalytic position emerges as uniquely homogeneous. The high proportion of psychoanalytically oriented practitioners who adhere to a pure psychoanalytic ideological position is somewhat surprising. Specifically, it is plausible to expect the most popular and prestigious orientation to embrace a larger number of variant perspectives and to receive the allegiance of more diverse adherents than less popular or visible positions. This would suggest that the proportion of psychoanalytically oriented practitioners who are ideological purists should be lower than the proportion of purists who adhere to other, less popular, and less generally familiar orientations. This line of reasoning seems to be discredited by our data. A possible alternative explanation is that the very popularity, visibility, and prestige of the psychoanalytic approach may have led many marginally involved and ideologically unsophisticated practitioners to have indicated sole allegiance to this orientation because they are unaware of others or because they viewed it as a desirable position with which to identify. Insofar as this explanation is valid, the unusual "purity" and exclusiveness of the psychoanalytic ideological positions is less a reflection of intensity and exclusiveness of ideological commitment than of the salience of their orientation and lack of awareness of others. Since limited awareness of alternative ideologies may well have an impact on choice of a professional role, "pure" psychoanalytically oriented practitioners will be analyzed separately from practitioners who indicated that the psychoanalytic position was the most important but not the only component of their therapeutic ideology. Of course, it would be desirable to distinguish purists from others in each of the various ideological positions but, as Table 9 reveals, the number of adherents to each of the therapeutic ideologies, except the psychoanalytic, is sufficiently small to preclude meaningful comparisons.

Table 9. DISTRIBUTION OF THERAPEUTIC ORIENTATIONS AMONG MENTAL HEALTH PROFESSIONALS

Type of Orientation	Distribution of Major Orientations Percent and (Base Number)	Questionnaire Responses Included in Category
Pure Psychoanalytic	31.0 (1061)	One of the following as major and also as *only* orientation: Freudian, Adlerian, Jungian, Alexander, Bettelheim, Classical Analytic
Psychoanalytic Major	27.8 (952)	One of the following as *major* orientation: Psychoanalytic, Freudian, Adlerian, Jungian, Alexander, Bettelheim, Classical Analytic
Neo-Freudian–Ego Psychological + Sullivanian	12.7 (433)	One of the following as *major* orientation: Ego Psychology, Neo-Freudian, Dynamic Psychiatric, Transactional, Fromm, Horney, Kleinian, Sullivanian, Interpersonal Psychiatry, William A. White
Rogerian + Existential	8.4 (290)	One of the following as *major* orientation: Rogerian, Client-centered, Nondirective, Neo-Rogerian, Existential, Experiential, Onto-analytic, Logo-therapy, Rollo May
Eclectic	4.6 (157)	One of the following as *major* orientation: Eclectic or Dynamically Oriented Eclecticism

Table 9. Distribution of Therapeutic Orientations Among
           Mental Health Professionals (cont.)

Social
  Psychiatric–
  Community
  Mental Health
	13.3
	(452)
		One of the following as *major*
		orientation: Social Psychiatric,
		Social-Community, Community
		Mental Health, Milieu Therapy,
		Group Dynamics, Anthropological,
		Social Environmental, Community
		Psychiatry, Sociotherapeutic,
		Ecological

Somatic–Organic– Pharmacologic	2.2 (74)	One of the following as *major* orientation: Organic, Somatic, Pharmacologic, Psychophysiological, Biopsychological, Psychopharma- cologic, Neuropsychiatric, Neurological, Medical Psychiatric
Total	100 (3419)	

It should be pointed out that what is being measured is not the substantive content of the therapeutic orientations, but rather certain generally agreed upon labels that refer to various sets of beliefs about mental illness and treatment. Undoubtedly, the various ideological positions differ with regard to such basic substantive issues as their conceptions of the bases of behavior and the nature of personality; their underlying theories concerning the etiology of mental illness and psychopathology; their views concerning appropriate treatment approaches, goals, and techniques; and their ideas as to which professional and institutional arrangements facilitate or optimize therapy. Unfortunately, the data do not permit us to examine the nature of these basic substantive differences between the various therapeutic ideologies, although they are almost certainly important determinants of the extent to which particular ideological positions are related to various professional roles.

However, we can examine other characteristics, associated with ideological positions, that do not involve substantive differences between the various positions but that may affect the relationships between ideologies and professional roles. These latter characteristics that distinguish various ideological positions include the extent to which they are capable of generating exclusive commitments for their adherents; the extent to which their adherents are a relatively homogeneous group in terms of their professional composition; and, of course, the extent to which they represent systematically articulated, explicitly formulated theoretical frameworks in contrast to amorphous "points of view" that represent an underlying value consensus on certain broad moral issues rather than a systematic theory. Thus, we are suggesting that, in addition to the possible effect of substantive differences, certain structural features of the ideologies may serve to predispose the practitioner to develop a commitment to a particular type of professional role. The plausibility of this line of reasoning is supported by the findings presented in Table 10, showing the relationship between therapeutic ideology and professional roles for each of the mental health professions.

Table 10 reveals that the four professional groups vary considerably in the extent to which they are ideologically homogeneous. As might be expected, psychoanalysts vary least in their ideological positions: nearly two-thirds of them are advocates of the pure psychoanalytic ideology, with the overwhelming majority of the remaining analysts claiming the psychoanalytic position as their major therapeutic orientation. There is considerably greater ideological variance among the members of the three remaining professional groups, although the popularity of some version of the psychoanalytic orientation is pronounced in each of them.

It is when we begin to consider the roles performed by adherents to various ideological positions in each of the professional groups that the structural features of ideologies become most clearly manifest. As noted earlier, the ideological orientation demonstrating the greatest capacity for eliciting exclusive commitment is, of course, the psychoanalytic. For each of the professional groups, practitioners who designate their therapeutic orientation as exclusively psychoanalytic manifest a pronounced tendency to specialize in the performance of one-to-one psychotherapy. That is, when the psychoanalyst and the individual psychotherapist roles are combined, they account for a much larger proportion of adherents to the pure psychoanalytic position than is the case for adherents to any other ideological group. More important, perhaps, is the fact that the pure psychoanalytic ideology is clearly segregated from other ideologies in all professions but social work. That is, among psychoanalysts, psychiatrists, and clinical psychologists, adherence to the pure psychoanalytic ideology is found predominantly among those engaged in one-to-one therapy and is not the preferred orientation of the majority of practitioners committed to other professional roles. A similar, albeit less pronounced, relationship exists among those who designate their major, but not exclusive, orientation as psychoanalytic. Like the other professionals, psychiatric social workers who designate their therapeutic orientation as

Table 10. RELATIONSHIP OF THERAPEUTIC IDEOLOGY TO PROFESSIONAL ROLES BY PROFESSION

PSYCHOANALYSTS

Professional Roles	THERAPEUTIC IDEOLOGY						
	Pure Psychoanalytic	Psychoanalytic Major	Neo-Freudian–Ego Psychological + Sullivanian	Rogerian + Existential	Eclectic	Social Community	Total
	Percent						
Group Therapist	1.7	2.4	2.3	—	—	6.7	2.0 (11)
Psychoanalyst	58.7	44.0	45.5	20.0	28.6	6.7	52.1 (284)
Diagnostician	0.3	0.8	4.5	—	—	—	0.7 (4)
Administrator	3.2	11.2	9.1	20.0	14.3	26.7	6.4 (35)
Academician	9.2	4.8	6.8	—	14.3	20.0	8.3 (45)
Individual Psychotherapist	24.1	30.4	25.0	20.0	42.9	26.7	25.9 (141)
Professional Educator	2.9	6.4	6.8	40.0	—	13.3	4.6 (25)
Total	100 (349)	100 (125)	100 (44)	100 (5)	100 (7)	100 (15)	100 (545)

PSYCHIATRISTS

Group Therapist	3.9	1.1	—	—	2.0	2.9	1.8 (10)
Psychoanalyst	4.7	1.1	31.6	—	—	—	5.8 (32)
Diagnostician	1.6	3.8	3.9	22.0	4.1	10.1	5.5 (30)
Administrator	10.2	11.4	7.9	12.2	26.5	30.4	14.4 (79)
Academician	4.7	9.7	7.9	34.1	8.2	14.5	10.6 (58)
Individual Psychotherapist	71.1	65.4	43.4	19.5	38.8	37.7	54.4 (298)
Professional Educator	3.9	7.6	5.3	12.2	20.4	4.3	7.5 (41)
Total	100 (128)	100 (185)	100 (76)	100 (41)	100 (49)	100 (69)	100 (548)

Table 10. Relationship of Therapeutic Ideology to Professional Roles by Profession (cont.)

THERAPEUTIC IDEOLOGY

Professional Roles	Pure Psychoanalytic	Psychoanalytic Major	Neo-Freudian–Ego Psychological + Sullivanian	Rogerian + Existential	Eclectic	Social Community	Total
			CLINICAL PSYCHOLOGISTS Percent				
Group Therapist	0.8	2.7	2.8	2.9	8.9	7.5	2.9 (31)
Psychoanalyst	18.5	5.4	12.0	—	3.6	1.5	8.9 (95)
Diagnostician	13.1	20.1	17.5	20.0	21.4	16.4	17.7 (190)
Administrator	12.0	13.2	11.1	20.7	16.1	25.4	14.4 (154)
Academician	17.8	16.5	21.2	27.9	12.5	23.9	19.5 (209)
Individual Psychotherapist	30.5	34.4	32.3	20.7	26.8	11.9	29.5 (316)
Professional Educator	7.3	7.8	3.2	7.9	10.7	13.4	7.3 (78)
Total	100 (259)	100 (334)	100 (217)	100 (140)	100 (56)	100 (67)	100 (1073)

Group Therapist	4.3	8.8	12.5	—	8.0	5.4	6.7 (68)
Psychoanalyst	1.8	1.9	—	—	—	—	1.2 (12)
Diagnostician	13.5	14.3	17.0	11.1	20.0	16.2	14.9 (151)
Administrator	31.1	31.2	33.0	44.4	28.0	42.3	34.2 (347)
Academician	5.8	5.2	8.0	11.1	4.0	8.8	6.6 (67)
Individual Psychotherapist	34.5	29.9	26.1	22.2	28.0	18.5	28.0 (284)
Professional Educator	8.9	8.8	3.4	11.1	12.0	8.8	8.5 (86)
Total	100 (325)	100 (308)	100 (88)	100 (9)	100 (25)	100 (260)	100 (1015)

psychoanalytic, whether pure or not, reveal a strong preference for the role of individual psychotherapist; but, unlike other practitioners, they express an equally strong preference for the role of administrator. The explanation for this deviation from the general professional pattern by psychiatric social workers may reside in the fact that administrative positions confer more status on members of this profession than on members of the other three professions. Indeed, the "folklore" of social work emphasizes the organization as the key to professional advancement to the point where practitioners "long for the day" when they will achieve administrative status. Since administrator is a prestigious role in social work, it is understandable that it would attract many of the most highly trained practitioners. Since advanced psychiatric training in social work most frequently entails exposure to psychoanalytic theory, it is not surprising that psychiatric social workers who espouse a psychoanalytic orientation are approximately equally divided among administrative and individual psychotherapeutic roles.

The affinity expressed by psychoanalytically oriented practitioners for the performance of individual psychotherapy warrants amplification because it provides an important clue in understanding the ways in which ideologies facilitate the development of an attachment to a professional role. The performance of one-to-one psychotherapy requires that the practitioner master a unique and highly specialized set of skills in social interaction. The application of these specialized skills occurs in a private, highly variable situation that is, by its very nature, fraught with uncertainty for the psychotherapist. Under such circumstances, it is understandable that a practitioner would be attracted to an ideological position that has been explicitly and systematically formulated. The psychoanalytic orientation obviously represents such an integrated ideological position. That is, unlike some other ideological positions, the psychoanalytic position has a theoretical fountainhead, and it has been subjected to a number of relatively widely accepted attempts to systematize and codify basic premises, approaches, and techniques. There is also a set of standard sources and references, which serve as basic theoretical and methodological guidelines for the ideological position. Thus, we are suggesting that adherence to a systematically formulated and explicit ideological position facilitates commitment to a specialized role. By implication, we are also suggesting that this line of reason not only is plausible for understanding the bases of commitment to individual psychotherapy but also has merit for explaining the relationship between mental health ideologies and professional roles at a general level. For example, it facilitates understanding the fit between the Rogerian–existential ideology and the role of academician. Next to the psychoanalytic position, the Rogerian–existential orientation represents, perhaps, the most clearly formulated and explicitly integrated of all the ideologies. Similarly, academicians are performing clearly defined, specialized roles for which they received considerable training during their years in professional schools. The fact that it is a specialized role, rather than a general organizational one, is probably a major reason why adherents to the Rogerian–existential ideological position show a pronounced tendency to become committed to the role of academician, at least in the two professions (psychiatry and clinical psychology) that have a sufficient number of practitioners espousing this orientation to make a meaningful comparison.

The social-community ideology stands in marked contrast to the psychoanalytic and Rogerian–existential positions. Unlike the latter two orientations, the social-community position does not have any single, authorative theoretical spokesman or small coterie of eminent practitioner-theorists whose writings definitely formulate the position. The fact that this ideological position reflects an amorphous "point of view" that represents an underlying value consensus on certain broad moral issues rather than systematic theory may help to explain why adherents to this ideology are not narrowly specialized in any particular role, except among social workers where they are concentrated in the organizational role of administrator.

Of the two remaining ideological positions, the eclectic is the most interesting theoretically. Since eclecticism means, in the present context, borrowing selected aspects from various orientations or perspectives, we would expect the adherence to this ideology to have a highly idiosyncratic influence on the choice of a professional role. This is indeed what the data show: among psychiatrists, clinical psychologists, and psychiatric social workers, eclectics are less likely to be individual psychotherapists than are adherents to a psychoanalytic orientation, less likely than social-community adherents to be administrators, and less likely than Rogerian–existentialists to be academicians. In short, both the structure of the eclectic orientation and its impact on professional roles is diffuse.

Neo-Freudian–ego psychological and/or Sullivanian adherents represent the only apparent exception to the proposition that the degree to which therapeutic ideologies are related to professional roles is dependent upon the extent to which there is a structural congruence between them. However, it is likely that this exception is more apparent than real. That is, the beliefs of several eminent psychodynamic theoreticians are contained in this ideological position (Fromm, Horney, Sullivan, Klein), and their views have undergone a considerable degree of codification and systematization. Thus, this ideological position actually consists of a number of separate and fairly well integrated orientations, each of which traces its origins to psychoanalytic theory and manifests a preoccupation with psychotherapy. Given these considerations, it is not surprising that, among adherents to the neo-Freudian–ego psychological–Sullivanian positions, actual departure from the psychoanalytic tradition is minimal, at least with regard to its influence on the choice of professional roles.

If the term *commitment* is used to refer to social constraints that serve to bind a person into an occupational role, then it is clear that, for mental health professionals, one important source of such influences emanates from adherence to a particular type of therapeutic ideology. Congruence between the structure of the ideological position and the structure of the professional role was the particular mechanism of cohesion we were able to identify. Previously we had documented the extent to which the dominant ethos of the professional training programs served to bind members of the four professions to various occupational roles. In discussing the influence of professional training programs it was pointed out that, in spite of the fact that it is no longer possible for any professional group to exercise exclusive jurisdiction over core functions, differences among the training programs still tend to produce a division of labor in the mental health field.

Roles and Work Setting

However, while professional skills tend to be restricted by professional training programs, the dominant sets of beliefs about mental illness and treatment are available to members of all four professions. Consequently, it is not surprising that adherence to different ideological positions serves to produce intraoccupational as well as interoccupational diversity in commitment to various practitioner roles. Thus, the general pattern of professional development appears to be a process in which the interests of individual professionals become progressively more refined and specialized. That is, most of our respondents began their professional education and training and became committed to a particular professional model before they became committed to a particular ideological position, and both preceded choice of a general practice setting and commitment to a specific professional role (Henry, Sims, and Spray, 1971). Given this portrait of the typical professional biography in the mental health field, these embryonic commitments to a professional role emerge as distinctly problematic. That is, in attempting to understand the basis of commitment to various professional roles it is impossible to ignore the evidence that clearly indicates that ideological stances and attachment to professional models of practice are frequently modified, if not entirely altered, in the course of performing specific roles in particular settings. The impact on therapeutic ideologies and professional identities is, of course, most likely to be mitigated when the roles are performed in organizational settings rather than in private practice. Thus, Strauss and others (1964) have noted that "professional philosophies brought from training centers are strengthened, muted, or transformed" in psychiatric institutions (p. 5). They have also noted that mental health institutions are both selective and productive in terms of ideologies: "They are selective in that only certain types of ideology can be tolerated or implemented within the limits set by both institutional necessities and the particular organization of treatment. . . . Institutions produce ideologies because the specific content of work conditions in which a particular ideological approach is applied leads to elaboration, further development, and modification in approach" (p. 360).

Thus, although the professional may attempt initially to select a work setting that provides support for his professional identity and therapeutic ideology, he may still undergo situational pressures during the course of performing his professional role which force him to alter his basis of commitment, if he desires to continue in the position. In private practice, the psychotherapist has no surveillance of his performance beyond that of his patients and he is relatively free to exercise personal decisions regarding his role. Organizational roles, however, require collaboration with others for their successful performance. To a certain extent, then, organizational employment means that the professional becomes dependent upon the institution, at least to some extent, for the provision of resources necessary for the application of his technical skills. Thus, the major distinction between organizational employment and private practice revolves around the extent to which institutional arrangements limit the degree to which professional philosophies and therapeutic ideologies get translated into the performance of professional roles.

Starting at the level of general organizational constraints, Table 11 makes it clear that the likelihood of performing a particular role in the mental health field is directly conditioned by the type of setting in which the professional finds employment. Specifically, the opportunity to perform one-to-one psychotherapy, either in the role of psychoanalyst or individual psychotherapist is more than twice as great in private practice as in any other type of institutional setting. Among organizations, psychiatric clinics have the largest proportion of professionals engaged in performing the role of individual psychotherapist. This is not surprising, since psychiatric clinics tend to be narrowly focused around the provision of treatment, usually individual psychotherapy, on an outpatient basis; and, as a result, they represent the type of organization most highly specialized in the provision of mental health treatment services. Of greater interest, perhaps, is the fact that, like the other types of institutions, psy-

Table 11. ROLE CLUSTERS BY TYPE OF WORK SETTING

Role Clusters	WORK SETTING							
	Health-related Organization[a]	General Hospital[b]	Mental Hospital[e]	Educational Organization[d]	Psychiatric Clinic[c]	Social Service Organization[f]	Private Practice	Total
	Percent							
Group Therapist	4.0	3.8	7.3	1.2	7.7	2.9	4.0	4.0
Psychoanalyst	—	1.9	1.8	4.3	2.3	0.9	30.4	12.6
Diagnostician	16.8	21.3	15.6	7.2	13.5	30.9	3.1	11.6
Administrator	42.3	28.2	40.4	24.8	29.0	28.5	1.3	19.4
Academician	9.8	11.7	13.7	41.4	7.0	11.2	4.6	13.2
Individual Psychotherapist	20.8	23.7	14.7	13.1	35.9	17.3	51.0	32.5
Professional Educationist	6.2	9.3	6.4	7.9	4.5	8.2	5.5	6.6
Total	100	100	100	100	100	100	100	100
	(274)	(418)	(109)	(580)	(482)	(340)	(1284)	(3487)

[a] Public and private homes for children and the elderly as well as health and mental health foundations and associations.
[b] Public and private hospitals not specializing in the treatment of mental illness.
[c] Public and private hospitals that are primarily specializing in the treatment and/or custody of the mentally ill.
[d] Colleges and universities as well as medical schools, counseling centers, and professional training institutes.
[e] Public and private clinics that provide (primarily outpatient) treatment, diagnostic testing, consulting, and referral services.
[f] A category composed of the following types of organizations: public and private schools, public and private welfare organizations, and public and private community service organizations.

chiatric clinics utilize the *majority* of mental health professionals in non-therapeutic roles, primarily that of administrator. Clearly, as a major professional role, psychotherapy is still the province of the private practitioner. Similarly, with regard to other professional roles, considerable specialization by type of institution is evident. The educational organization is the most prevalent site for the academician while the other type of organization that is not primarily concerned with care of the mentally ill, the social service organization, has mental health professionals performing the roles of diagnostician and administrator with equal frequency. Mental hospitals, which serve both custodial and therapeutic functions and tend to emphasize inpatient care, are most likely to utilize their professional personnel in the role of administrator. Health-related organizations, which are also concerned with custodial responsibilities and with problems of health and illness that are not restricted to intensive, individual treatment approaches, also use mental health professionals primarily as administrators. Finally, general hospitals, which are concerned with treating illness in general, are the least specialized of all the institutions, in that mental health professionals have approximately the same likelihood of performing any one of three roles—diagnostician, administrator, or individual psychotherapist.

The availability of professional roles clearly differs by type of institution. Since the ability to translate various ideological perspectives and professional philosophies into professional practices is dependent upon the range of roles available to the practitioner, it is necessary to examine the extent to which the differential distribution of roles is due to differences in the professional composition of the various types of organization. Table 12 reveals that the probability of a psychoanalyst, psychiatrist, clinical psychologist, or psychiatric social worker performing any particular role varies by type of work setting.

In terms of the extent to which professional philosophies and therapeutic ideologies find expression through professional roles, it is clear that the organizational context of practice is least salient to psychoanalysts and most salient to psychiatric social workers, with psychiatrists and clinical psychologists holding some intermediate position. By avoiding organizational employment, the vast majority of psychoanalysts are able to integrate their professional techniques and their Freudian-based therapeutic ideology into the role of psychoanalyst or individual psychotherapist. Even among the small minority of psychoanalysts who do accept organizational employment, most manage to confine their participation to individual therapy or to the nearly equally congruent role of academician. Analysts achieve this specialized occupational profile primarily through the judicious selection of work settings, a selection process that appears to

Table 12. Role Clusters by Profession and Type of Work Setting

WORK SETTING[a]

PSYCHOANALYSTS

Percent

Role Clusters	Health-related Organization	General Hospital	Mental Hospital	Educational Organization	Psychiatric Clinic	Social Service Organization	Private Practice	Total
Group Therapist	—	—	—	1.5	4.3	—	2.0	1.9
Psychoanalyst	—	22.7	25.0	24.2	26.1	16.7	58.6	50.3
Diagnostician	—	—	—	—	—	16.7	0.4	0.5
Administrator	62.5	13.6	50.0	19.7	26.1	16.7	1.6	6.8
Academician	25.0	27.3	25.0	33.3	17.4	16.7	3.4	9.1
Individual Psychotherapist	12.5	18.2	—	9.1	21.7	33.2	29.8	26.0
Professional Educationist	—	18.2	—	12.1	4.3	—	4.1	5.4
Total	100 (8)	100 (22)	100 (8)	100 (66)	100 (23)	100 (6)	100 (440)	100 (573)
Proportion of all Psychoanalysts	1.4	3.8	1.4	11.5	4.0	1.0	76.8	

PSYCHIATRISTS

Group Therapist	7.1	—	—	1.5	7.7	—	2.4	2.4
Psychoanalyst	—	1.6	—	1.5	2.5	—	11.1	6.7
Diagnostician	3.6	17.8	11.9	1.5	7.7	36.8	3.0	5.4
Administrator	42.8	31.2	50.0	26.5	10.2	10.5	0.6	13.3
Academician	7.1	17.2	9.5	38.2	12.8	10.5	3.6	10.5
Individual Psychotherapist	35.7	28.1	16.7	22.0	53.8	31.6	73.3	54.1
Professional Educationist	3.6	14.1	11.9	8.8	5.1	10.5	6.0	7.6
Total	100 (28)	100 (64)	100 (42)	100 (68)	100 (39)	100 (19)	100 (333)	100 (593)
Proportion of all Psychiatrists	4.7	10.8	7.1	11.5	6.6	3.2	56.1	

* For a description of the specific organizations listed under each category, see notes of Table 11.

Table 12. Role Clusters by Profession and Type of Work Setting (cont.)

WORK SETTING[a]

CLINICAL PSYCHOLOGISTS

Percent

Role Clusters	Health-related Organization	General Hospital	Mental Hospital	Educational Organization	Psychiatric Clinic	Social Service Organization	Private Practice	Total
Group Therapist	—	3.6	18.9	0.3	2.2	2.4	5.7	3.4
Psychoanalyst	—	1.8	—	2.1	2.2	0.9	20.2	7.6
Diagnostician	23.9	31.8	27.0	9.2	22.9	34.5	5.9	16.8
Administrator	31.0	17.3	21.6	18.5	20.7	25.1	1.4	14.9
Academician	16.9	23.6	24.3	48.3	5.8	13.8	6.9	21.5
Individual Psychotherapist	21.1	15.4	5.4	13.5	34.0	14.3	52.6	28.7
Professional Educationist	7.0	6.3	2.7	8.0	3.7	8.9	7.1	7.1
Total	100 (71)	100 (110)	100 (37)	100 (325)	100 (135)	100 (203)	100 (420)	100 (1301)
Proportion of All Clinical Psychologists	5.4	8.4	2.8	25.0	10.4	15.6	32.3	

Psychiatric Social Workers

Group Therapist	5.4	5.4	4.5	3.3	10.5	4.4	12.1	7.1
Psychoanalyst	—	—	—	0.8	0.3	—	10.9	1.2
Diagnostician	16.7	22.0	9.1	9.1	10.9	24.1	3.3	14.8
Administrator	46.1	34.2	50.0	43.8	35.8	38.4	2.2	35.7
Academician	6.6	2.7	—	28.9	2.1	6.2	3.3	6.7
Individual Psychotherapist	18.6	27.0	31.8	9.1	35.4	19.6	64.8	28.5
Professional Educationist	6.6	8.5	4.5	4.9	4.9	7.1	3.3	6.1
Total	100 (167)	100 (222)	100 (22)	100 (121)	100 (285)	100 (112)	100 (91)	100 (1020)
Proportion of All Psychiatric Social Workers	16.4	21.8	2.1	11.8	27.9	11.0	6.1	

a For a description of the specific organizations listed under each category, see notes of Table 11.

be based more on therapeutic ideology than on professional affiliation. That is, in the process of becoming a certified psychoanalyst, attraction to the psychoanalytic ideology is what led many practitioners to decide to specialize in psychiatry while interest in therapeutic technique led them to undergo additional analytic training. Since approximately nine out of every ten practicing analysts still claim allegiance to the psychoanalytic ideology, it is clear that the opportunity to practice their profession in accordance with the precepts of this orientation underlies their willingness or unwillingness to perform various occupational roles.

Virtually to the same extent that psychoanalysts are specialists in solo office practice, psychiatric social workers are specialists in organizational practice. Social work has the largest concentration of practitioners in organizations in general (more than 90 percent) and the most pronounced specialization in one particular type of organization of any of the four professions. Similarly, next to psychoanalysis, psychiatric social work has the largest proportion of members claiming allegiance to some version of the psychoanalytic ideology. Also, like psychoanalysts, the overwhelming majority of psychiatric social workers in private practice are adherents to the psychoanalytic ideology. Unlike psychoanalysts, however, ideological adherence appears to have little impact on the roles performed by psychiatric social workers in the various types of organizations. The social-community ideology represents the only popular alternative to the psychoanalytic orientation in social work, and we earlier noted that social-community adherents had a somewhat greater probability of being administrators than was true of adherents to other positions. However, social-community adherents are approximately uniformly distributed among several different types of organizations so that when type of setting is taken into account they emerge as no more likely than their psychoanalytically oriented colleagues to be administrators. In fact, since the proportion of psychiatric social workers who are administrators exceeds the proportion performing any other single role in five of the six types of organizations, psychoanalytically oriented social workers are apparently quite willing to adopt this explicitly organizational role. In all the other professions, the psychoanalytic ideology is much more strongly related to treatment roles than to organizational administration. The atypical pattern of social workers in this regard, therefore, warrants explanation. In order to provide a tentative explanation, it should be noted, at the outset, that the role of administrator is composed of two sets of activities: administration and the training and supervision of trainees. In our earlier discussion of interprofessional relations, it was noted that psychiatric social workers hold the psychiatric profession, and particularly psychoanalytic theory, in high esteem. In social work, the supervisory relationship is analogous, in many respects, to the training analysis and incorporates, both implicitly and explicitly, many elements of this socialization procedure—most notably, the psychoanalytic ideology. Finally, there is considerable prestige associated with the supervisory role per se, partially because of the prestige of the psychoanalytic ideology and method that underlie the process of supervision, partially because of the prestige attached to the psychiatric model of professional practice, and partially because of the tangible rewards of power and income associated with the role. Thus, while the role of administrator may be incongruent with respect to the individual treatment emphasis of the psychoanalytic ideology, the role appears to mesh nicely with the professional philosophy of social work.

The prevalence of psychiatric social workers in the administrator role is also undoubtedly a reflection of the fact that the career structure of social work is based on the hierarchical structure of organizations, with the high-status positions being supervision, teaching, and administration, rather than actual practice. In such a situation, the normal distinction between professional roles and organizational roles becomes blurred. That is, where occupational advancement results in psychiatric social workers becoming primarily involved in supervising members of their own profession, the professional may not be forced to relinquish his professional philosophy and become preoccupied with organizational concerns. Perhaps this is why psychiatric social workers are more likely to accept employment in psychiatric clinics, as well as being more willing to perform the role of administrator in this treatment-oriented type of organization than is true of other professionals. Similarly, more than one-half of the mental health professionals working in health-related organizations and general hospitals are psychiatric social workers, a fact that may be related to their somewhat greater likelihood of becoming administrators in these organizations than is true for members of the other professions. In general, then, it appears that, with regard to the role of administrator, the primary function of the organization has less of an impact on psychiatric social workers than the professional composition of the institution. The crucial distinction, of course, is whether or not social workers are working mainly with members of their own profession. The importance of this condition is reflected in the fact that, except for educational organizations, the vast majority of psychiatric social workers in each type of organization are accounted for by only two roles: administrator and individual psychotherapist. The role of academician is largely unavailable to psychiatric social workers employed outside of educational organizations. The pragmatic, social-action concerns of the social work profession are clearly reflected in the fact that a comparatively small proportion of psychiatric social workers choose to work in educational organizations.

The professional philosophy of psychiatry emphasizes the application of technical skills, primarily those involved in the treatment of mental illness. Since the setting most conducive to the intensive treatment of mental illness is private practice, it is not surprising that the majority of psychiatrists become solo practitioners. Nor is it surprising that, given their concern for the application of occupational skills, the type of institution in which the psychiatrist is employed is a much stronger determinant of the role he performs than is his therapeutic ideology. To a certain extent, of course, this outcome reflects the fact that the majority of psychiatrists claim allegiance to the psychoanalytic orientation. To a much greater extent, however, this pattern of practice reflects the fact that psychiatrists are drawn to specific roles that permit them to exercise their technical expertise. The specific occupational roles available to psychiatrists vary according to the type of employing organization. The specialized role available to psychiatrists in psychiatric clinics is, of course, that of individual psychotherapist. The role of academician represents the specialized role most attractive to psychiatrists in educational organizations, while the role of diagnostician is the most preferred role in social service organizations. The custodial function of mental hospitals in combination with the restriction of legal responsibility for patient care to those with the M.D. degree and the reliance on social workers and other ancillary personnel for the provision of treatment, all add up to the fact that the specialized skills of the psychiatrist are most often utilized in the role of administrator. The type of organization that has placed greatest emphasis on community mental health approaches and related programs is what is termed health-related organizations here; and this fact, in combination with the custodial functions performed by some of these organizations, undoubtedly accounts for psychiatrists' preferences for the role of administrator in these institutions. Finally, in general hospitals, psychiatrists are almost as likely to be individual psychotherapists as administrators. General hospitals have been the site of a good deal of experimentation in the attempt to find solutions to the problem of providing treatment to hospitalized mental patients in the absence of a sufficient number of professionally trained therapists. As a result, various forms of milieu and group therapy have been used in these settings in an attempt to provide inpatient treatment on a more efficient basis than is possible using intensive individual psychotherapy. As a result of these developments, psychiatrists are apparently about as likely to end up administering innovations as conducting standard forms of psychotherapeutic treatment. In either case, the roles tend to be quite specialized. In sum, strong identification with occupational skills enables psychiatrists to give expression to their professional philosophy in a variety of organizational roles.

Clinical psychology is the profession with the least specialized professional philosophy and manifests the least exclusive reliance on the psychoanalytic ideology for guidelines to action. As in the other professions,
clinical psychologists who go into private practice tend to be psychoanalytically oriented. Although the factors associated with entry into
private practice appear to be the same in both groups, it is considerably
easier for clinical psychologists to enter private practice than is the case
for psychiatric social workers. Several states have established licensing and
certification procedures for clinical psychologists doing psychotherapy in
private practice; and a number of associations have been formed to
represent their interests—such as Psychologists Interested in the Advancement of Psychotherapy, Psychologists in Private Practice, and the American Academy of Psychotherapists. These developments are reflected in
the fact that the proportion of clinical psychologists in private practice
is much larger than the proportion of psychiatric social workers in solo
practice. Although clinical psychologists are more likely to engage in the
private practice of individual psychotherapy than is true of psychiatric
social workers, the same cannot be said for the performance of individual
psychotherapy in organizations. In fact, psychiatric social workers have a
somewhat greater likelihood than clinical psychologists of performing the
role of individual psychotherapist in three of the six organizations with
the other institutions revealing little difference between the two groups in
this regard.

We earlier pointed out that the ethos of clinical psychology re-
volved around reliance on the scientific method to develop explanatory
statements about human behavior. Like psychoanalysts, clinical psychologists in private practice can reconcile their conceptual concerns with
their therapeutic responsibilities by using their clinical experiences to
elaborate on extant psychoanalytic literature. For organizational psychologists, the most appropriate way to translate the professional philosophy
into an occupational role is to become an academician. Since the role of
academician is much more available in educational organizations than
anywhere else, fully one-quarter of the clinical psychologists accept employment in such settings. However, the number of academicians needed
in other types of organizations is apparently quite restricted, so only about
one-fifth of all clinical psychologists end up in the role. Similarly, a fair
number of organizational psychologists perform the role of individual
psychotherapist, but only in psychiatric clinics is the likelihood of performing this role greater than the likelihood of performing some other role. If
a clinical psychologist accepts employment in a health-related organization, he is more likely to be utilized as an administrator than anything else,
although only a very small proportion of psychologists enter such organi-

zations. In general hospitals, mental hospitals, and social service organizations, the scientific ethos of clinical psychology apparently finds applied expression in the role of the diagnostician. To the extent that the philosophy of the profession emphasizes reliance on objective measures to develop causal statements, the role of diagnostician may well represent the "applied science" of clinical psychology. In this regard, it should be noted that the opportunity for performing individual psychotherapy is quite limited in these three settings so that if the professional desired to *practice* clinical psychology rather than teach it, the only role readily available is that of diagnostician.

When these findings concerning the distribution of professional roles in the various organizations employing mental health professionals are summarized, the conclusion that emerges is that the translation of professional philosophies and therapeutic ideologies into professional roles is constrained by institutions in at least two ways. First, the character of the organization determines the extent to which various roles are available to members of the four mental health professions. Second, the professional composition of the organization determines the extent to which the performance of various roles requires active collaboration with graduates of different training programs and/or adherents to different ideological positions. The assumption is, of course, that frequent contact with representatives of other traditions and perspectives will serve to weaken professional ties and ideological allegiances. Thus, from the standpoint of the practitioner, professional autonomy can be maximized by choosing to go into private practice, rather than accept organizational employment. If organizational employment is accepted, then choice of a role that requires minimal collaboration with and dependence on other types of professionals for its performance constitutes the most effective defense of professional identity. Conversely, maximum organizational constraint is experienced by those practitioners who accept an organizational role that may be performed by affiliates of various professions and that requires the application of skills not acquired in professional schools.

Personal Psychotherapy of Practitioners

Although members of the four mental health professions have graduated from clearly differentiated and highly specialized training programs, they have all received extensive training in the skills deemed necessary for the successful performance of psychotherapy. Undergoing personal analysis or psychotherapy is an integral part of this training in psychotherapeutic skills in all four professions, although it is formally required only of psychoanalysts. Psychiatrists, clinical psychologists, and psychiatric social workers are encouraged by their professional trainers to undergo psychotherapy because it is believed that the experience provides the practitioner with personal insights instrumental to the development of his therapeutic skills. This uniquely intense socialization process—involving changes in attitudes, values, motivations, and identifications—has both personal and professional objectives. In recognition of this fact, Levinson has observed: "The socializing experience brings about changes in certain personal charcteristics; these affect the student's subsequent career and are in turn affected by it" (Levinson, 1967, p. 258). Given the nature of the therapeutic experience, we would expect it to produce strong, binding commitment to the psychotherapeutic skill system on the part of the recipient. If this is one way in which personal psychotherapy affects the practitioner's career, then we would expect the increased professional commitment to be reflected in the choice of private practice as the preferred work setting and individual psychotherapist or psychoanalyst as the preferred professional role. Table 13 reveals that those who are performing therapeutic roles are indeed more likely to have received therapy than those who are engaged in nontreatment roles. Psychoanalysts, who are formally required to undergo a training analysis, represent the only professional group that deviates from this pattern. To a certain extent, commitment to the role of individual psychotherapist or psychoanalyst also means commitment to private rather than organizational practice. That this is particularly true for psychoanalysts and psychiatrists is attested to by the fact that virtually all analysts and 72 percent of the private-practicing psychiatrists have received psychotherapy. The comparable figure for organizational psychiatrists is 56 percent. The pattern also holds for clinical psychologists and psychiatric social workers: 90 percent of the psychologists in private practice have had therapy compared to 67 percent of their organizational colleagues; 88 percent of private-practicing social workers have experienced personal psychotherapy compared to 58 percent of their colleagues employed by organizations. Thus, for each of the professions, those who have had therapy are most likely to be performing therapy, a relationship that strongly suggests that personal commitment to psychotherapeutic skills is a major tie binding the practitioner to the role of individual psychotherapist or psychoanalyst. Since the pattern holds for all four professions, it is clearly psychotherapeutic skills and not professional techniques that link practitioners to therapeutic roles. That is, professional socialization in all four professions is designed, in part, to ensure that students develop a commitment to some scientific explanation of human behavior. All four professions consider personal psychotherapy to be a major mechanism for bringing about the desired belief in psychological determinism. Similarly, willingness to undergo personal psychotherapy is indicative of a predisposition to the logic of psychodynamics and

Table 13.   Proportion of Practitioners in Each Role Who
Have Received Personal Psychotherapy, by Profession

| Professional Roles | PROFESSION | | | |
	Psychoanalyst	Psychiatrist	Clinical Psychologist	Psychiatric Social Worker
	Percent and (Base Number)			
Group Therapist	100.0 (11)	86.7 (15)	82.6 (46)	74.7 (75)
Psychoanalyst	99.7 (292)	100.0 (41)	100.0 (100)	100.0 (13)
Diagnostician	100.0 (4)	46.9 (32)	65.5 (193)	58.3 (156)
Administrator	92.5 (40)	44.6 (83)	60.6 (193)	56.6 (373)
Academician	98.1 (52)	60.0 (65)	71.8 (294)	61.3 (75)
Individual Psychotherapist	98.0 (151)	74.4 (328)	88.7 (387)	78.5 (297)
Educationist	88.9 (45)	55.1 (89)	66.7 (144)	55.2 (105)
All Practitioners	97.8 (595)	67.1 (653)	75.8 (1387)	64.7 (1094)

since therapy is not required in three of the four training programs, the experience is an expression more of personal choice than of professional identity in the mental health professions.

Religiocultural Affinities

In an earlier volume (Henry, Sims, and Spray, 1971), we noted that, although the four professions vary in the extent to which they emphasize the principle of psychological determinism, the factors that surround the practitioner's acceptance of personal psychotherapy and psychodynamic explanatory systems were the same in all four professional groups. Among the range of factors examined in this regard, Jewish religiocultural tradition places fewer restrictions on the acceptance of psychological determinism than is true of Catholic or Protestant religious traditions. At the same time, the Jewish tradition does not provide the individual with the social and psychological supports obtained from intense commitment to a dogmatic religious belief system. If it is assumed that individuals have a basic psychological need for stable commitment to a systematically and explicitly formulated belief system, then we would expect individuals reared in the Jewish culture tradition to be both more receptive to and/or more in search of an alternative belief system, such as psychological determinism. We earlier used this line of reasoning to account for the religiocultural composition of the mental health professions. We are now proposing that the argument holds not only for choice of a profession but also for choice of an occupational role in the mental health field. Specifically, this would seem to be the most parsimonious explanation of the association between the practitioner's religiocultural affinity and his occupational role revealed in Table 14. To be sure, the relationship between religiocultural affinity and professional roles is less pronounced than the relationship between personal therapy and roles, the significant differences do form a consistent pattern. That is, practitioners who claim a Jewish cultural affinity are more likely than their Christian colleagues to be performing individual psychotherapy, as measured by combining the roles of psychoanalyst and individual psychotherapist. Similarly, in each profession both those who claim a Jewish cultural affinity and those who claim to have no cultural affinity are more likely to be

Table 14. PROFESSION BY CULTURAL AFFINITY AND OCCUPATIONAL ROLE

Role Cluster	CULTURAL AFFINITY			
	Christians[a]	Jewish	None	*Total*
		Percent		
PSYCHOANALYSTS				
Group Therapist	0.8	1.9	1.8	1.7
Psychoanalyst	42.2	48.0	48.6	47.0
Individual Psychotherapist	26.3	26.3	17.1	24.6
Diagnostician	0.8	0.5	—	0.5
Administrator	10.5	4.9	8.2	6.6
Academician	7.9	8.1	10.8	8.6
Educationist	11.5	10.3	13.5	11.0
Totals	100	100	100	100
	(114)	(369)	(111)	(594)
PSYCHIATRISTS				
Group Therapist	2.4	2.2	2.8	2.3
Psychoanalyst	2.0	9.4	4.2	6.1

Table 14. PROFESSION BY CULTURAL AFFINITY AND OCCUPATIONAL ROLE (cont.)

Role Cluster	CULTURAL AFFINITY			
	Christians[a]	Jewish	None	*Total*
	Percent			
Individual Psychotherapist	48.2	49.2	55.5	49.5
Diagnostician	6.1	4.9	1.4	5.0
Administrator	13.8	10.7	16.7	12.5
Academician	10.9	9.4	4.2	9.4
Educationist	16.6	14.2	15.2	15.2
Totals	100	100	100	100
	(247)	(327)	(72)	(646)
CLINICAL PSYCHOLOGISTS				
Group Therapist	3.8	3.4	2.6	3.5
Psychoanalyst	3.2	8.9	10.5	7.0
Individual Psychotherapist	22.3	31.8	28.3	27.9
Diagnostician	20.4	15.2	9.4	16.2
Administrator	17.8	10.8	15.7	14.0
Academician	22.0	20.4	22.5	21.3
Educationist	10.5	9.5	11.0	10.1
Totals	100	100	100	100
	(471)	(669)	(191)	(1331)
PSYCHIATRIC SOCIAL WORKERS				
Group Therapist	7.7	6.8	4.6	7.0
Psychoanalyst	0.4	1.4	3.6	1.1
Individual Psychotherapist	20.9	32.5	30.2	27.3
Diagnostician	16.2	12.9	11.6	14.3
Administrator	38.8	29.5	31.4	33.7
Academician	5.5	7.6	10.4	6.9
Educationist	10.5	9.3	8.2	9.7
Totals	100	100	100	100
	(455)	(511)	(86)	(1052)

[a] This category is composed of those who claimed either a Protestant or Catholic cultural affinity.

performing the role of psychoanalyst than is true for those with a Christian cultural affinity. Finally, for all groups except psychoanalysts, those with a Christian affinity are less likely to be individual psychotherapists than is true for those claiming no affinity or a Jewish affinity. In fact, it is only for the roles of administrator and diagnostician that the proportion of Christians consistently exceeds the proportion of those with a Jewish affinity.

Perhaps the primary significance of these relationships between cultural traditions and professional roles resides in the implication that commitment to a particular type of practitioner role is based, to a certain extent, on preprofessional and/or extraprofessional experience. That is, different professional roles tend to recruit different kinds of people. That persons with varied interests should have varied backgrounds is not surprising; nonetheless, this dimension is frequently ignored in the manifold discussions of professional conflict within the mental health field. In rejecting the notion that considerable homogeneity in identities, values, and interests exists among members of a given profession, Bucher and Strauss (1961) argue that professions are made of "segments." To the extent that homogeneous clusters of activities can be taken to represent segments, our findings certainly support this view of professions. We have also been able to extend this line of reasoning by demonstrating that these intraprofessional segments tend to recruit persons from different sociocultural backgrounds. Finally, if these observations are placed in the context of the process of becoming a mental health professional, the resulting conclusion is that segments may be composed of practitioners drawn from different professions. That is, the critical vocational decisions that resulted in separating the respondents of our present sample into professional training routes (that is, the medical school–residency route for psychiatrists and psychoanalysts, the university route for clinical psychologists, and the professional school for psychiatric social workers) are made, by the great majority of recruits, by late adolescence or early adulthood. That is, the positive or negative decisions for a career in the professional field took place before there existed a differentiated commitment to the specialized professional roles of individual psychotherapist, diagnostician, administrator, academician, and so forth. To the extent that specific roles within the mental health field are responsible for professional recruitment profiles and to the extent that a "premature" segregation in training occurred before these roles were fully manifest, it becomes plausible to expect that persons performing the same specialized role will be more alike in background across professions than like their professional colleagues who are performing different roles.

4

The Therapeutic Community

Our survey in Chicago, Los Angeles, and New York City revealed that there were 74,595 patients receiving treatment from 3204 psychotherapists in our sample. Those established therapeutic relationships were the end product of a variety of social processes involving decisions on the part of both professionals and patients. For the mental health professional, the therapeutic encounter represents the culmination of a long series of personal experiences. The first were the early experiences that led him to the initial choice of a career in medicine, psychology, or social work and subsequently resulted in commitment to a therapeutic speciality within one of these professions; the second set of experiences were those that occurred during professional preparation and that culminated in his official certification as a professional psychotherapist. Pursuit of a particular type of professional career that led the practitioner to accept a particular role in a particular type of work setting constitutes the third general set of experiences. The final set of experiences conditioning the practitioner's decision to accept or refuse to engage in a therapeutic encounter consists of the residue of past treatment relationships and is reflected in the way in which the professional performs the role of therapist or, in brief, his *therapeutic style.*

With regard to the clients' decisions, Kadushin (1969) suggests that in order for a potential patient to meet a psychotherapist the person must go through a process that includes "the realization of a problem, discussion of the problem with friends and relatives, choice of the type of professional healer to attend (such as a doctor, a psychiatrist, a psychologist, or a faith healer), and selection of a particular practitioner" (p. 12). Of course, the potential patient may not be accepted by the therapist of his choice and may, therefore, be forced to repeat the process several times. Similarly, should the potential patient, either willingly or unwillingly, come to the attention of various community agencies, he may have his freedom to make decisions concerning treatment limited or removed by the institutions at any stage of the process, including the initial recognition of a problem. When this latter event occurs, it may lead to the patient receiving treatment but, if so, it is invariably dispensed through some mental health institution.

Professionals conducting therapy in private practice exercise a great deal more control over the type of patients they encounter than is true for their institutionally based colleagues. Private psychotherapists conduct the intake interview and decide on the basis of information gained personally, whether or not to accept the potential patient into psychotherapy. Patients receiving psychotherapy in institutions go through a somewhat different process. In institutions, the intake interview is frequently conducted by a social worker or someone other than the psychotherapist who eventually ends up treating the patient. Thus, the initial institutional screening process, which is designed to assess compatibility between the patient's needs and abilities and the resources and goals of the institution, occurs before the patient meets the therapist. The institutional screening of potential patients is a relatively formal, standardized procedure, which undoubtedly affects the types of patients initially seen by organizationally based psychotherapists. Furthermore, institutional screening mechanisms as well as resources influence the criteria in terms of which organizational therapists select patients. The availability of various evaluative and diagnostic tools for therapists in organizations presumably enables them to rely heavily on assessment of such factors as the patient's psychological-mindedness or his verbal ability, whereas psychotherapists in private practice necessarily rely to a much greater extent on their own judgment as to whether or not patients should be accepted for psychotherapy. Although the method of selection varies by type of practice setting, there is ample evidence indicating that the two processes together produce differential rates of participation in psychotherapy among various social groups (Myers and Schafer, 1954; Rosenthal and Frank, 1958). Group variation in the rates of entry into psychotherapy suggests that professional specialization in the mental health field exists not only in terms of functions performed but also in terms of clientele served. It is important to determine the extent to which this is true, because the processes surrounding the successful establishment of a therapeutic relationship indicate that the selective matching of patients and psychotherapists are based on *social* as well as *technical* criteria. The technical criteria for specialization are based on the limited area of professional practice for which the practitioner has received intensive training and for which he can claim special competence. The social criteria for professional specialization revolve around the social attributes of the practitioner, which, although not necessarily directly linked to his technical expertise, influence the way he performs the role of professional psychotherapist. Both types of specialization provide the practitioner with a professionally acceptable solution to the problem of having to assume responsibility for treating all persons who seek his professional services. That is, specialization serves to restrict the range of patients for whom the practitioner can legitimately be held accountable. Identifying himself as a specialist enables the practitioner not only to affirm publicly his interest in particular types of patients but also to announce his lack of interest in all other types of patients who might potentially come to his professional attention. Obviously, the particular criteria used for defining the professional specialty affects the kinds of patients that the practitioner finds acceptable or unacceptable. Thus, variations among psychotherapists in the type of clientele served should be related to differences in the "mix" of technical and social criteria used by practitioners to define their professional specialty in the mental health field.

Although social criteria play a prominent role in defining specialties in all the "healing" professions, those groups specializing in verbal therapy must, of necessity, place greater reliance on social factors than is true of groups concerned with physical functioning. In medicine, practitioners can specialize in a limited range of illness, thereby avoiding having to assume responsibility for a relationship with the patient as a person. This type of professional neutrality is difficult for psychotherapists to maintain, since psychotherapy, as a mode of treatment, is based on the establishment of a dyadic relationship that enables the therapist to help reorient the patient to the everyday world. Thus, to the extent that patients are not viewed as basically unmotivated systems or biologic reactors, heavy reliance must be placed on social criteria to provide guidelines for the selection of clients.

Performance of the role of psychotherapist, like the performance of other social roles, requires that the incumbent become involved not only in a set of activities but also in a set of social expectations held by the participants in the relationship. The distinctive nature of the role of psychotherapist derives from the fact that the performance of verbal therapy requires the possession of a unique and highly specialized set of skills for managing social interaction. That is, in order to achieve the professional goal of alleviating mental distress through therapeutic practice, the practitioner is trained to use a particular kind of controlled but emotionally based relationship to patients. Thus, in order to become certified as a psychotherapist, a person must master what Blum and Rosenberg (1968) have termed the "psychotherapeutic skill system." These skills are highly technical and require a personal-social orientation quite different from that deemed appropriate for normal, everyday social interaction. Since the professional skills are highly technical, professional schools have developed rationally organized, scientifically grounded programs of professional training in an attempt to ensure uniformity and predictability in their performance. Thus, in preparation for his professional role, the psychotherapist goes through a series of training experiences designed to provide him with the appropriate professional norms and expectations. He also is subjected to a range of experiences that are designed to allow him to acquire the specific information and theoretical knowledge necessary for the achievement of therapeutic goals. Finally, he undergoes a series of experiences designed to socialize aspects of his own attitudes, values, and cognitions so that he will conduct himself in a professionally appropriate manner in problematic and uncertain situations.

Although the formal training programs designed to facilitate mastery of therapeutic skills are extensive in each of the four mental health professions, qualified practitioners generally acknowledge that the potential for becoming a competent psychotherapist depends upon the presence of certain personal qualities. On the basis of Holt and Luborsky's (1958) summary of expert opinion concerning the qualities sought in applicants for psychiatric training and in established practitioners, a competent psychotherapist should possess three qualities: an introspective orientation, an intellectual predisposition, and a relativistic perspective.

The act of observing the patient's inner life is the major endeavor of psychotherapy. Both therapist and patient are engaged in the observation of the latter's inner experiences in an effort to uncover thoughts and emotions that usually are inaccessible to him. The peeling away of the patient's defensive structures comes through the process of continually recording what he is thinking about and what is happening to his feeling states. In order for this process to succeed, the therapist must be committed to the principles of self-observation and self-disclosure. On the basis of his own personal experiences, the therapist must know that self-understanding is based on self-observation (Erikson, 1965). The therapist's own introspective processes also serve to delineate any personal reactions that might interfer with his task of understanding and guiding the patient. Fromm-Reichmann (1960, p. 3) emphasizes this necessity for the psychotherapist to be in touch with his inner states: "Unless the psychiatrist is widely aware of his own interpersonal processes so that he can handle them for the benefit of the patient in their interpersonal therapeutic dealings with each other, no successful psychotherapy can eventuate." Thus, if the therapist believes that personal problems are created in large part by the inner reactions, defenses, and distortions of individuals, then he must subscribe to the observation and revelation of these phenomena in himself as well as in others.

A second personal attribute necessary for the competent performance of psychotherapy is an intellectual approach to the patient's inner experience. The therapeutic observation of others must be complemented by self-analysis—the rational, dispassionate examination and evaluation of one's own thoughts, feelings, and behavior. The psychotherapeutic process engages both the patient and therapist in the exploration of psychological events and their deeper meanings in relating these separate experiences to each other and to the therapeutic objectives. Intellectual examination represents one part of an effort to bring understanding to the patient by probing and questioning the meaning of particular inner experiences. This attempt to locate and identify specific psychological determinants of behavior has been referred to at various times as the ability to understand the unconscious, the ability to focus attention on the problem at hand, psychological-mindedness, and ability to gain insight. Regardless of the particular term used, the general point is that the therapist must have a pervasive, ineluctible tendency to engage in analysis of his own and others' inner lives (Holt and Luborsky, 1958).

A third important characteristic of psychotherapists is a relativistic perspective; that is, the ability to accept and tolerate individual as well as cultural deviance and differences. The capacity of the therapist to understand the patient requires a nonjudgmental, relativistic, and empathic view of the patient. The therapist must suspend moral judgment in order to be a "bearer of understanding" (Greenson, 1961). In this sense, the therapist must be able to deal tolerantly and constructively with the patient's differing views of himself and the world and see them as having intrinsic validity and underlying meaning. He must impartially mediate the patient's groping for the new perceptions and values offered to him in therapy and must tolerate the patient's wish to defensively retain his old emotional structures. He must be able to identify with both his own and his patient's perspective on living without becoming dogmatically entrenched in either position. Edward Bibring describes the essence of the relativistic perspective in the following definition of objectivity: "The ability to understand another without being handicapped by one's own attitude, to be empathic but not to be subjective. To understand a person's attitudes toward life without being influenced by one's own attitudes, this is objectivity" (Holt and Luborsky, 1958, p. 344).

In sum, the personal characteristics appropriate for psychotherapists involve: the tendency to observe inner experiences, to introspect; intellectually critical tendencies in approaching understanding of human behavior; and a sense of the relativity of each individual's experience—withholding judgment of another person's behavior and outlook in order to understand their meaning. Thus, qualified psychotherapists are individuals who are extremely concerned about their own inner lives and view their own personal dynamics as crucial equipment for understanding others. This concern for personal intrapsychic processes sets the psychotherapeutic relationship apart from other social encounters. Specifically, by agreeing to accept a patient into psychotherapy, the therapist assumes responsibility for helping him achieve greater self-knowledge in order to cope more effectively with the everyday world.

The therapist is faced with the problem of attempting to use a highly personalized procedure focusing on intrapsychic processes to alleviate interpersonally felt problems of social adjustment in the patient. Since the bond between the therapist and the patient consists of both mutual sympathies and common perspectives, the psychotherapist can facilitate this relationship by selecting for treatment only those persons to whom he can relate and who can easily relate to him affectively, as well as on a cognitive level. The ability to experience, understand, and express affect is obviously not something that a psychotherapist can assess on initial contact with a potential patient. However, to the extent that feelings are the product of personal experiences, the therapist can indirectly assess the extent of emotional compatibility between them by determining the extent to which the potential patient's experiential background falls within the range of experiences that are meaningful to him. Since the potential patient's social attributes constitute the most accessible, albeit crude, index of the patient's experiential background, the therapist can use them as clues to whether or not he will be able to meet the person's need for assistance in various dimensions of his personal life. Thus, to the extent that the social attributes of the potential patient reflect his experiential background, they are meaningful to the therapist in terms of both his technical and his social specialization. That is, the psychotherapist is equipped to handle a certain range of experiences by virtue of his professional training. The technical and the social dimensions of specialization become fused in the patient screening process with the outcome being a specialized type of therapeutic practice.

Psychotherapy and Professional Identity

In the course of professional preparation, the novice practitioner is supposed to master the technical skills of psychotherapy. Considering the different emphases placed by the four different training routes upon particular techniques and explanatory systems, it might well be expected that therapists from these four routes would find themselves dealing with rather different kinds of patients. However, we earlier noted that in the autonomous setting of private practice there is a high degree of uniformity among members of the four professions in terms of the types of mental distress experienced by those receiving treatment. In fact, interprofessional differences in types of clientele apparently do not reflect differences in professional preferences for various types of patients or techniques but rather reflect differences in the distribution of practitioners by type of practice setting. As a result, professional differences in types of patients treated are largely confined to institutional practices. Interprofessional homogeneity in clientele is, therefore, directly related to the degree of professional autonomy in the selection of patients.

Professional specialization in the alleviation of mental distress is mediated by interprofessional differences in the setting in which psychotherapy is dispensed. Members of the four professional groups vary not only in terms of their general reliance on private practice as a treatment setting, but also, as Table 15 reveals, in their utilization of the private office for treating specific types of mental distress. Most notable in this regard is the fact that the severity of the illness does not produce a uniform pattern across the professions. Specifically, psychoanalysts are as likely to treat those diagnosed as psychotic in private practice as psychiatrists are to treat either the relatively healthy or those suffering from a character disorder. Similarly, clinical psychologists have about the same likelihood of treating those suffering from psychosomatic illness in private offices as psychiatrists of treating relatively healthy patients in private practice. Psychiatrists and clinical psychologists also see about the same proportion of addicts and alcoholics in private practice. Finally, the principal private clientele for psychiatric social workers comes from the psychoneurotic group but the proportion of such patients treated in private practice by social workers does not exceed proportions of psychotics and addicts and alcoholics treated by clinical psychologists outside of institutions.

When these findings are placed in the context of our earlier finding

Table 15. Proportion of Patients in Each Diagnostic Category Receiving Treatment in Private Practice, by Profession

Diagnostic Category	PROFESSION				
	Psychoanalyst	Psychiatrist	Clinical Psychologist	Psychiatric Social Worker	Total
	Percent and (Base Number)				
Relatively Healthy	78.2 (678)	63.2 (1209)	37.5 (4203)	13.3 (2418)	36.8 (8508)
Psychoneurotic	93.6 (4719)	80.1 (6291)	63.7 (8518)	29.9 (4527)	67.5 (24,055)
Character Disorder	86.0 (4003)	64.3 (4042)	58.6 (5643)	26.2 (4096)	58.6 (17,784)
Psychosomatic Illness	87.4 (652)	70.0 (1602)	61.3 (1158)	17.7 (768)	60.7 (4180)
Functional and Organic Psychoses	63.5 (1927)	41.6 (5759)	30.9 (3285)	8.6 (2664)	35.7 (13,635)
Addicts and Alcoholics	54.6 (359)	37.7 (820)	33.1 (718)	8.2 (546)	32.2 (2444)
Patients Treated in Private Practice	84.1 (12,338)	62.0 (19,723)	52.1 (23,525)	21.0 (15,020)	53.9 (70,606)

of remarkable similarity in the distribution of types of patients treated in private practice by members of the professions, we are led to conclude that the professional groups differ not only in terms of the extent to which they specialize in private practice but also in terms of the type of mental distress they attempt to alleviate in mental health institutions. Since mental health organizations differ in terms of the clientele they serve, it is possible that professional variation in types of patients treated is due more to selective institutional recruitment of practitioners than to differences among members of the four professional groups with regard to the types of mental illness they specialize in treating. At a general level, of course, psychotherapists specialize in the treatment of psychoneurosis and character disorders, in the sense that the majority of patients treated by members of each profession fall into these two diagnostic categories. Therefore, an important clue to understanding organizational influences on therapists' patterns of patient selection can be gleaned from observing the extent to which organizational personnel are utilized in treating psychological disturbances other than those labeled as psychoneurosis or character disorders.

If this line of reasoning is pursued, it comes as no surprise to find, in Table 16, that the general form of patient specialization manifested by the private-practicing members of the four professional groups also holds in most types of mental health institutions. The general pattern is modified, of course, in hospitals that have a large proportion of the patient population composed of severely disturbed persons. Thus, psychoanalysts are much more likely to treat either those suffering from character disorders or from psychoneurosis than any other type of patient in all kinds of mental health institutions except general and mental hospitals. A similar pattern of patient specialization is exhibited by psychiatric social workers. Clinical psychologists manifest an exception to the specific pattern of patient specialization but do not constitute a deviation from the general principle. Clinical psychologists are exceptional in that they are more likely to specialize in treating the relatively healthy than any other type of patient in both educational and social service organizations. They are also exceptional in that they are more likely to treat character disorders than any other kind of patient in general hospitals. As was the case in private practice, psychiatrists represent the professional group having the largest proportion of practitioners treating patients diagnosed as psychotic. Given their medical training, this pattern is not, in itself, unexpected. What is striking about the pattern of patient specialization manifested by psychiatrists is that it is not confined to hospitals but, rather, holds for all types of mental health organizations. In fact, clinical psychologists are as likely as psychiatrists to treat psychotics in mental hospitals, and analysts are similarly comparable to psychiatrists in general hospitals. As a result, the extent to which psychiatrists specialize in treating the severely disturbed in psychiatric clinics and in social service, educational, and health-related organizations distinguishes them from other mental health professionals. Since all types of organizations, except hospitals, permit psychoanalysts, clinical psychologists, and psychiatric social workers to specialize to a considerable degree in the treatment of those less severely disturbed than psychotics, we can only conclude that it is not organizational constraints but rather professional identity that results in psychiatrists' specializing in the treatment of psychotics.

Although it is certainly true that professional differences in types of mental distress treated are largely confined to mental health institutions, our findings also make it clear that professional specialization in the various categories of mental illness is remarkably resistant to organizational characteristics, except perhaps in hospitals. To be sure, selective recruitment to mental health organizations differing in objectives and kind of clientele served does produce greater intraprofessional variability in the types of patients treated by organizational practitioners than was observed among private practitioners. Institutional recruitment patterns did little to accentuate the few interprofessional differences in the kinds of patients accepted into therapy by the autonomous private practitioners. Since we earlier documented the fact that members of all four professional groups identified the same range of experiences as being of strategic importance to their mastery of psychotherapeutic skills, it is not surprising that, given the free-choice situation of private practice, there would be a general tendency to select the same kinds of patients. Nor is it difficult to understand why the medical training of psychiatrists would result in their "overselection," relative to the other professionals, of severely disturbed patients. These preferences are all reflections of the fact that members of the four professional groups went through a series of training experiences that prepared them to specialize in the alleviation of certain types of mental illness. That is, during the course of professional training, practitioners develop embryonic commitments to specialized types of patients and practices. The acquisition of these commitments generally precedes the development of institutional preferences and affiliations.

In the context of this developmental process the striking thing about our findings is that they give little indication of subsequent modification of professional commitments during the course of the psychotherapist's organizational practice, with the exception, again, of those who are employed in general or mental hospitals. In sum, the evidence clearly implies that specialization in clientele is based in part on mastery of technical skills during training. It also suggests that those attributes of

Table 16. Distribution by Diagnostic Categories of Patients Seen in Organizations, by Profession

Diagnostic Categories	TYPE OF ORGANIZATION						
	Health-related Organization	General Hospital	Mental Hospital	Educational Organization Percent	Psychiatric Clinic	Social Service Organization	Total
PSYCHOANALYSTS							
Relatively Healthy	4.6	5.4	5.2	10.2	6.0	8.2	5.1
Psychoneurotic	22.0	13.7	13.0	9.4	27.6	22.0	15.9
Character Disorder	39.4	23.1	30.4	21.5	25.0	31.2	26.7
Psychosomatic	—	8.8	—	5.7	6.4	—	3.8
Functional and Organic Psychoses	9.2	24.6	30.7	26.7	16.4	10.5	26.0
Addicts and Alcoholics	7.3	4.4	13.3	15.6	9.9	4.4	10.4
Other Than Above	—	—	—	6.1	0.4	—	1.8
Totals	100	100	100	100	100	100	100
PSYCHIATRISTS							
Relatively Healthy	5.1	5.8	2.0	9.2	5.4	6.5	5.3
Psychoneurotic	12.3	16.0	7.4	19.1	20.1	12.5	14.6
Character Disorder	24.1	17.6	12.3	25.2	14.2	25.8	18.3
Psychosomatic	2.9	7.6	2.8	8.7	4.1	3.3	5.0
Functional and Organic Psychoses	49.5	35.7	53.7	32.1	45.8	38.9	43.6
Addicts and Alcoholics	0.7	6.7	8.7	4.4	4.9	8.0	5.6
Other Than Above	4.3	10.4	13.0	1.1	5.3	5.0	7.5
Totals	100	100	100	100	100	100	100

CLINICAL PSYCHOLOGISTS

Relatively Healthy	13.3	9.2	1.9	44.5	9.4	37.3	22.5
Psychoneurotic	30.7	20.0	7.3	31.9	37.6	25.7	26.3
Character Disorder	22.2	30.1	13.4	13.1	25.1	16.2	19.5
Psychosomatic	3.1	6.6	2.9	2.8	2.8	3.4	3.6
Functional and Organic Psychoses	17.1	21.8	62.6	5.4	18.3	11.8	20.3
Addicts and Alcoholics	5.9	9.8	4.2	2.2	2.4	3.2	4.3
Other Than Above	7.5	2.3	7.6	—	4.3	2.3	3.4
Totals	100	100	100	100	100	100	100

PSYCHIATRIC SOCIAL WORKERS

Relatively Healthy	20.1	12.7	4.2	22.0	15.3	29.6	17.2
Psychoneurotic	26.8	19.9	20.9	24.5	25.7	28.5	24.4
Character Disorder	20.7	19.0	18.8	20.8	29.0	29.0	24.0
Psychosomatic	4.4	7.6	3.1	4.7	3.6	5.5	5.1
Functional and Organic Psychoses	16.4	29.7	48.8	24.8	18.6	4.1	20.2
Addicts and Alcoholics	4.1	6.5	3.5	8.6	2.4	1.7	4.2
Other Than Above	7.1	4.5	0.7	4.4	5.1	1.5	4.7
Totals	100	100	100	100	100	100	100

patients that serve as foci for technical training in the mental health professions should also serve as the basis for professional specialization in the
practice of psychotherapy. In addition to diagnostic categories, chronological age serves as the basis for specialized training in the mental health
professions. Thus, to the extent that there is a differential emphasis both
within and among the four professions with regard to preparing the
psychotherapist to handle the psychological problems of various age groupings in society, we would expect differences among practitioners in the
extent to which they specialize in treating children, adolescents, young
adults, and the elderly.

If we again assume that the clientele of the private practitioner
represents the unrestrained expression of professional preferences for types
of patients, we find in Table 17 that children are the least preferred and
adults twenty-one to thirty-nine years of age are the most preferred patients. This is true in all four professions and, as a result, children constitute only 8 percent of all the patients treated by our sample of psychotherapists. In light of current composition of the United States population
this pattern of patient selection represents a pronounced negative specialization. That is, just before our survey, the population of the United States
was estimated to be 196 million, with children under the age of fourteen
constituting approximately 30 percent of the total. Since it has been
estimated that somewhere between 10 and 12 percent of the nation's
school children are suffering from some type of emotional problem, it
does not seem likely that they are underrepresented in patient populations
being treated by psychotherapists because they are healthier than adults.
A more plausible explanation is simply that relatively few psychotherapists receive specialized training in the treatment of emotionally disturbed
children. Thus, in 1968 fewer than 500 psychiatrists claimed to be
specialists in the treatment of children's psychological problems. Similarly,
in 1970 the Education and Training Board of the American Psychological
Association reported that there were only seventeen child-guidance training centers that were approved as sites for graduate psychologists to take
their clinical internships. Since few psychotherapists have training experiences that prepare them to treat children, the result is that practitioners
infrequently select them for private treatment. Thus, to the extent that
children are seen by psychotherapists, it is primarily within an institutional context. However, the particular type of institutional context in
which children receive therapy depends upon the professional affiliation
of the therapist. That is, there are interprofessional differences with regard to the extent to which children are treated in each of the six different types of mental health institutions.

Specifically, the differences among the four professional groups

Table 17. Distribution by Age Categories of Patients Seen in Organizations, by Professions

Patient Age Categories	TYPE OF ORGANIZATION						
	Health-related Organization	General Hospital	Mental Hospital	Educational Organization	Psychiatric Clinic	Social Service Organization	Total
	Percent						
PSYCHOANALYSTS							
21 to 39 Years	50.2	48.2	43.9	55.1	54.7	7.8	45.5
40 Years and Over	42.9	26.9	16.9	38.3	25.7	5.5	27.0
Adolescents	4.8	12.2	37.5	5.1	13.3	80.1	22.5
Children	2.0	12.5	1.7	1.5	6.2	5.5	5.0
Totals	100	100	100	100	100	100	100
PSYCHIATRISTS							
21 to 39 Years	48.8	36.4	41.7	19.2	36.6	26.1	36.8
40 Years and Over	28.4	41.3	42.5	34.5	31.4	6.3	33.5
Adolescents	13.9	11.3	9.7	34.3	14.6	57.7	19.4
Children	8.9	11.0	6.5	11.9	17.3	9.8	10.1
Totals	100	100	100	100	100	100	100
CLINICAL PSYCHOLOGISTS							
21 to 39 Years	43.4	44.6	47.8	39.9	39.0	31.5	39.6
40 Years and Over	21.2	41.9	38.5	8.4	28.6	22.5	25.2
Adolescents	25.9	6.5	9.4	41.6	20.7	27.4	23.9
Children	9.4	6.9	4.3	10.1	11.7	18.5	11.3
Totals	100	100	100	100	100	100	100
PSYCHIATRIC SOCIAL WORKERS							
21 to 39 Years	40.2	42.2	34.3	50.1	43.6	30.4	41.5
40 Years and Over	26.9	43.3	40.3	28.0	21.5	15.6	28.5
Adolescents	16.2	9.2	13.2	20.6	19.9	30.7	17.3
Children	16.6	5.3	12.1	5.5	15.0	23.5	12.7
Totals	100	100	100	100	100	100	100

directly reflects their differential willingness to accept children into private therapy. For example, psychoanalysts accept the smallest proportion of children into private practice of any of the professional groups and they confine their institutional treatment of children mainly to general hospitals. This strongly suggests that the children analysts see in institutions are those who have experienced a sudden and severe psychological disturbance. Psychiatrists, on the other hand, see more children and also utilize a wider range of institutions for treating children than is true of psychoanalysts. Specifically, the population of patients treated by psychiatrists in psychiatric clinics, general hospitals, and educational organizations all contain sizable proportions of children. Clinical psychologists not only treat proportionally more children in private practice than either group of physicians, they are also more willing to include children among the clientele they treat in organizations devoted primarily to outpatient, rather than inpatient care. Finally, psychiatric social workers demonstrate the greatest willingness to accept children into private practice and also include sizable proportions of them in the therapeutic practices they establish in mental hospitals, psychiatric clinics, and social service and health-related organizations. Psychiatric social workers thus constitute the only group for which the proportion of children included in the patient population does not differ systematically between organizations devoted primarily to inpatient care and those focusing primarily on outpatient treatment.

The pattern of institutional treatment of adolescents reveals somewhat less professional variability. For psychiatrists and psychoanalysts, adolescents constitute the largest proportion of patients treated in social service organizations. Also, the proportion of adolescents treated by psychiatric social workers is greater in social service organizations than in any other type of institution. Educational organizations constitute the site where adolescents are most likely to be treated by clinical psychologists. Thus, adolescents, who are somewhat more preferred as private patients than is true for children, are also more heavily concentrated in social service and educational organizations. The social service organizations include schools, and the heavy concentration of adolescent patients in this type of organization suggests that the older students are receiving the bulk of therapeutic attention in such institutions.

Finally, the pattern for adult patients reveals somewhat less variability, both by type of institution and by type of profession than was true for the younger patients. Adults twenty-one to thirty-nine years of age are clearly preferred by private-practicing members of all four professional groups and they have the most uniform distribution among the various types of institutions for all professions, except psychoanalysts. For analysts there is somewhat less institutional variability among patients forty years of age and older, primarily because they treat very few younger adults in social service organizations.

These findings provide clear documentation that during professional training psychotherapists develop a strong commitment to the treatment of adults. Although psychoanalysts, psychiatrists, clinical psychologists, and psychiatric social workers are differentially distributed between private and organizational practice, the largest proportion of patients treated in both types of settings by all four professional groups are adults twenty-one to thirty-nine years of age. More importantly, this professional specialization in this age group is less sensitive to influences emanating from different types of mental health institutions than is true for age groups having lower rates of treatment by professional psychotherapists. Children constitute the age group least frequently serviced by mental health professions, and it is the one that has the largest variation in professional treatment rates by type of institution. Similarly, adolescents have somewhat less variation in treatment rates by types of institution and are more frequently treated by therapists than is true of children. In sum, chronological age is an important basis for professional specialization in the practice of psychotherapy.

When the findings presented thus far are summarized, the general conclusion that emerges is that the attributes of patients that serve as the foci for the technical training of the psychotherapist also provide the basis for specialization in therapeutic practice. Thus, specialized professional training is organized around both diagnostic categories and age groupings with the result that practitioners develop technical skills for alleviating certain types of mental distress in patients who are at certain stages in the life cycle. Indirectly, then, diagnostic categories and age groups provide the basis for specialization in the practice of psychotherapy. Although these technical criteria of specialization provide a professionally legitimate way for the practitioner to avoid having to treat the full range of persons who might seek his services, they serve to distinguish only broad categories of patients.

However, the therapeutic relationship is highly personal, and greater precision than that afforded by technical criteria is often desired by the psychotherapist. To gain such added precision, the therapist often scrutinizes the patient's social background for clues to the kinds of experiences the person has had that might be relevant to establishing a therapeutic relationship. In this way, social criteria come to be integrated with technical criteria and ultimately produce a specialized type of therapeutic practice. Having already examined the technical bases we will now turn to the social bases of specialization.

Psychotherapy and Social Class

Knowledge of the potential patient's social-class origins provides an important clue to his experiential background. Since the extent to which a potential patient's experiential background falls within the range of experiences that are meaningful to the therapist, it is not surprising that there is a vast literature documenting the relationship between social-class origins and differential participation in psychotherapy. The striking social-class differences in socialization and communication patterns as well as adult values and behaviors have led several investigators to suggest that participation in psychotherapy is inversely related to the extent of the class discrepancy between psychotherapists and potential patients. This interpretation assumes that the discrepancies in the social-class character-istics of therapists and patients reflect equally marked differences in education, verbal ability, values, and psychological-mindedness, which, in turn, result in mutual decision-making processes that produce an underrepresentation of lower-class participants. Indirect evidence that the bond between therapist and patient is based on shared social experiences comes from a study by Rowden and others (1970, p. 52), designed to investigate the "influence of social class, insight–verbal ability, and thera-pists' social-class origins on therapists' judgments regarding the use of psychotherapy as a treatment modality." The general conclusion of the study was that, of all the factors examined, the personality characteristics of the patient, including his insight, intelligence, and verbal ability, most strongly influenced the therapist's decision to recommend psychotherapy. To the extent that cognitive attributes reflect particular socialization experiences or communication patterns acquired early in life which, in turn, influence present-day perspectives, it is plausible to assume that the meaning ascribed to them depends primarily on the therapist's own back-log of social experiences. Thus, the impact of these cognitive character-istics on the therapist's decision to recommend psychotherapy can be considered a specific instance of the general tendency for social relation-ships to be facilitated by the presence of shared experiences.

In general, the extant literature makes it clear that psychothera-pists engage in selective recruitment of patients from various social cate-gories. Similarily, the relevant evidence uniformly suggests that the selective recruitment of psychotherapy patients is based on the mutual sharing by therapists and patients of certain social characteristics. Con-siderably less clarity exists with regard to the specific characteristics that, when shared by patient and therapist, bind the two parties into a psychotherapeutic relationship. Finally, the evidence regarding the extent to which the crucial attributes are related to the social-class origins of therapists and the current social-class position of patients is ambiguous and incomplete. To be sure, the studies do indicate that psychotherapists who come from upper-class backgrounds and who have, therefore, not experienced upward social mobility, do tend to overselect patients whose current status is commensurate with the therapist's present socioeconomic position. However, for lower-class background psychotherapists who have experienced upward social mobility, the basis for selectively recruiting patients has not been systematically specified. Since the issue is crucial to our understanding of the extent to which social class origins serve as the basis for developing specialized clientele in the mental health professions, we will focus on the relationship between the social-class background of psychotherapists and two components of the patient's current social class position: namely, the level of education achieved by the patient and the annual yearly income of the patient and/or his family. Although patients' education and income are clearly related, the two dimensions of social class were analyzed separately because it was felt that they might have a differential impact on the operation of the selective recruitment process. In particular, education would seem to be much more directly related to such factors as insight and verbal ability and, therefore, might contribute more to the establishment of therapeutic relationships based on shared values than would be true for income. Conversely, any significant relationships between social class origins of therapists and income levels of patients would enable us to specify the nature of economic discrimination, if any, existing among mental health practitioners.

In order to determine the social class origins of our sample of psychotherapists, the Hollingshead two-factor index of social position was used to determine the social class level of the respondent's father (Hollingshead and Redlich, 1958). This index is based on father's occupation and education, which are ranked separately. These two independent dimensions are differentially weighted and then combined to obtain the final class ranking. The scale produces the following five classes, as defined by Hollingshead: *Class I*, upper class, is composed of major professionals such as physicians, lawyers, engineers, architects, most of whom are in private practice, and major executives and officeholders in large financial, industrial, and manufacturing corporations. *Class II*, upper-middle class, is composed mainly of business managers, proprietors of middle-sized businesses, and salaried professionals, such as teachers, social workers, pharmacists, and accountants. *Class III*, intermediate-middle class, is composed primarily of owners of small businesses, semiprofessionals, technicians, salaried administrative and clerical personnel, supervisors, and skilled manual workers; the typical level of education is that of high school graduate. *Class IV,* lower-middle class, is composed primarily of semi-skilled manual employees, clerical and sales workers, and small shop-keepers; most people in this category attended high school, but did not graduate. *Class V,* lower class, is composed mainly of unskilled or semi-skilled manual workers and low-paid service workers; most of the persons in this category do not have a grade-school diploma.

Psychotherapists' current social class positions, based on their occu-pational ranking, education, and income, are all ranked as Class II or above. Since the major distinctions between Classes I and II revolve around such symbolic factors as lineage, residential area, and club mem-berships, it is not possible for us to distinguish between these two class levels with the available data. Hence, the two top classes will be considered as representatives of the professionals' current class standing, and practi-tioners coming from backgrounds of Class III and below will be con-sidered to have been upwardly mobile one or more class levels.

It should be noted that our examination of the social bases of clientele selection uses therapists' responses both as a basis for classifying their own social class origins and as a basis for classifying their patients' income and educational levels. That is, the measure of the therapists' social class background is not independent of the measure of the patients' current class characteristics—both sets of characteristics are based on the therapists' responses to various questionnaire items. This reliance on data obtained solely from therapists to classify both therapists and patients with respect to social-class characteristics raises a number of methodological issues. For example, exactly how reliable are therapists' descriptions of their patients' characteristics; to what extent do the therapists' own characteristics bias their perceptions and/or descriptions of the charac-teristics of their patients? In short, to what extent does exclusive reliance on data obtained from therapists bias any findings that either support, disconfirm, or specify the social bases of patient selection? These questions obviously cannot be dismissed lightly.

In methodologically evaluating the appropriateness of these data, several considerations are important. One concerns the question of the reliability of therapists' descriptions of their patients. All our previous analyses, as well as our impressions based on intensive interviews with mental health professionals, suggest that therapists' commitment to ob-jective analyses of themselves as well as their patients and their extensive and accurate knowledge of the social characteristics of their patients mitigate the gravity of this methodological limitation. More important, any biases with respect to supporting or disconfirming the existence of social factors in clientele selection should not affect the relative influence of patients' income and education. Furthermore, one advantage of using data obtained from psychotherapists' descriptions of their own and of their patients' characteristics to assess the nature of therapeutic specialization is that these data describe relationships that have actually been established rather than merely expressions of preference for certain types of patients.

To what extent do social-class characteristics enter into the process of establishing therapeutic encounters in the mental health field? The extent to which economic considerations serve to bind the two parties into a psychotherapeutic relationship is revealed in Table 18.

Although private-practicing psychotherapists do tend to selectively recruit patients from certain economic strata, the evidence does not support the view that social class origins of the therapist affect the rate at which he accepts patients from various income groups. With regard to differential recruitment of patients, it is clear that private psychotherapists do tend to give selective preference to persons in the higher income brackets. Specifically, relative to their proportional representation in the society as a whole, persons with incomes of $20,000 or more are markedly over-represented in the patient populations treated by private-practicing members of all four professional groups. Similarly, while approximately one-half of the adult population in the United States had an income of less than $10,000 in 1961, the proportion of patients having comparable incomes in the private practices of each of the mental health professions is considerably smaller. However, the social class origins of the psychotherapist, whether he be an analyst, psychiatrist, clinical psychologist, or psychiatric social worker, do not affect this pattern of preferential treatment. That is, psychotherapists from lower social class origins are no more likely to carry low-income patients than are their professional colleagues with higher class origins. Even more important, perhaps, is the fact that upwardly mobile psychotherapists differ very little from their socially stable colleagues with regard to the selection of patients from the wealthiest social categories. Psychotherapists coming from Class III, IV, and V backgrounds have themselves had to overcome a series of financial, social, and psychological obstacles in order to achieve their current high professional and economic status. Since one might well expect persons possessing both the ability and the motivation to move upward one or more class levels to place greater emphasis on the financial rewards of professional status than persons who have inherited their professional standing, it is reassuring to note that this is not the case for private-practicing psychotherapists.

In general, the findings contained in Table 18 suggest that the probability of being accepted into treatment by a private psychotherapist is only partially related to financial standing. To be sure, it would appear that a minimum level of income is necessary for a person to have a reason-

Table 18. Social Class Origins of Psychotherapists by Income of Patients Seen in Private Practice

SOCIAL CLASS ORIGINS OF PRACTITIONERS

Income of Patients	Class I	Class II	Class III	Class IV	Class V	Total
			Percent			
PSYCHOANALYSTS						
Less Than $5000	6.7	3.5	3.9	2.8	4.6	3.6
$5000 to $10,000	27.8	20.6	19.0	22.2	29.6	21.4
$10,000 to $20,000	31.2	20.7	31.1	33.5	26.0	32.0
$20,000 and More	25.2	35.7	32.6	35.3	29.6	33.6
Income Unknown	8.9	8.3	13.4	6.2	10.2	9.3
Totals	100	100	100	100	100	100
	(682)	(1999)	(2892)	(3356)	(196)	(9125)
PSYCHIATRISTS						
Less Than $5000	7.4	8.7	9.9	6.7	5.3	7.9
$5000 to $10,000	34.9	31.8	29.6	30.0	28.6	30.7
$10,000 to $20,000	23.4	34.9	32.6	33.2	38.8	32.9
$20,000 and More	16.2	15.9	17.2	12.6	21.9	15.2

CLINICAL PSYCHOLOGISTS

Income Unknown	13.0	8.6	10.7	17.6	5.3	13.3
Totals	100	100	100	100	100	100
	(917)	(2827)	(2517)	(4429)	(451)	(11,141)
Less Than $5000	13.5	5.9	6.8	6.3	4.0	6.5
$5000 to $10,000	31.1	39.8	35.1	35.1	25.1	34.9
$10,000 to $20,000	35.9	27.8	32.4	34.2	35.7	32.9
$20,000 and More	11.0	10.8	12.8	14.1	28.8	14.1
Income Unknown	11.4	15.7	12.8	10.2	6.3	11.5
Totals	100	100	100	100	100	100
	(839)	(1704)	(3031)	(5217)	(823)	(11,644)

PSYCHIATRIC SOCIAL WORKERS

Less Than $5000	7.5	4.3	5.0	6.2	11.7	6.3
$5000 to $10,000	35.1	28.9	33.5	37.0	43.7	35.6
$10,000 to $20,000	45.6	44.0	41.3	36.7	33.3	39.1
$20,000 and More	10.9	18.2	19.1	10.2	11.0	13.7
Income Unknown	0.8	4.3	0.9	9.9	0.3	5.3
Totals	100	100	100	100	100	100
	(239)	(418)	(736)	(1323)	(300)	(3016)

able chance of being accepted into psychotherapy, but beyond that level the chances of receiving therapy do not improve with wealth. In sum, there is little evidence to support the contention that the selective recruitment of patients by private psychotherapists is based primarily on financial considerations.

The findings concerning therapeutic encounters that occur in mental health institutions are similar to those that occur in private practice, except that the patients are concentrated at the lower end of the income hierarchy. That is, among the population of patients receiving treatment in organizations, 70 percent of those seen by psychoanalysts, 68 percent of those seen by psychiatrists, 64 percent of those seen by clinical psychologists, and 77 percent of those seen by psychiatric social workers have annual family incomes of less than $10,000. The social class origins of the psychotherapists, of course, have no effect on this pattern of patient allocation. Thus, the difference between private and organizational practice serves to distinguish among patients according to their economic standing, but does not serve to distinguish psychotherapists with regard to specialized clientele.

When placed in the context of our earlier discussion of the social bases of client specialization in psychotherapy, the finding of no consistent relationship between therapist's social class origins and patient's current level of income supports the suggestion that shared experiences and values, rather than similarity in current social status, constitute the bond between particular therapists and their patients. That is, current income is not an accurate reflection of the biographical characteristics of the patient and is a weak indicator of social class related values. Thus, to the extent that shared experiences are in some way implicated in the establishment of psychotherapeutic relationships, there is little reason to expect the social-class backgrounds of therapists to have any effect on the selection of patients from various income groups. Current income is, therefore, an important but indirect measure of the social bases for the selective recruitment of patients by psychotherapists.

In contrast, an assessment of the educational level of patients provides a direct measure of the influence of social experiences on the allocation of patients to psychotherapists. That is, level of educational attainment represents a powerful indicator of current social values as well as reflecting a wide range of biographical characteristics. Thus, by comparing the current educational level of patients with the social class origins of therapists, it is possible to examine the extent to which the residue of early socialization experiences, summarized in a set of social values, binds particular patients to particular psychotherapists (see Table 19). It is not surprising to find that the educational level of patients treated in private practice binds them to particular psychotherapists. College graduates are preferred over any other specific level of educational attainment by each of the four groups of private-practicing psychotherapists. However, it is surprising to find that the educational level of patients treated in private practice varies with the psychotherapist's social class origins only for clinical psychologists and psychoanalysts. Clinical psychologists most clearly fit the expected pattern, in that therapists from the higher social class backgrounds tend to have a much greater concentration of college graduates as patients than is true for their professional colleagues from lower-class backgrounds. Psychoanalysts have a similar pattern of selective recruitment but differences are much less pronounced than is the case for psychologists.

Although the extent to which college graduates are preferred as patients clearly distinguishes clinical psychologists who have experienced upward social mobility from their socially stable colleagues in private practice, psychologists resemble the other professional groups in that practitioners from the lower three social classes reveal no tendency to select patients whose current educational level most closely approximates the therapist's class background. However, the same cannot be said for practitioners treating patients in organizational settings. That is, the relationship between therapists' social-class origins and patients' level of educational attainment is uniform in three of the four professional groups. For clinical psychologists and psychiatric social workers the relationship is direct: the lower the social class origins of the therapists, the larger the proportion of patients having less than a high school education. The relationship for psychiatrists is uniform but inverse: the lower the social-class origins of the therapists, the smaller the proportion of patients having less than a high school education. In light of the fact that these psychotherapeutic relationships occur in institutions in which patients are required to go through organizational screening processes before they initially meet their therapists, these findings are truly remarkable. In fact, only psychoanalysts, who exhibit no consistent relationship between class origins of therapists and level of educational attainment of patients, fit the expected pattern of patient allocation in mental health institutions. The importance of these findings warrants additional examination.

Perhaps the most intriguing pattern of patient selection by organizational practitioners is the one occurring among psychiatrists. Variation in class background makes no consistent difference in the way patients are allocated to psychiatrists in organizations as long as the patients have at least graduated from high school. However, variation in class background does produce differences not only in the proportion of patients having less than a high school education, but also the proportion of patients whose

Table 19. SOCIAL CLASS ORIGINS OF PSYCHOTHERAPISTS BY EDUCATIONAL LEVEL OF PATIENTS AND SETTING OF PRACTICE

Educational Level of Patients	SOCIAL CLASS ORIGINS OF PRACTITIONERS					
	Class I	Class II	Class III	Class IV	Class V	Total
			Percent			
PSYCHOANALYSTS IN PRIVATE PRACTICE						
Less Than High School	9.4	6.9	8.2	8.8	12.8	8.4
High School Graduate	15.7	14.2	14.6	17.5	19.4	15.8
Some College	15.4	14.0	14.1	17.0	33.9	15.8
College Graduate	58.3	59.6	56.3	54.0	31.4	55.7
Education Unknown	1.1	5.2	6.8	2.7	2.5	4.4
Totals	99.9	100	100	100	100	100
	(679)	(2077)	(2862)	(3565)	(242)	(9425)
PSYCHIATRISTS IN PRIVATE PRACTICE						
Less Than High School	7.2	14.0	12.1	15.8	15.1	13.7
High School Graduate	16.9	29.1	23.3	28.6	28.0	26.5
Some College	18.7	18.1	24.2	20.2	14.7	20.2

College Graduate	51.4	36.0	35.8	25.9	38.9	33.6
Education Unknown	5.7	2.7	4.7	9.3	3.3	6.1
Totals	100 (1044)	99.9 (2835)	100 (2583)	100 (4536)	100 (457)	100 (11,455)

CLINICAL PSYCHOLOGISTS IN PRIVATE PRACTICE

Less Than High School	16.6	10.0	15.1	14.0	9.8	13.3
High School Graduate	20.3	15.0	25.3	20.9	16.7	20.3
Some College	3.4	13.7	19.1	21.3	24.4	18.3
College Graduate	59.0	59.6	38.1	39.9	41.2	44.9
Education Unknown	0.6	1.7	2.4	3.9	7.8	3.1
Totals	100 (701)	100 (2662)	100 (2596)	100 (5657)	100 (634)	100 (12,250)

PSYCHIATRIC SOCIAL WORKERS IN PRIVATE PRACTICE

Less Than High School	18.2	23.8	18.6	13.5	30.4	18.1
High School Graduate	20.8	19.7	20.8	25.9	29.4	23.7
Some College	30.7	16.8	21.0	23.7	11.8	21.5
College Graduate	26.8	34.1	36.2	33.9	18.7	32.6
Education Unknown	3.5	5.5	3.4	2.9	9.7	4.1
Totals	100 (231)	100 (416)	100 (818)	100 (1370)	100 (289)	100 (3124±)

Table 19. SOCIAL CLASS ORIGINS OF PSYCHOTHERAPISTS BY EDUCATIONAL LEVEL OF PATIENTS AND SETTING OF PRACTICE (Cont.)

Educational Level of Patients	SOCIAL CLASS ORIGINS OF PRACTITIONERS					
	Class I	Class II	Class III	Class IV	Class V	Total
			Percent			
PSYCHOANALYSTS IN ORGANIZATIONS						
Less Than High School	30.0	34.9	49.3	29.7	75.7	39.3
High School Graduate	16.7	20.2	20.0	37.0	9.1	25.7
Some College	15.5	8.7	7.0	10.7	6.1	9.0
College Graduate	37.8	21.0	8.3	18.7	9.1	15.6
Education Unknown	—	15.2	15.4	3.8	—	10.4
Totals	100	100	100	100	100	100
	(90)	(415)	(883)	(764)	(33)	(2185)
PSYCHIATRISTS IN ORGANIZATIONS						
Less Than High School	50.9	46.8	43.6	37.3	27.6	42.4
High School Graduate	16.0	28.6	25.7	15.1	2.0	15.4
Some College	10.8	13.3	10.9	9.6	6.4	10.9

College Graduate	10.2	7.9	6.2	9.3	8.8	8.3
Education Unknown	12.0	3.3	13.6	28.7	55.2	17.7
Totals	100 (756)	100 (1759)	100 (1506)	100 (2561)	100 (203)	100 (6785)

CLINICAL PSYCHOLOGISTS IN ORGANIZATIONS

Less Than High School	17.1	29.1	34.1	36.4	46.0	34.1
High School Graduate	36.5	20.2	21.5	23.3	22.3	23.0
Some College	23.1	15.3	20.3	16.6	14.5	17.4
College Graduate	16.9	7.5	18.5	15.2	27.8	14.3
Education Unknown	6.5	27.9	5.6	8.4	5.2	11.1
Totals	100 (650)	100 (2062)	100 (2409)	100 (4730)	100 (848)	100 (10,699)

PSYCHIATRIC SOCIAL WORKERS IN ORGANIZATIONS

Less Than High School	39.2	35.2	37.5	45.2	60.1	42.2
High School Graduate	25.6	22.8	28.9	26.6	23.3	25.9
Some College	9.1	15.8	12.8	18.8	4.9	11.5
College Graduate	16.9	16.2	13.2	18.2	3.4	10.3
Education Unknown	9.1	9.9	7.5	7.7	8.4	8.3
Totals	100 (790)	100 (2731)	100 (2557)	100 (4733)	100 (1087)	100 (11,898)

educational background is unknown to the psychotherapist. That is, organizational psychiatrists from Classes III, IV, and V have proportionally more patients with unknown educational backgrounds and proportionally fewer patients with less than a high school education than is true of their colleagues coming from the upper two classes. Taken together, these two patterns strongly suggest that psychiatrists do not attempt to select patients whose current educational level most closely matches their own social class background. In combination, the two patterns also suggest that, for psychiatrists, the relationship between patients' level of educational attainment and therapists' social class origins is more a reflection of selective organizational recruitment than selective recruitment of patients by practitioners. Support for this assertion is found in the fact that, for psychiatrists, 64 percent of the institution's patients with less than a high school education receive their treatment in either a general or a mental hospital. Both types of institutions provide inpatient care for the severely disturbed but they differ in that mental hospitals also allocate major resources to the custody and management of long-term patients. The two types of mental health organizations also differ in terms of their patterns of recruitment of mental health professionals. That is, mental hospitals recruit proportionally more professionals from the lower social classes than is true of other types of mental health institutions. In our sample of psychotherapists, the characteristics of the mental hospital are reflected in the fact that psychiatrists from Classes III, IV, and V are less likely to know the level of educational attainment of their patients than is true of their colleagues from Classes I and II. Psychiatrists who have limited knowledge of their patients probably do not frequently encounter them in psychotherapeutic relationships—this too is consistent with the conventional view of mental hospitals as sites for professional practice.

The types of institutions in which treatment occurs also provide a clue to understanding the relationship of social class origins of therapists and level of educational attainment of patients that exists among clinical psychologists and psychiatric social workers. That is, among clinical psychologists, eight out of every ten patients who come to therapeutic encounters having less than a high school education receive their treatment in an institution primarily concerned with outpatient care. The comparable figure for organizationally based psychiatric social workers is seven out of every ten patients. The patient populations served by such organizations as schools and psychiatric clinics include persons with varying levels of educational attainment while the focus on outpatient care provides the professional practitioner with some freedom to select patients. Thus, the relationship between the practitioners' social-class origins and the patients' level of educational attainment exhibited by clinical psychologists and psychiatric social workers reflects the combined influences of selective organizational recruitment of professionals and selective recruitment of patients by professionals.

When our findings regarding the relationship between social-class origins of psychotherapists and the educational level of patients are summarized, it becomes clear that client specialization is based to only a limited degree on social class characteristics. For private practitioners, the general tendency is to select patients who most closely approximate the psychotherapist's current social standing. With the notable exception of clinical psychology, this pattern of patient recruitment holds regardless of the class background of the psychotherapist. For psychotherapists in organizational practice, class background is related to the type of institution in which the practitioner meets patients. The characteristics of the employing institution also affect the availability of various types of patients as well as the degree to which the psychotherapist can select his patients. Where the opportunity structures permit, some professionals do select their patients in such a way that the resulting clientele is more or less congruent with the practitioner's own class background. The general conclusion emerging from these findings is that psychotherapeutic relationships tend to be established on much the same bases as other social relationships, at least with regard to social class characteristics. Unless organizational constraints interfere, psychotherapists from the upper class tend to select patients who have social characteristics similar to their own. Psychotherapists of lower-class origins are more likely to recruit patients who have characteristics that match their current social standing than to recruit patients who have characteristics that match their original class position. Where organizational factors increase the range of educational attainment represented by potential patients, psychotherapists do show a tendency to select persons with whom they have some social-class affinity as patients.

Cultural Affinity and Psychotherapy

The essential structure of the psychotherapeutic relationship is based on the patient's need for help with certain personal problems and the therapist's ability to provide help in ameliorating or coping with these problems. In this respect, the psychotherapist-patient relationship involves an asymmetrical flow of help: regardless of whether it is in the form of interpretation, understanding, listening, reflecting, or stimulating, help proceeds from therapist to patient. In order for the psychotherapist to be able to meet the patient's need for assistance in various dimensions of his personal life, the therapist must be able to understand, accept, and identify with both his own and the patient's perspective on living. Thus, the decision to accept a person into psychotherapy rests, in part, on the therapist's judgment as to whether or not the potential patient's perspective is compatible with the therapist's own perspective and range of experience.

Given our biographical perspective on the formation and maintenance of the psychotherapist's perspectives, we have assumed that the home world acquired during the period of preprofessional socialization has a lasting impact on the individual. This home world is never totally reconstructed during professional training, and its concomitant perspective has equally lasting biographical importance. Thus, to the extent that one of the defining characteristics of a professional role is that it requires a heavy investment of self, it is plausible to assume that in performing this role the individual will rely heavily on affective criteria—religiocultural criteria—values and attitudes that formed the cultural context of the practitioner's preprofessional experiences. Therefore, by using religiocultural background as a criterion for patient selection, the therapist can attempt to insure the sharing of at least some social values and experiences.

In order to explore this working hypothesis, psychotherapists in our sample were asked to respond to the following questionnaire item: "For you, your spouse, and your parents, indicate whether you or they share a cultural affinity with one of these religious groups even though there may be no adherence to its religious position: Protestant, Catholic, Jewish, None, Other." The respondents were also asked to indicate the religiocultural background of their patients, separately for those seen in private practice and those treated in organizations, by using the first three of the above categories. The results obtained when religiocultural backgrounds of therapists are compared with those of their patients are contained in Table 20.

For therapeutic encounters conducted in private practice, the uniformity across all four professional groups in the congruence of therapists' and patients' religiocultural backgrounds provides strong empirical support for the view that patient selection is based, in part, on the relationship between these biographical characteristics. Thus, regardless of professional affiliation, private-practicing Protestant psychotherapists are much more likely to select patients with a Protestant religiocultural background than patients having any other cultural affinity. Similarly, psychotherapists having a Jewish cultural affinity are much more likely to select patients who also have a Jewish cultural background than patients coming from either Protestant or Catholic backgrounds. The same pattern of cultural congruence is exhibited by Catholic therapists and patients for private-practicing psychiatrists and clinical psychologists, but not for members of the other two professional groups. Actually, psychiatric social workers constitute the only meaningful deviation from the pattern of cultural congruence between therapists and patients. Catholic social workers in private practice exhibit a preference for Jewish patients rather than for patients coming from either one of the two Christian traditions; Catholic psychoanalysts, on the other hand, tend to prefer Protestants rather than Catholics or Jews as patients. Finally, the psychotherapists having the most erratic pattern of patient selection are, of course, those who claim no cultural affinity. The absence of any binding religiocultural conviction leads these uncommitted practitioners to select patients from the various cultural groups at a rate that is commensurate with the proportional distribution of the religiocultural groups within each of the profession's patient populations.

The emphasis on religiocultural background is obviously consistent with psychotherapeutic ideologies (for example, psychoanalytic, neo-Freudian) that emphasize the influence of early childhood experiences on adult attitudes and behaviors. Since the overwhelming majority of professionals adhere to therapeutic ideologies that focus on early childhood experiences, there is a direct link between the psychotherapeutic subculture and practitioners' religiocultural origins. In a very real sense, then, the various social forms of patient specialization result from the various patterns of background cultural conditioning experienced by psychotherapists. The home world of the patient also plays a significant role in allocation of clientele to psychotherapists in private practice. That is, the establishment of the psychotherapeutic relationship requires that both therapist and patient accept a psychological view of man. For most psychotherapists, this broad psychological perspective is embedded in a general psychoanalytic theoretical perspective. Regardless of the particular therapeutic orientation espoused by practitioners, potential patients from a Jewish background are more willing to accept the professional psychological perspective of psychotherapists than are individuals from other religiocultural groupings. This is reflected in the fact that more than 40 percent of all patients seen by our sample of private-practicing psychotherapists come from Jewish backgrounds, with Protestant patients constituting the next most prevalent, followed by a much smaller proportion of patients with Catholic backgrounds. This representation of religiocultural groups in the patient population matches the representation of cultural backgrounds among psychotherapists, who are disproportionately composed of Jews and those who eschew traditional religious allegiances. In short, religiocultural background strongly affects the types of persons who seek out psychotherapists as well as the types of psychotherapists who are available to offer treatment in private practice. Thus, religiocultural background

Table 20. RELIGIOCULTURAL AFFINITY OF PSYCHOTHERAPISTS AND RELIGIOCULTURAL BACKGROUND OF PATIENTS, BY TYPE OF TREATMENT SETTING

Religiocultural Background of Patients	RELIGIOCULTURAL AFFINITY OF PSYCHOTHERAPISTS				
	Protestant	Catholic	Jew Percent	None	Total
PSYCHOANALYSTS IN PRIVATE PRACTICE					
Protestant	46.2	39.2	26.4	36.3	31.5
Catholic	14.4	25.1	10.0	11.8	11.4
Jew	35.3	27.4	59.4	46.9	52.6
Religion Unknown	4.2	8.2	4.2	5.0	4.4
Totals	100 (1629)	100 (255)	100 (6497)	100 (1595)	100 (9976)
PSYCHIATRISTS IN PRIVATE PRACTICE					
Protestant	43.8	29.4	26.5	36.5	32.7
Catholic	23.5	46.1	17.2	22.5	22.6

Jew	19.9	13.9	48.3	20.8	33.7
Religion Unknown	12.8	10.6	8.0	20.6	11.1
Totals	100 (3152)	100 (1237)	100 (5861)	100 (1375)	100 (11,625)

CLINICAL PSYCHOLOGISTS IN PRIVATE PRACTICE

Protestant	49.2	33.0	26.2	32.9	32.8
Catholic	16.3	38.6	13.1	13.4	15.1
Jew	25.3	23.4	54.2	46.2	45.0
Religion Unknown	9.1	4.9	6.+	7.5	7.1
Totals	100 (2681)	100 (551)	100 (6749)	100 (2049)	100 (12,030)

PSYCHIATRIC SOCIAL WORKERS IN PRIVATE PRACTICE

Protestant	50.7	24.6	25.7	46.8	33.6
Catholic	19.4	19.7	9.2	12.9	12.3
Jew	26.0	37.1	55.0	35.6	45.6
Religion Unknown	3.9	18.6	10.1	4.3	8.5
Totals	100 (639)	100 (183)	100 (1955)	100 (474)	100 (3251)

Table 20. RELIGIOCULTURAL AFFINITY OF PSYCHOTHERAPISTS AND RELIGIOCULTURAL BACKGROUND OF PATIENTS, BY TYPE OF TREATMENT SETTING (Cont.)

Religiocultural Background of Patients	RELIGIOCULTURAL AFFINITY OF PSYCHOTHERAPISTS				
	Protestant	Catholic	Jew Percent	None	*Total*
PSYCHOANALYSTS IN ORGANIZATIONS					
Protestant	43.9	15.8	27.7	22.4	28.6
Catholic	12.1	15.8	19.0	14.5	17.1
Jew	20.0	15.8	20.4	25.8	21.5
Religion Unknown	23.9	52.6	32.9	37.2	32.8
Totals	100 (280)	100 (19)	100 (1305)	100 (441)	100 (2045)
PSYCHOLOGISTS IN ORGANIZATIONS					
Protestant	44.8	39.9	26.6	28.8	33.9
Catholic	21.4	35.5	25.2	19.1	24.8

Jew	13.4	19.6	16.8	16.9	16.3
Religion Unknown	20.4	4.9	31.4	35.2	25.0
Totals	100 (2053)	100 (1125)	100 (3184)	100 (1170)	100 (7532)

CLINICAL PSYCHOLOGISTS IN ORGANIZATIONS

Protestant	34.3	20.6	25.3	26.1	27.1
Catholic	17.0	38.4	20.9	18.6	22.2
Jew	15.5	9.2	28.5	19.3	21.1
Religion Unknown	33.2	31.7	25.3	35.9	29.6
Totals	100 (2851)	100 (1603)	100 (5061)	100 (1304)	100 (10,819)

PSYCHIATRIC SOCIAL WORKERS IN ORGANIZATIONS

Protestant	43.7	26.0	29.9	37.4	33.7
Catholic	21.9	35.0	17.4	19.5	21.6
Jew	20.3	19.7	40.0	27.0	30.3
Religion Unknown	14.1	19.3	12.6	16.0	14.3
Totals	100 (3595)	100 (1960)	100 (6071)	100 (711)	100 (12,337)

not only tends to filter and screen potential participants in a private psychotherapeutic relationship but also serves as a crucial mechanism for selectively allocating particular patients to particular therapists.

Psychotherapeutic encounters that occur in organizational contexts result from a screening process that is quite different from that occurring in private practice. Consequently, it is not surprising to find that the participants to the therapeutic relationship occurring in organizations differ from those occurring in private practice. Specifically, the organizational clientele includes more patients with a Protestant than a Jewish religiocultural background. Also, the proportion of Catholic patients is much larger in organizations than in private practice. Equally important is the fact that organizations also contain more Protestant and Catholic psychotherapists than is true for private practice. Due to similarity in the patterns of patient and practitioner recruitment into organizations, it is possible for religiocultural background to serve as one basis for establishing therapeutic relationships in mental health institutions. To be sure, the organizational context diminishes the degree of fit between the religiocultural backgrounds of therapists and patients, but the relationship is clearly visible. Specifically, for clinical psychologists the pattern is clearly one of mutual congruence between religiocultural background of therapists and patients. Patient-therapist congruence is also the pattern for psychiatric social workers, except in the case of those practitioners who claim no cultural affinity. Because Jewish psychiatrists and those with no cultural affinity have a pronounced tendency to not know the religiocultural backgrounds of their patients, the pattern of congruence does not obtain for these organizational practitioners. However, since the vast majority of organizational patients treated by psychiatrists with these cultural backgrounds are seen either in general or mental hospitals, it is understandable that these medically trained psychotherapists would not know the details of their clients' backgrounds. The same institutional features also account for the fact that psychoanalysts do not know the religiocultural backgrounds of a sizable proportion of the patients they see in organizations. Thus, except for institutions specializing in inpatient care of severely disturbed patients, patient-therapist congruence on religiocultural background serves as a mechanism for allocating patients to therapists regardless of the treatment setting.

On the basis of all our findings concerning the technical and social basis of patient specialization, it appears that the several factors at issue take on their significance from the degree to which they relate to the final therapeutic activity. Thus, the professional training the practitioner received that equipped him to handle patients placed in certain diagnostic categories, is both therapeutically specific and refers to the professional's participation in current therapeutic encounters. Patient age, on the other hand, indicates much less about the patient's suitability for treatment by a particular therapist and provides fewer guidelines for the conduct of the therapeutic encounter than is true for diagnostic labels. Consequently, it is understandable that age of patient was not as directly linked to professional training as was true for diagnostic label. Similarly, with regard to social attributes, congruence in religiocultural background was found to be more strongly related to clientele specialization than was the relationship between social-class origins of the therapists and either the patient's level of income or level of educational attainment. Not only is religiocultural affinity directly related to the psychological bases of therapy, it also is a characteristic of the therapist that is both current and personal. In sum, the way in which professional and social attributes are related to the psychotherapeutic relationship determines whether or not they will become fused in the patient screening process to produce a specialized type of therapeutic practice.

Therapeutic Styles

On the basis of our discussion of the therapeutic community, it appears that psychotherapists rely on an individualistic orientation to cope with problems encountered in the course of their work. They approach the problem of professional responsibility for treating all persons who seek their therapeutic services by selectively recruiting patients according to whether or not they possess attributes that are personally meaningful to the therapist. Hence, we may well ask whether or not the *way* they perform psychotherapy is also informed by their individualistic orientation. That is, in our discussion of the variability in roles performed and clientele served, we have, upon occasion, taken note of the importance of situational factors in accounting for differences in behavior. However, when we focus on only one action situation, psychotherapy, these situational factors are held constant and variations in behavior must then be considered a function of differences among individual practitioners—who they are and what they bring to the therapeutic encounter.

What psychotherapists bring to the therapeutic encounter is determined in part by their professional preparation. The training of mental health professionals includes both the transmission of theoretical knowledge and the opportunity to obtain therapeutic skills through practice. It incorporates a system designed to instill professionally appropriate behaviors, with a set of procedures that give the trainee the understanding requisite for his practice. The objective of these training programs is to enable mental health professionals to "profess" their knowledge of an ability to act upon a certain body of phenomena, namely, mental problems. At the conclusion of his training program, the professional must be able to treat these problems successfully. In contrast to other professions, however, he cannot be given a formal and standardized body of knowledge and accepted techniques. He is presented with a number of theoretic formulations and is trained to use a number of techniques that rest primarily on his own personality for their effectiveness. He cannot rely on scientific tests to prove the worth of his knowledge, nor yet on shared dogma. Thus, in forming his belief system concerning the nature of the subject matter he must deal with, he recognizes the necessity that he will have to act, but will have little fact on which to base his action.

It is the necessity for action in the face of uncertainty that gives rise to the possibility of the practitioner developing an ideology; that is, a set of beliefs that are coherent and integrated and that provide him with a basis for action. In elaborating his ideology the therapist may simply accept the tenets of a theoretical school as they are taught; he may select from one or among several schools in an eclectic fashion; or he may interpret, translate, and modify until he reaches a satisfactory personal synthesis. This latter alternative is, of course, most consistent with the individualistic orientation with which we have characterized psychotherapists in our sample.

The nature of the psychotherapeutic relationship also raises the possibility that the behavior exhibited by the therapist will not directly correspond to the techniques the practitioner was exposed to during his professional training. That is, the therapist deals with an interpersonal relationship in which the most important tool is himself and there is no rule book that can fully govern the situation in which he happens to find himself. No test can be applied to determine if the "right" material has been covered, and even the objective determination of the results of his actions is exceedingly difficult. Thus, what the therapist does and how he does it must, of necessity, be an amalgamation of the techniques he has been taught and his personal responses, his perception of the situation and its requirements. His decision to act or not at any given moment must be made spontaneously. The results of hundreds of such decisions over long periods of time form his therapeutic style. It is clear that it cannot be assumed that this style will be identical to the techniques that the therapist has been exposed to during his training.

In order to assess the possibility that individualism permeates not only the mental health professional's choice of whom he performs therapy on, but also how he goes about conducting a psychotherapeutic relationship, a set of items was developed to tap behavioral practices. Each respondent was rated on every item in the set from his statements in the interview. The technique used was to read the entire interview, marking out those portions that contained information relevant to therapeutic practices. Rating was then performed on the second reading of the relevant sections. Each item received only one score. Therefore, when an issue was addressed more than once in an interview, the two statements were compared and the final score reflected agreement between them. Truly contradictory statements appeared very infrequently, but in such cases, if no additional evidence was found to confirm a clear decision, no score was given to the item. The entire coding process was then repeated for items of ideological conceptualizations.

The first step in deriving the items consisted of a content analysis of the ninety-six items devised by Sundland and Barker (1962). They state that their items were accumulated after an extensive perusal of the theoretical literature pertaining to therapy and include all major shades of opinion on many issues. Approximately three-fifths of the items could be classified as dealing with therapeutic ideological issues, and the remainder concerned behaviors. A number of items from the original set were deleted because they did not deal with matters of specifically therapeutic concern, or because they were too specific to be rated from the interview data at hand. In addition, a number of items were added on the basis of their appearance in the interview protocols; and, conversely, several items were dropped due to their infrequent appearance.

It should be noted that in the case of coding behavioral items, care was taken to refer very specifically to methods and techniques actually used by the therapist, with minimal reliance upon technical concepts.

For example, if a respondent discussed his practice of analyzing the patient's "transference," it was coded in terms of his discussing the therapeutic relationship. If he mentioned "analysis of the countertransference," it was coded as his recognition of his own responses as sources of data and/or as use of his own responses as therapeutic tools if this was relevant. In this way the coding procedure was designed to avoid the common confounding of ideological positions and actual behaviors, the error of confusing theory and practice.

Similarly, the ideological items were also designed to be free from specific theory-bound concepts. This was often achieved by referring a conceptual statement found in an interview only to an ideological item with which it most specifically dealt. For example, a respondent might say that he was primarily concerned with having his patient come to grips with the essence of the human encounter. Such a statement was only coded into the category dealing with concern about interpersonal relationships. It was recognized, however, that implicit in such a statement are a number of ideas concerning the representation and behavior of the therapist, the nature of personality, and the goals of therapy. It was decided, however, that attempting to code implicit meaning instead of only the explicit would lead first to multiple coding of single statements and further to subjectivity and unreliability.

The end product of this series of steps was a set of fifty behavioral items and fifty ideological issues. Table 21 presents the percentage of respondents agreeing to each of the behavioral items, according to their professional affiliation and self-designated therapeutic orientation. Since the vast majority of professionals are adherents of the psychoanalytic ideology, we have dichotomized therapeutic orientation into psychoanalytic and other.

Although the training programs maintained by the four mental health professions are standardized and clearly distinguishable, the therapeutic encounter is private and constantly variable. Perhaps that is why the findings contained in Table 21 can be accurately summarized by the level of agreement practicing psychotherapists expressed for item number 42; the highest level of agreement with the statement that the therapist relies primarily on his formally learned skills and techniques is the figure of 17 percent, found among psychoanalytically oriented social workers. In addition to indicating the limited utility of the therapeutic techniques acquired during professional training, the response to this item also serves to illustrate several other important generalizations contained in these data. First, the percentage of agreement with all the behavioral items tends to be low. To be sure, many items in the set elicit a higher level of positive endorsement than is true of item 42, but in only four cases did more than half of the members of a particular group of practitioners express agreement with a behavioral item. In other words, no items stand out as being core techniques around which therapists organize their style of therapy. The second generalization to be noted is that there are very few significant interprofessional differences in the rates at which various items of behavior are utilized in therapeutic relationships. This is true for both practitioners who designate their therapeutic orientation as being psychoanalytic as well as those who claim adherence to some other type of therapeutic orientation. Third, within each profession, self-designated therapeutic ideology makes no consistent differences in the therapeutic behavior employed by psychotherapists. There are, of course, differences between psychoanalytically oriented practitioners and those who subscribed to some other therapeutic orientation with regard to their utilization of specific items of behavior, but these differences do not systematically distinguish between the members of any one of the four professional groups. In combination, the three factors strongly suggest that the combinations of behaviors actually used by practicing psychotherapists reflect the individual's own synthesis of techniques much more than they reflect the therapeutic skills or theoretical orientation acquired during professional training.

Commensurate with the individualistic manner in which therapeutic behaviors are organized, psychotherapists exhibit an equally pronounced tendency to develop an idiosyncratic ideological belief system concerning their practices. If it is assumed that therapists develop a belief system based on the theoretical conceptions learned in training, then the finding contained in Table 22 indicates that the practitioner extensively modifies and adapts these formally learned tenets to suit his own situation. As was true for therapeutic behaviors, the rate of endorsement of specific ideology items is variable but characteristically low. Moreover, the variation in the acceptance of various ideological beliefs does not flow along the lines of either professional affiliation or therapeutic orientation. In sum, psychotherapists tend to develop idiosyncratic belief systems to provide them with guidelines for engaging in therapeutic action in situations of uncertainty.

On the basis of these findings, it seems safe to conclude that an individualistic orientation permeates not only the screening processes that psychotherapists use to selectively recruit patients, but also the set of beliefs that they develop about the nature of psychotherapy and the set of techniques that become organized into their therapeutic styles.

Conclusion

In the everyday social world "birds of a feather flock together," presumably because in part they talk the same language and, hence, can feel comfortable not only with the terminology used, but with the trend and flow of conversation and with the cognitive and intellectual processes used in deriving conclusions. Since psychotherapists specialize in the performance of verbal therapy, it is not surprising that they prefer patients who can talk their own language. However, the psychotherapeutic relationship, particularly when the therapist focuses on intrapsychic processes, differs radically from other social relationships. In particular, the psychotherapeutic encounter is set apart from other social encounters by its peculiar reliance on affective communication. Since the therapeutic relationship is not like other encounters, it is understandable that its establishment takes a unique form. Specifically, since affect constitutes the bond that connects therapist and patient in a therapeutic encounter, such interpersonal factors as similar intellectual abilities and cognitive styles are necessary, but not sufficient conditions for the endurance of the relationship. What is needed in addition is a commonality of feeling states. The presence or absence of emotional mutuality cannot be determined directly by the therapist. However, the therapist can determine the extent

Table 21. Percentage of Psychotherapists Agreeing with Each Behavior Item, by Profession, and Therapeutic Orientation

Behavior Items	Psychoanalysts		Psychiatrists		Psychologists		Psychiatric Social Workers	
	Psycho-analytic	Other	Psycho-analytic	Other	Psycho-analytic	Other	Psycho-analytic	Other
				Percent				
1. The therapist relies on intellectual interpretation of the patient's behavior as his main therapeutic tool.	41	23	46	47	33	43	56	23
2. The therapist bases his techniques on the individual personality of the patient.	41	31	39	63	53	34	37	29
3. The therapist maintains constant attention to everything being said by the patient.	33	23	43	42	47	41	27	41
4. The therapist adapts his techniques according to the diagnostic categorization of the patient.	37	23	39	53	28	21	37	23
5. Social family, group, or milieu therapies are often used.	33	8	25	53	33	31	37	41
6. The therapist uses supportive techniques.	30	54	43	42	25	14	42	29
7. All aspects of the therapeutic relationship are conceptualized and analyzed by the therapist.	37	23	32	21	33	38	27	23

8. Therapy focuses primarily on the demands of reality on the patients.	26	15	32	21	28	28	46	29
9. The therapist will lay down specific rules for behavior or offer suggestions and advice.	18	23	25	37	42	14	31	47
10. Therapy focuses primarily on present functioning of the patient.	26	31	25	42	33	24	27	35
11. The therapist relies on his own internal responses to the patient as guides to help him modify his own behavior.	15	54	29	16	22	35	33	35
12. The therapist describes his technique as "generally analytic."	48	23	36	16	36	14	15	12
13. The goals of therapy are set by the patient.	41	15	25	26	28	14	27	18
14. The therapist will use outside consultants and personal analysis regularly or with particular problem patients.	15	—	21	26	28	31	35	12
15. Therapy focuses primarily on the patient's relationship with others.	26	23	32	26	19	21	21	35
16. The therapist attempts to be empathically "with" the patient at all times, offering the strength of his own personality.	30	23	32	42	8	21	19	23
17. Therapist generally interprets dreams.	22	31	21	16	22	34	19	18
18. The therapist considers himself "active."	18	23	14	21	19	28	23	23

Table 21. Percentage of Psychotherapists Agreeing with Each Behavior Item, by Profession, and Therapeutic Orientation (cont.)

Behavior Items	Psychoanalysts		Psychiatrists		Psychologists		Psychiatric Social Workers	
	Psycho-analytic	Other	Psycho-analytic	Other	Psycho-analytic	Other	Psycho-analytic	Other
				Percent				
19. The goals of therapy are set by the therapist.	26	8	21	21	31	14	29	6
20. Drugs, shock, and/or hypnosis are often used.	37	46	39	42	3	7	4	6
21. Therapy focuses primarily on the patient's needs and desires.	18	—	—	16	25	38	31	—
22. The therapeutic relationship is examined with the patient.	22	8	25	21	31	24	19	23
23. The therapist will sometimes use innovation or experimental techniques with patients.	30	31	7	16	25	24	12	18
24. The therapist takes a genetic approach using the childhood experiences of the patient as illustrative or explanatory.	30	—	18	21	22	17	12	6
25. The therapist will sometimes reveal his personal responses to the patient.	15	23	14	10	14	38	19	12
26. The relationship between patient and therapist is always formally structured.	18	8	32	16	17	21	21	—

27. The therapist will see the family or friends of the patient as part of the treatment process.	15	—	21	26	6	7	17	29
28. The therapist relies primarily on his own personality as a therapeutic tool.	26	15	14	10	19	27	6	12
29. The therapist relies on his own internal responses to the patient as guides to help him modify his own behavior.	15	15	11	21	17	24	15	12
30. The therapist will sometimes attempt to manipulate the (unhospitalized) patient's environment.	15	23	7	21	11	10	25	12
31. The primary technique used in therapy is probing, directing attention, and pointing out areas of concern.	11	—	18	16	14	17	19	18
32. The therapist attempts to suppress all internal experiences while he is conducting therapy.	26	—	11	5	14	17	15	18
33. Therapist generally uses free association.	30	15	21	5	5	14	10	12
34. The primary technique used in therapy is neutral commentary, nondirective verbalization, and reflection.	30	—	21	21	6	21	10	6
35. The therapist will sometimes use "confrontation" techniques.	7	8	18	5	17	17	12	6

Table 21. Percentage of Psychotherapists Agreeing with Each Behavior Item, by Profession, and Therapeutic Orientation (cont.)

Behavior Items	Psychoanalysts		Psychiatrists		Psychologists		Psychiatric Social Workers	
	Psycho-analytic	Other	Psycho-analytic	Other	Psycho-analytic	Other	Psycho-analytic	Other
				Percent				
36. Interpersonal distance from the patient is always maintained.	22	—	7	21	17	14	8	12
37. The therapist will generally insist on the couch.	22	8	14	10	14	10	6	6
38. Intensive involvement is maintained in therapy through frequent visits (three or more per week).	15	15	18	5	11	10	4	—
39. The therapist will often express direct approval of the patient's thoughts, behaviors, etc.	15	—	21	5	8	14	15	18
40. All therapy is designed to permit the patient's free expression, acting out, etc., is permitted.	7	15	11	16	11	21	10	—
41. The therapist will arrange or conduct exploratory interviews to obtain a full background history of the patient.	4	8	4	16	8	—	10	18
42. The therapist relies primarily on his formally learned skills and techniques.	7	15	7	5	6	—	17	6

43. The therapist will sometimes "role-play," acting out the role of a significant other in the patient's life.	15	23	14	5	8	7	4	6
44. The goal and ends of therapy are discussed and explained to establish what both the patient and therapist have conceptualized.	4	—	7	5	2	10	6	12
45. Sometimes the therapist will reveal completely spontaneous reactions to the patient.	—	—	—	—	19	21	6	—
46. The therapist may express sympathy, etc., toward the patient but maintains complete inactivity at all times.	11	—	3	5	8	3	6	12
47. Therapy focuses primarily on the working through of particular emotional problems.	7	—	7	—	—	3	4	—
48. Therapy focuses primarily on specific traumatic events in the patient's life.	7	—	7	—	5	—	8	6
49. The therapist has conceptualized an ideal image of the therapeutic role and strives to conform to this image.	4	—	7	—	6	—	4	—
50. The therapist uses the therapeutic relationship to to guide and control the patient's behavior through the creation of guilt.	—	—	7	5	—	3	2	6
Total Number of Practitioners	27	13	28	19	36	29	48	17

Table 22. Percentage of Psychotherapists Agreeing with Each Ideology Items, by Professional and Therapeutic Orientation

Ideology Items	Psychoanalysts		Psychiatrists		Clinical Psychologists		Psychiatric Social Workers	
	Psycho-analytic	Other	Psycho-analytic	Other	Psycho-analytic	Other	Psycho-analytic	Other
	Percent							
1. The aim of therapy is to enable the patient to function within a social context, to adapt and adjust.	52	46	46	74	41	41	54	47
2. The therapist's responsibility is to diagnose and analyze the problems of the patient.	44	38	54	47	36	24	35	41
3. The aim of therapy is that the patient comes to understand his own behavior, achieving self-insight (intellectual).	41	8	39	58	42	34	40	53
4. The therapist must operate from within a coherent conceptual scheme to guide his understanding and behavior.	52	31	29	26	50	41	40	12
5. The therapist considers the interpersonal relationship the most important aspect of therapy.	26	38	43	42	25	55	44	23
6. Individual and social dynamics are intimately connected and both must be understood to effect therapeutic gains.	27	23	39	42	36	24	31	23

7. Each patient is different from every other.	41	8	18	10	39	24	37	23
8. The therapist considers his own internal response to the patient as important source of data.	33	23	25	26	31	41	35	23
9. The aim of therapy is the reduction of anxiety and alleviation of other symptoms.	56	31	39	42	25	21	23	12
10. The therapist must himself undergo analysis to learn how to control his own personality in the relationship.	30	38	21	21	19	31	40	18
11. The aim of therapy is that the patient achieve self-awareness and self-acceptance, the ability to experience and express emotion.	22	8	32	10	31	28	25	29
12. The aim of therapy is that the patient develop ego strength, self-acceptance and esteem, a sense of identity.	18	15	21	16	44	31	33	18
13. The aim of therapy is that the patient achieves social acceptance, social interaction and communication, new or better relationships.	22	23	21	16	22	31	27	29
14. Treatment is complete when the precipitating crises are resolved.	26	23	18	32	22	21	12	23
15. Therapy is considered fundamentally a learning experience, for the patient, and is designed as a corrective emotional experience.	11	31	14	—	19	34	19	23

Table 22. Percentage of Psychotherapists Agreeing with Each Ideology Items, by Professional and Therapeutic Orientation (cont.)

Ideology Items	Psychoanalysts		Psychiatrists		Clinical Psychologists		Psychiatric Social Workers	
	Psycho-analytic	Other	Psycho-analytic	Other	Psycho-analytic	Other	Psycho-analytic	Other
				Percent				
16. The therapist must see the intimate connections among the psychological, physiological, genetic, and constitutional aspects of the patient.	4	—	4	—	—	3	4	6
17. The aim of therapy is recognizing and coping with internal conflicts.	11	23	18	5	19	14	15	12
18. Therapeutic gains are assumed to be contingent upon the patient's obtaining an understanding of therapeutic processes and his relationship with the therapist.	22	8	14	21	22	21	10	18
19. Mental illness is personal unhappiness or discomfort.	22	8	7	32	11	14	10	18
20. Individuals are characterized by their internal resources and potential.	22	8	7	16	11	14	17	18
21. Therapy is considered to be a new type of interpersonal experience for the patient, which is based on empathy and trust.	4	31	18	10	19	21	10	6

22. Some patients simply cannot be helped by therapy.	30	—	14	5	22	10	8	6
23. Therapy is considered the application of a series of tools and techniques, which are formerly learned.	15	8	11	10	11	10	17	12
24. The responsibility for achieving the goals of therapy rests with the patient rather than the therapist.	22	8	7	21	17	14	12	—
25. The therapist recognizes the interpersonal power inherent in the therapeutic relationship and is concerned about its use and control.	18	—	7	21	17	14	10	—
26. The healthy personality is characterized by the capacity to choose.	7	8	11	16	22	21	4	6
27. Therapy is designed as an arena for the patient's free expression of himself and his problems.	4	—	14	10	17	14	15	—
28. Therapy is considered fundamentally as an inter-action between two individual personalities, and dependent upon the compatibility of those personalities.	18	8	7	—	11	7	10	6
29. The aim of therapy is to allow the patient to develop his own personality (self-actualization).	—	8	11	—	6	21	12	12
30. The therapist assumes that his effectiveness is a result of the patient's identification with aspects of the therapist's personality.	15	38	4	5	3	—	4	6

Table 22. Percentage of Psychotherapists Agreeing with Each Ideology Items, by Professional and Therapeutic Orientation (cont.)

Ideology Items	Psychoanalysts		Psychiatrists		Clinical Psychologists		Psychiatric Social Workers	
	Psycho-analytic	Other	Psycho-analytic	Other	Psycho-analytic	Other	Psycho-analytic	Other
31. Nonverbal as well as verbal communication must be interpreted by the therapist.	7	8	4	5	14	14	2	6
32. Symptoms can only be relieved through the patient's experience of emotional insight.	4	8	11	—	8	10	8	—
33. Man is basically an irrational, impulsive being.	15	—	14	—	6	17	—	—
34. The aim of therapy is that the patient comes to recognize his reality situation.	—	15	7	—	6	—	8	12
35. Mental problems should be treated in conjunction with medical supervision.	15	8	11	10	6	3	8	6
36. The therapist's personal responses to the patient are considered to have an important effect on the outcome of therapy.	11	—	4	26	6	10	—	—
37. Mental illness is the inability to control impulses and emotions.	15	—	11	—	17	3	—	—
38. Mental illness is self-destructive tendencies.	7	—	3	—	6	7	2	17
39. Mental illness is the distortion of reality.	4	—	—	10	6	7	6	6

Statement	1	2	3	4	5	6	7	8
40. Mental illness is the inability to act on impulses and emotions.	11	—	4	—	3	14	2	6
41. Mental problems must be treated in purely psychological terms.	4	—	—	10	11	7	2	—
42. The aim of therapy is that the patient changes his attitudes and values.	—	—	7	10	6	3	2	—
43. Ego control must always be maintained to prevent the disruption of functioning.	4	—	7	—	8	7	—	—
44. Therapy is expected to consist of a reenactment of past experiences of the patient.	4	—	4	—	—	3	4	6
45. All illnesses are conceptualized as lying along a single continuum, with no qualitative differences among them.	4	—	—	—	3	10	—	6
46. Mental illness is a function of the breakdown or defect in personality structure.	4	—	4	—	—	7	—	6
47. Mental illness is characterized by inappropriate emotional responses.	11	—	—	—	—	3	2	—
48. No acting out or irrationality is expected of a healthy personality.	—	8	7	5	—	3	2	—
49. All individuals have a natural (unconscious) propensity toward health.	4	—	—	—	3	3	—	—
50. The aim of therapy is personality growth and the achievement of maturity, personality reorganization and development.	—	—	—	—	—	7	2	—
Total Number of Practitioners	26 / 27	23 / 13	29 / 28	37 / 19	31 / 36	24 / 29	23 / 48	35 / 17

to which the patient's experiential background is one which he shares and/or understands, at least at a level sufficient for him to alleviate the person's mental distress. Since the psychotherapist's professional training has equipped him to deal with a certain range of human experience, the practitioner can use such attributes as diagnostic categories and chronological age as an index of the personal *technical* suitability for psychotherapy. However, to the extent that social-class standing accurately reflects social values and interpersonal skills the therapist can use the patient's class position as an index of his *social* suitability for psychotherapy. However, with regard to the patient's emotional suitability for psychotherapy, the practitioners in our sample apparently find the degree of fit between the therapist's and patient's religiocultural affinity to be the best screening device. In sum, social-class characteristics seem to be related to those dimensions of the psychotherapeutic role that pertain to intellectual understanding of human behavior in general, and particularly to the relativity of each individual patient's experiences. Religiocultural affinity, on the other hand, seems to be a direct expression of the emotional and introspective dimensions of the psychotherapist's role. Since religiocultural congruence is a basic factor in the selective matching of therapists and patients, we can only conclude that psychotherapy is primarily an affective rather than an intellectual venture. Perhaps that is why psychotherapists rely so heavily upon their own personalized, idiosyncratic set of beliefs and practices to conduct such relationships.

5

The Contemporary
Family

The assumption that persons and professions mutually attract each other rests on a solid empirical foundation in the mental health field. On the one hand, considerable evidence suggests that certain biographical characteristics of the person result in a set of attitudes and values that find expression more easily in the mental health professions than in many other fields. On the other hand, there is little doubt but that the mental health professions select as trainees individuals whose values and attitudes are in harmony with core professional functions. In an earlier volume (Henry, Sims, and Spray, 1971), we documented the way in which these two reciprocal processes interacted to produce a remarkable uniformity in the social and cultural characteristics of psychotherapists. Specifically, we found a marked tendency for psychotherapists to be second-generation Jewish persons who had rejected, in adolescence, the religious beliefs and political views of their parents and who had experienced intergenerational upward social mobility.

The close fit between biographical characteristics and professional identity not only serves to identify who becomes a psychotherapist but also highlights the possibility that biographical experiences may be implicated in styles of professional practice. For mental health professions, this

is a distinct possibility, since the symbolic core of professional identity revolves around psychotherapeutic skills in such a manner that the practitioner must focus his attention on personal roles and behaviors—those of
the patient as well as those of the therapist himself. In our earlier discussion of the public lives of psychotherapists (Henry, Sims, and Spray,
1971), we documented several points at which the close linkage of occupational and personal perspectives produced an orientation toward work
that strongly reflected the biographical experiences of the practitioners.
For example, we noted that sociocultural characteristics of therapists were
associated with their choice of a practice setting, the type of functions they
were performing in various types of settings, and the kinds of persons they
accepted as private psychotherapy patients.

On the basis of our previous findings, it is clear that the blurring
of the distinction between occupational and personal roles, which is
generally characteristic of professional life styles, is accentuated for psychotherapists. This heightens the possibility that life outside the profession
is partially shaped by influences generated within the professional therapeutic community. It also raises the possibility that early psychodynamic
experiences, as distinct from the sets of values and attitudes imbedded in
sociocultural characteristics, may also be implicated in both vocational
choice and style of practice in the mental health professions. We will
examine the first possibility by examining the manner in which the
psychotherapist relates to his spouse and children. The second possibility
will be examined in the context of the evidence we gathered on the
psychotherapist's relationships with parents and sibs, as well as data on
the therapist's early social, sexual, and intellectual development.

Bases of Mate Selection

A key for understanding the relation of personal and professional
roles resides in whom the psychotherapist chooses to marry and why. The
literature is replete with findings that document the overwhelming influence of social origins on mate selection and the predominance of
homogamous mating in this society. It would be expected that with mental health professionals, too, the impact of social characteristics traditionally acquired through early childhood socialization will have a strong
affect on choice of a spouse. At the same time, it is important to recognize
the extensive involvement in professional or other non-family-related
activities may tend to undermine the traditional social constraints placed
on choice of a spouse. The degree of professional involvement may also
affect the relationship the individual practitioner chooses to make between
his work world and his marital status. Thus, the distinctive nature of the
system of professional preparation undergone by psychotherapists may

serve to decrease both the level of social homogamy in mate selection and the rate of marital disruption. In particular, receipt of personal psychotherapy by the professional undoubtedly serves to increase the degree of commitment to the psychotherapeutic skill system and the psychodynamic explanatory system while at the same time integrating professional and personal change into one unified process. That is, at one level, undergoing personal psychotherapy represents training for a professional role and emphasizes changing the individual professionally. At another level, receiving psychotherapy involves the learning of one's own personal dynamics, thereby bringing about personal change. There is sound reason, therefore, for expecting the change-oriented nature of the professionalization process to affect both the level of social congruence and the amount of marital disruption characterizing the marriages of mental health professionals.

In order to examine these issues, the 3992 mental health professionals constituting the survey sample were asked to designate their current marital status. The resulting findings: single, 17 percent; married, 61 percent; remarried following divorce, 11 percent; remarried following widowhood, 1 percent; separated, 1 percent; divorced, 6 percent; and widowed, 3 percent. For the analyses to be presented here, these categories were combined as follows: First, remarried following divorce and remarried following widowhood were combined; almost nine out of every ten remarried practitioners had remarried following divorce. Second, the currently separated, divorced, and widowed categories were combined. Thus, the data on the current marital status of psychotherapists were finally classified into four categories: single (never married), 17 percent; married (first marriages), 61 percent; remarried (following divorce or widowhood), 12 percent; unremarried (not remarried following separation, divorce, or widowhood), 10 percent. These figures do not depart substantially from those describing the marital status of the white male population of the United States in the 1960 census.

With regard to the social bases of marriage, mental health professionals reveal the expected pattern of therapist-spouse congruence on important social characteristics. Specifically, professional-spouse congruence was measured on three social attributes—religious adherence, cultural affinity, and political orientation. For each of these factors on which the respondents and spouses were identical, respondents received a score of 1; for each dimension on which respondents and spouses differed, respondents received a score of 0. This procedure generated four possible scores: 0, indicating that the respondents and spouses were incongruent on all three variables; 1, indicating congruence on only one out of the three social variables; 2, indicating congruence on two of the three characteristics; and 3, indicating practitioner-spouse congruence on all three attributes. Respondents with a score of 0 were designated as having low marital congruence; those with a score of 3 were designated as having high marital congruence; and those with scores of 1 or 2 were considered to have moderate marital congruence. Using this typology, the evidence revealed that fully half of the total sample (53 percent) manifest high marital congruence while fewer than one-fifth (18 percent) were classified as having low marital congruence. However, a comparison between married and remarried practitioners revealed that there was a definite relationship between social homogamy and marital stability. Within each profession, married practitioners are much more likely to have a highly congruent marriage than is true for remarried practitioners. For the total sample, 55 percent of the married scored high on marital congruence while the comparable figure for the remarried was 41 percent. There was no significant interprofessional difference in this relationship. Conversely, remarried practitioners have a higher proportion of incongruent marriages (27 percent) than is true for stably married practitioners (16 percent).

In general, these findings are consistent with the extant literature, which indicates that there is a greater divergence between remarried husbands and wives on various social characteristics than is the case for those married only once. It is also important to note that while married and remarried psychotherapists differ significantly with regard to their marital congruence scores, it is not clear whether marital convergence is the *basis* for marriage or the *product* of marital interaction. That is, it is possible that agreement on religion, cultural affinity, and political orientation emerges out of marital interaction rather than being the basis for the initial selection of a mate. Since psychotherapists represent a highly educated and articulate group in which companionship norms of marriage are frequently held, the possibility that the marital partners "grow together" over time cannot be readily dismissed. However, whether the difference between married and remarried practitioners is due to differences in the length of their marriages or to differences in the initial basis of mate selection, the fact is that remarried psychotherapists less frequently base their marriage on value consensus derived from the sharing of similar religious, cultural, and political views, than is true for their once-married colleagues.

While it is not possible, with the available data, to assert that second and subsequent marriages of psychotherapists tend to be based on personal complementarity while first marriages tend to be based on value consensus, it is clear that marital status is related to receipt of personal psychotherapy (see Table 23). Specifically, in the sample as a whole, and in each profession except social work, a larger proportion of married than

Table 23. PROPORTION OF EACH PROFESSION WHO HAVE RECEIVED
PERSONAL PSYCHOTHERAPY, BY MARITAL STATUS

Marital Status	Psychiatrists[a]	Clinical Psychologists	Psychiatric Social Workers	*Total*
	Percent and (Base Number)			
Single	74.7 (99)	66.1 (192)	65.7 (379)	67.2 (670)
Married	79.9 (947)	72.4 (889)	57.7 (530)	72.1 (2366)
Remarried	84.5 (175)	83.6 (195)	76.6 (94)	82.3 (464)
Unremarried	83.0 (100)	82.7 (172)	77.9 (145)	83.0 (417)

[a] This column also includes psychoanalysts.

single professionals have experienced psychotherapy. This difference is not
the result of single respondents being younger, as the finding holds when
the data are controlled for age. The respondents themselves, as may be
seen later, suggest a reason for this difference; namely, that one function
frequently served by psychotherapy is the resolution of emotional and
interpersonal difficulties that otherwise would prevent marriage.

A second, and for our purposes here, more striking difference revealed in Table 23 is that between respondents who are stably married
and those who have experienced marital disruption. Practitioners who
have been divorced (or, infrequently, widowed), those who have subsequently remarried as well as those who have not, are much more likely
to have received psychotherapy than either those who have remained
married to their first spouse or those who are single. Both marital disruption and remarriage appear to be strongly related to psychotherapy—a
socialization experience that undoubtedly produces a more binding commitment to the psychodynamic explanatory system. In short, receiving
psychotherapy is strongly related to remarriage while high marital congruence is strongly related to first marriage.

The remaining issue to be resolved is whether personal psychotherapy and marital congruence represent independent or overlapping
influences on marital status. To explore this issue, we examined the relationship between personal psychotherapy and marital status for each level
of marital congruence. The results indicated that, for each level of con-

gruence, remarried practitioners are much more likely to have received therapy than married practitioners. Thus, personal psychotherapy is strongly related to marital status irrespective of some crucial characteristics of the marriage relationship. We can conclude that personal psychotherapy exercises an independent influence on second and subsequent marriages.

When these findings are summarized they suggest that the impact of personal psychotherapy is inversely related to marital stability. Thus, the interpenetration of therapeutic experiences and marital patterns occurs primarily among professionals who have experienced marital disruption. On the other hand, early socialization experiences, as reflected in congruence on social characteristics, have the greatest impact on first marriages. While there is no basis for inferring that psychotherapy either leads to or is precipitated by marital disruption, the evidence does support the conclusion that the interdependence of professional and personal roles is much greater for remarried than for once-married practitioners.

This chapter began with the questions whom and why does the psychotherapist marry? In turning to the data derived from interviews, we have the opportunity to answer these questions using more specific, more complex, and more subtle dimensions. We can, for example, now ask psychotherapists whom did they marry in terms of character and personality; and we can ask them why in terms of motivation.

However, the analysis of interview data concerning psychotherapists' relationships with their spouses and children must be preceded by some comment on the quality and tone of the discussions elicited by the series of questions directed at the psychotherapist's current family life. Of course, fifteen open-ended questions produced a great deal of material. But generally, compared with the richness of data and the free flow of its delivery when the respondents discussed former relationships with their parents or current relationships with their patients, discussion of their marital and parental relationships was relatively sparse and restricted. The topic, once begun, was not self-propelling.

Although we can only speculate as to why this was the case, several possibilities deserve discussion. The first of these may be termed a defense. There is a general expectation in the mental health field that those who perform psychotherapy, who aid the emotionally distressed, should themselves be psychically healthy, should have worked out their own problems. "Good" relationships with one's spouse and children are seen as constituting a kind of proof of such an achievement. Conversely, difficulties in these relationships make one vulnerable to the admonition "Physician, heal thyself." It is embarrassing not to be able to practice what one preaches. Prolonged discussion of family relationships, inevitably revealing imperfections, may be seen as self-incriminating and, in turn, as threatening to one's sense of professional legitimacy. Thus, in defense, a cursory generalization may be substituted for an easy, unrestrained, and extensive characterization of one's family life.

However, not only were there differences in the quantity and quality of *what* was said about current family relationships in comparison with discussions of relationships with parents and patients, but also interviewers emphasized the ephemeral differences in delivery—in expression, gesture, and tone of voice—that characterized these various discussions. The typical affective posture of the psychotherapist when speaking of his spouse or children was one of cool placidity, in striking contrast to the involved excitement that distinguished discussion both of the family relationships of childhood and of the current patient-therapist relationships.

It suggests that the intense and intimate engagement characteristic of the therapeutic encounter may be balanced by relatively moderate and distant interpersonal interaction in private life. Why? Occasionally a respondent will identify this lesser intensity of private relationships as a needed "relief" from therapeutic interaction. More rarely, a psychotherapist suggests that the intimacy of therapeutic interaction is a substitute for the lack of, or inability for, intimacy in one's personal life. These are stated as the respondents' own speculations. What is certain is that psychotherapists' discussions of current personal relationships with spouses and children are often characterized by brevity of response, by generality, and by a relatively less intense emotional style.

However, it should be stressed that such characteristics were by no means universally evident. Some respondents did indeed discuss their relationships with their spouses and children freely, expansively, and in intensely emotional terms. It is only as a group, and in comparison with discussion of either their *past* private life (parent and sibling relations) or their current *professional* life (therapeutic relations) that the relative affective diminution of their *current* private life (spouse and child relations) becomes apparent.

Relationship with Spouse

When controlled for sex and age, analysis of the data on the respondents' spouses yielded few interprofessional differences. Even *within* each sex, that is, viewing *only* husbands *or* wives, there were but few distinctions among the four professional groups of therapists. Accordingly, most of the data presented are for the sample as a whole, without professional breaks. Naturally, on those variables for which there are statistically significant interprofessional differences, or clear trends, they will be noted.

The first question asked about the respondent was "What kind of family did your wife (husband) come from? In particular, what was her (his) father's education and occupation?" The original intent of this question was to get the respondent's estimate of his spouse's social-class origins; and indeed, it served that purpose (see Table 24). In addition, however, it frequently elicited a characterization of what might be called the emotional climate of the spouse's family home. For example, one therapist says, "My wife had destructive parents," while another praises her husband's parents—"His folks are fine people, intelligent and kind." There were no interprofessional differences in the frequency with which positive and negative characterizations were offered by the respondents.

Table 24. FAMILY ORIGINS OF SPOUSES OF PSYCHOTHERAPISTS

	PROFESSION				
Father of Spouse	Psycho-analysts	Psychi-atrists	Clinical Psychol-ogists	Psychi-atric Social Workers	*Total*
		Percent			
OCCUPATION OF SPOUSE'S FATHER (N = 144)					
Occupation					
Business	39	41	54	39	44
Professional	39	33	23	15	28
Other	22	26	23	46	28
Total	100	100	100	100	100
	(33)	(39)	(39)	(33)	(144)
EDUCATION OF SPOUSE'S FATHER (N = 71)					
Educational Level					
Less Than High School	28	21	21	40	27
High School	22	26	47	20	30
More Than High School	50	53	32	40	43
Total	100	100	100	100	100
	(18)	(19)	(19)	(15)	(71)

Although not statistically significant, the percentage differences among the professions on occupation and education of spouse's father follow expected trends. Social workers especially and, to a considerable degree, also clinical psychologists are differentiated from the medical professions in that fewer of their spouses' fathers were professionals. There is a correlative tendency for the fathers of the spouses of social workers and psychologists to be less educated than those of psychiatrists and analysts. These findings are congruous with those characterizing the fathers of the respondents themselves and provide further evidence of the similarity of background between psychotherapist and spouse shown earlier.

The findings regarding the emotional climate of the spouse's home are noteworthy—more than half (55 percent) of the sixty-nine respondents who commented on this factor offered a negative characterization. Of course, strictly speaking, this is volunteered information; no question was designed specifically to explore this issue. Since it is probable that the subject would more likely be raised if "negative," this finding must be viewed cautiously. Furthermore, even if this figure was truly representative of the total sample, it is not clear that it would distinguish mental health professionals from other professional groups. Nevertheless, it is impossible to resist speculating about the possibility that with a greater-than-chance frequency mental health professionals marry persons who were raised in unhappy family situations. The hypothetical dynamics of such a mutual selection process might be the respondent's "desire-need" to nurture and treat meshing with the spouse's "desire-need" for succor and healing. As will be seen, such a formula was frequently implicitly given by the respondents in such remarks as "I guess I married my first 'patient.'"

Such self-diagnosis constituted one type of response to the question "Tell us about your decision to marry." Generally, the reasons given for getting married could be classified into four categories. The first is *romance*—love, sexual attraction, or the desire for intimacy. Examples of this fairly straightforward classification are "It was love at first sight," or "It began as a passionate, violent, sexual affair."

A second reason given for marriage is *propitious circumstance*—the respondent reports that he was psychologically and socially "ready" for marriage, the "time had come." In these cases, the prospective spouse is seen as meeting general requirements rather than being uniquely attractive; for example, "I decided to marry and this girl was a good person to marry—she was ready to get married also."

The third "explanation" for marriage identified by psychotherapists is *psychotherapy* itself. Although other factors are assumed to be at work, such as mutual attraction, the point made here by some respondents is the cruciality of therapy to the marriage; for example: "If not for my analysis I would have broken off, the only thing that kept us going was my analysis. We were both very cagey about getting involved."

Finally, there is an explanation of marriage that we have labeled *obligation,* in which the prospective spouse is perceived as having pressured the somewhat reluctant respondent to marry. The pressure may have been direct or indirect and consciously or unconsciously felt; for example: "My first marriage was a rescue mission, I married a 'patient' "; or "He threatened me with the fact that he would go away to war and didn't know what would happen."

These data, presented in Table 25, present some difficulties in that the four categories coded are not conceptually mutually exclusive; there is some overlap. For example, those respondents who emphasized the crucial

Table 25. Interprofessional Comparison: Most Important Factor in Effecting Marriage

Reason for Marriage	PROFESSION				
	Psycho-analysts	Psychi-atrists	Clinical Psychol-ogists	Psychi-atric Social Workers	Total
	Percent				
Romance	87	68	76	46	68
Propitious Circumstance	—	16	14	25	15
Therapy	13	12	7	8	10
Obligation	—	4	3	21	7
	100	100	100	100	100
	(15)	(25)	(29)	(24)	(93)

NOTE: N = 93.

role played by therapy and are consequently coded, may, nevertheless, certainly have married for love as well, but are not coded under romance. Thus, in examining these data, it is necessary to stress that the only dimension coded was what the respondent brought up as the single *most important* factor in accounting for his marriage.

With that caution in mind, it is nonetheless most interesting to see that a third of the entire sample point to something other than romantic feelings as the *most* important determinant of their marriage, Thus, 15 percent describe themselves as having reached a psychosexual-social stage of readiness for marriage at which time any person meeting certain general criteria constituted an appropriate potential spouse; another 7 percent identify the dynamic of obligation, saying, essentially, that they had married under pressure; and finally, 10 percent see their marriages as the consequence of their experience in therapy.

Interprofessional differences appear on three of the four dimensions coded. First, the four professional groups rank themselves on the category romance as follows: analysts, 87 percent; psychologists 76 percent; psychiatrists 68 percent; social workers 46 percent. While there are meaningful differences among the first three professions as listed, the most notable difference on this dimension is that between social workers and all three of the other groups of professionals. Thus, less than half of the social workers identify romantic feelings as the most important factor in effecting their marriage in contrast to at least two-thirds of all other professions who do so.

The second interprofessional difference in Table 25 contrasts psychiatrists (16 percent), psychologists (14 percent) and especially social workers (25 percent) with analysts (0 percent) on the dimension of propitious circumstance. The third difference, on the dimension of obligation, opposes social workers (21 percent) against all of the other three groups who show only minimal percentages.

When the interprofessional differences on the three dimensions are juxtaposed, it is the social workers who stand out most clearly: Romance (love, passion, intimacy) was far less salient a factor in their marriages, and correspondingly, they more frequently describe their marriages as having resulted from either feelings of obligation (evoked by the potential spouse) or feelings of nonspecific readiness ("I wanted to get married. It was time I settled down. And she came along.").

One part of this picture of social workers, namely, the greater frequency with which they reported marrying because of propitious circumstances, might be explained by the fact that they finish their training earlier than the other professional groups and thereby are earlier exposed to the external and internal expectations that dictate that the "time to get married" has arrived. Analysts, psychiatrists, and psychologists, who are longer in training, are, as it were, still in school, and singleness is seen as appropriate to the student role. Marriage during training, then, would be less likely to be in response to the feelings that one *ought* to be married or that one was *ready* to be married but would rather be a response to *being in love.*

It is more difficult to suggest a rationale for the fact that almost a quarter (21 percent) of the social work respondents identify feelings of obligation as the major factor effecting their decision to marry, whereas the figures for psychiatrists, psychologists, and analysts are only 4 percent, 3 percent, and 0 percent respectively. However, since many of the responses coded under this rubric refer to what the respondents now perceive as their constrained reaction to neurotic cries for help (the "I married my first patient" syndrome), it is instructive to note that social workers were also distinguished from the other professional groups by the higher frequency with which they mentioned the desire to help people as a motive active in determining professional choice (Henry, Sims, and Spray, 1971).

The first question directed at describing the life style of the psychotherapist's spouse concerned their employment status. On the first dimension—amount of time employed—there is a clear interprofessional difference along medical-nonmedical lines. That is, almost twice as many spouses of psychologists and social workers work full-time as do spouses of psychiatrists and psychoanalysts (the figures are 49 percent, 53 percent, 29 percent, and 25 percent respectively). As would be expected, these figures of interprofessional differences in employment time of wives can be attributed to interprofessional differences in educational level of wives. Only 33 percent of psychiatrists' wives have gone beyond college in their education, whereas the figures for graduate training of the wives of analysts, psychologists, and social workers are 47 percent, 46 percent, and 54 percent respectively. The fact then, that almost twice as many social workers' wives as psychiatrists' wives are employed full-time may be, in considerable part, a function of a greater proportion of them having experienced graduate training.

But this argument cannot account for the difference in employment time between wives of analysts and wives of psychologists, for in this case, the educational level of the two groups is virtually identical. Why then do twice as many psychologists' wives work full-time as do the wives of analysts? It may be that this is related to differences in family income. The economic status of the analysts (*and* of the other medical professional, the psychiatrist) is dramatically higher than that of the psychologist (*and* of the other nonmedical professional, the social worker). Survey data reveal the following average yearly income figures for "major job activity": psychoanalysts, $37,000; psychiatrists, $28,000; clinical psychologists, $17,000; psychiatric social workers, $11,000.

When the kinds of work done by spouses are categorized, the figures are: professional (general), 40 percent; mental health professional, 27 percent; clerical-sales, 14 percent; the arts, 13 percent; and other 6 percent. Although there are no statistically significant interprofessional differences regarding type of work done by spouse, male or female, it is true that almost double the percentage of social workers' wives are themselves employed as mental health professionals as are the wives of the other three professional groups.

What the respondents perceive to be the principal interests and activities of their spouses are shown in Table 26. It should be emphasized that only those interests and activities were coded that the respondents reported as being somewhat emotionally involving for their spouses. Thus, for example, the affective response "She loves being a homemaker, cooking and cleaning" would be coded here, whereas the neutral response "She spends some time keeping house" would not.

Table 26. DISTRIBUTION OF INTERESTS AND ACTIVITIES OF SPOUSE

Interest/Activity	Percent
Professional (e.g., holding office in professional organization)	40
Familial (e.g., helping children with homework)	32
Artistic (e.g., painting)	32
Civic and Charitable (e.g., hospital volunteer work)	19
Cultural (e.g., attending the theater)	18
Intellectual (e.g., participating in a study group)	17
Political (e.g., membership in A.C.L.U.)	16
Reading (e.g., reading of nonprofessional literature)	13
Domestic (e.g., house cleaning, cooking)	12

NOTE: N = 174.

On six of the nine dimensions there are no interprofessional differences; generally, the various interests and activities of both wives and husbands are distributed similarly within each of the four groups of mental health professionals.

For the sample as a whole, *professional* matters are seen as constituting the most salient area of interest-activity of the spouse. Does the importance of this dimension hold for each sex, that is, for both husbands and wives? Fifty-eight percent of female psychotherapists mention the professional interests and activities of their husbands, whereas only 35 percent of male therapists cite the professional interests and activities of their wives. However, it should be noted that only one other area of interest, that of family concerns, is reported more frequently in the description of wives, and the figure there is but 40 percent. Thus, virtually as many male respondents mention their wives' involvement in work as in family affairs.* Professional matters then, constitute a salient area of interest and activity for the spouses, whether husband or wife, of mental health professionals.

This is not the case for the second dimension shown in Table 26—familial interests and activities. In fact, the sex difference is quite striking; 40 percent of male respondents mention their wives' involvement with family matters in contrast to but 5 percent of female respondents who so characterize their husbands. It would appear that the typical, indeed stereotypic, male-female division of involvement that characterizes American middle-class society is repeated here—the husband's preoccupation with work, the wife's (even the *professional* wife's) greater concern with family.

For the remaining seven categories listed in Table 26, no substantial sex differences for the total sample appear. However, there are three sex-related interprofessional differences. First, the wives of the four professional groups manifest different degrees of artistic interest and activity, which rank as follows: psychiatrists, 49 percent; psychologists, 35 percent; analysts, 25 percent; and social workers, 14 percent. Further, more of the husbands of social workers than the husbands of the other three groups of professional women are described as having cultural interests and engaging in nonprofessional reading.

With the data presented in Table 27, we move from those interests and activities that respondents associate especially with their spouses to those interests and activities that the respondents *share* with their husbands and wives.

There are no interprofessional differences on seven of the eight categories of interests-activities presented in Table 27; the concerns that members of all four mental health professions share with their husbands or wives are, with one exception, substantially the same.

The most salient area, mentioned by almost three-quarters of the total sample, is that of socializing—interaction with friends. This activity holds its first-rank position, incidentally, for both sexes; that is, it is the most frequently mentioned activity of both male and female respondents describing what they share with their husbands or wives.

The second most salient area of shared concerns—familial, is

* Although not statistically significant, more male psychologists and social workers mention their wives' involvement in professional affairs than do psychiatrists and analysts. This is in line with the findings that about twice as many wives of psychologists and social workers are employed as those of psychiatrists and analysts.

Table 27. DISTRIBUTION OF INTERESTS AND ACTIVITIES SHARED
WITH SPOUSE

Shared Interest/Activity	Percent
Socializing with Friends	73
Familial	58
Cultural	45
Professional	24
Athletic	18
Travel	16
Cinematic	15
Manual	11

NOTE: N = 184.

mentioned by 58 percent of the sample. Although somewhat more than half of the total sample identify family concerns as shared concerns, the figure of 58 percent represents a considerable drop from the 73 percent who mentioned shared socializing.

It is on this dimension—family matters—that the single inter-professional difference in the table appears: male social workers are distinguished from male psychologists by the higher frequency (81 percent compared with 63 percent) with which they report sharing familial interests and activities with their wives. However, both of these groups, male psychologists as well as male social workers, are in turn distinguished by their more frequent mention of shared family concerns from male psychiatrists and analysts (the figures for these latter groups are 43 percent and 49 percent respectively). There is, then, a medical-nonmedical professional difference here, as well as a difference between the two nonmedical professions.

The survey data provide the following figures on the length of the average work week for the four groups of therapists: psychoanalysts, 57 hours; psychiatrists, 52 hours; psychologists, 47 hours; and social workers, 49 hours. Since this pattern of interprofessional differences in amount-of-time-devoted-to-work is strikingly the inverse of the pattern of interprofessional differences in family-activities-shared-with-spouse described above, it would seem reasonable to conclude that more social workers and psychologists than analysts and psychiatrists share familial interests and activities with their spouses because they have more free time. However, data on the amount of time spent with spouse contradicts this logic. There are *no* interprofessional differences regarding how much time the psychotherapist spends with his wife (or her husband). The figures for the sample as a whole are: little time together, 33 percent; a moderate amount of time together, 41 percent; much time together, 26 percent. Thus, the greater sharing of family activities with their wives by social workers first and psychologists second, as opposed to analysts and psychiatrists, is not a result of a greater availability of time, but a reflection of the greater value they place upon familial interaction.

A two-part question initiated general discussion of the therapist's view of his spouse as a person: "How would you describe your wife (husband)? What kind of a person is she (he)?" As one would expect, such open-ended inquiry elicited an enormous variety of response. This gallery of portraits of wives and husbands would have constituted a formidable task of inductive coding. Fortunately, Henry Murray's dictionary of personality dynamics seemed particularly appropriate to these data; it was both sufficiently specific and comprehensive. General definitions of the eighteen terms used are found in *Explorations in Personality* (Murray and others, 1938). We illustrate them here with quotations from the interviews. Every spouse was coded as to whether each of the following traits was mentioned or not.

1. *need Acquisition:* "She said, 'Ridiculous, if you can only see some people while you're recovering, you should see your best-paying patients.' Money, my wife is always worried, always concerned and anxious about it."

2. *need Achievement:* "She's industrious, she is extremely persistent. She can't give up anything that she starts."

   "She wrote several textbooks, then she wrote a novel . . . she is always busy writing another novel."

3. *need Competence:* "Very skillful in everything he does. If he does something, he does it well."

4. *need Infavoidance:* "She's shy and reserved in her opinions, anxious."

5. *need Dominance:* "She's a strong person in many ways . . . she will be domineering if there is someone she can be domineering to."

   "He's a good manager of me and sees that I get my work done and that it is channeled in the proper directions."

6. *need Autonomy:* "She is a person with a very independent mind and has a great integrity of thought."

7. *need Aggression:* "My husband is really aggressive."

   "She can be sharp and very telling, direct."

8. *need Abasement:* "I think she's afraid of me."

"She can't manage her mother, won't even smoke in front of her."

9. *need Blamavoidance (Conflict):* "My wife, you see, is a perfectionist, and I keep telling her 'Good enough must do.' "

10. *need Blamavoidance (Integration):* "She's very honest and loyal."

11. *need Affiliation (Diffuse):* "He is very close to a lot of people; he has many friends; he makes up our social life."

12. *need Affiliation (Focal):* "My wife lives for me, through me. In fact, we live like twins."

13. *need Nurturance:* "I would say that he is much more giving than I."

"She is furiously protective."

14. *need Understanding:* "She enjoys learning."

"He's a bright man, quite an intellectual."

15. *need Sentience:* "She's an extremely sensitive person with a very fine aesthetic perception."

16. *need Activity:* "He's active, he does many things. That's one of the things that attracted me to him. He's very enthusiastic about a lot of things and maintains this enthusiasm over a long period of time."

17. *need Create:* "He is a very creative man, a writer."

18. *need Understand People:* "She's psychologically insightful."

In Table 28 the respondents' descriptions of their spouses are presented in terms of these eighteen personality variables. The overall point made in Table 28 is that members of the four mental health professions characterize their spouses similarly; there are no interprofessional differences on fourteen out of the eighteen dimensions coded.

On the four dimensions for which professional differences do occur, two are restricted to *wives* only and two to *husbands* only. Looking first at *need Affiliation (Diffuse)*, we see that in both cases the wives of analysts are more frequently characterized (46 percent) than are the wives of psychiatrists (23 percent), the wives of clinical psychologists (19 percent), or the wives of social workers (12 percent). That is, they are more active in general and more active socially in particular. On *need Aggression* and *need Dominance* the interprofessional differences refer to *husbands* and are more complex: 75 percent of female psychiatrists characterize their husbands as aggressive, in contrast to 40 percent and 42 percent of female analysts and psychologists respectively, in further contrast to but 9 percent of female social workers. Regarding the dimension of *need Dominance,* the important difference is between husbands of

Table 28. Descriptions of Spouse in Murray's Need
Terminology

Characteristic	Percent
Understanding (Intelligent)	49
Competence	48
Nurturant	34
Blamavoidant (Integration)	29
Affiliative (Diffuse)	29
Aggressive	28
Active	24
Affiliative (Focal)	24
Achieving	20
Autonomous	19
Sentient	16
Understanding of People	15
Infavoidant	15
Creative	13
Abasing	13
Dominating	13
Acquisitive	11
Blamavoidant (Conflict)	11

NOTE: N = 208.

women with and without M.D.s; 67 percent of the female psychiatrists
and 50 percent of the female analysts describe their husbands as dominating, in contrast to 8 percent and 17 percent of female psychologists and
social workers respectively.

The eighteen personality variables in Table 28 are arranged in
rank order; since so few interprofessional or between-sex differences
appear, a study of the figures reveals that characteristics of spouses (both
husbands and wives) are seen as more or less salient by all four professional groups.

Two dimensions are mentioned by virtually half of the entire
sample—*need Understanding* (meaning both capable of, and engaging in,
intellectual activity) and *need Competence* (meaning the display of skill
and ability in activity). It should be noted that, denotatively, neither of
these most salient characteristics of the spouse is affective in nature. Although they undoubtedly have an emotional valence, intelligence and skill

are not affective qualities of the same order as, say, *need Nurturance* or *need Affiliation*. Borrowing from Talcott Parson's vocabulary, intelligence and skill may be described as universalistic dimensions, that is, appropriate to the evaluation and description of anyone, regardless of one's relationship with them, and as opposed to a particularistic dimension, such as affection, which would be appropriate only to persons with whom one was intimate (Parsons, 1951).

While "most frequent" does not necessarily mean "most important" or "most valued," the data make clear that the frequency with which the qualities coded as *need Understanding* and *need Competence* were mentioned reflects not only the fact that their spouses are indeed bright and able, but also the fact that such attributes are highly prized.

The single question "How would you describe your current relationship with your wife (husband)?" elicited data of two kinds. The first was general in nature and involved a comprehensive, overall evaluation of the marriage relationship. These could be classified into three categories, which are illustrated by interview quotes:

1. *Very satisfying:* "We've been married twenty-two years. I think we're very happy. We kind of fit together. It's a good, healthy relationship."

2. *Moderately satisfying:* "Oh, it is rather up and down. Basically, I think it's a good marriage. We have a lot of respect for one another. Unfortunately, we really have very little in common."

3. *Unsatisfying:* "It's not really a good marriage—I get sabotaged by her, and I think she's afraid of me."

But such general summaries usually preceded further characterizations of the marriage that were much more elaborate, detailed and specific, and required a fairly extensive code. The fourteen categories used are defined by illustration below.

1. *Compatible:* "We have a comfortable marriage, a nonstressful type of relationship."

2. *Incompatible:* "There is continuous friction."

3. *Shared work interests important to relationship:* "We have much in common with a psychiatric basis; we do research together."

4. *Shared nonwork interests important to relationship:* "We have the same interests, like the same friends, do things together."

5. *Enjoyment of each other is stressed:* "We enjoy each other's company."

6. *Respect for one another is stressed:* "She allows me to live the kind of life I want to; we have a lot of respect for each other."

7. *Intimacy is stressed:* "Our sexual and emotional relationship was the turning point of my life."

8. *Sensitivity to one another is stressed:* "I think we really understand each other—a glance suffices."

9. *Influence of spouse is stressed:* "He opened up the whole intellectual world for me."

10. *Independence of each partner is stressed:* "We lead individual and separate lives."

11. *Dependency of one partner is stressed:* "My basic tendency is to be dependent, and he pushes me."

12. *Closeness of the relationship is stressed:* "We live like twins, we'd gotten closer and closer as the years go on."

13. *Supportiveness of the spouse is stressed:* "He is endlessly helpful in my thinking and my living and personal problems."

14. *Shared interests in children important to relationship:* "We meet in the context of the family—our best relationship is through the children."

In Table 29 the psychotherapist's relationship with his spouse is described in terms of these fourteen categories.

As there are interprofessional differences on only two of the fourteen dimensions coded, the four groups of therapists are extremely similar in characterizing their current spousal relationships. It is of great interest that the most frequently offered description and, in fact, the only one to be mentioned by as much as half the sample, denotes a primarily intellectual mode of interaction—the sharing of work interests. And indeed, the next most frequently given characterization also defines a relatively unemotional area—the sharing of nonwork interests. It is not until one reaches the category of "intimacy" which is third in rank and mentioned by somewhat less than a third of the respondents, that husband-wife interaction is encountered that is clearly affective in nature.

Looked at as a whole, the table presents an extremely positive characterization of spousal relationships. Only one dimension is negative—incompatible, and that is mentioned by less than a quarter of the sample. One must look carefully, however, at the wide variety of definitions of what constitutes a positive spousal relationship. They range from intimate ("We have always been very much in love") through compatible (". . . a comfortable marriage, a nonstressful type of relationship") to independence ("We are careful to allow each other to go our own ways").

As would be expected from these descriptions, the great majority of respondents, both male and female, and equally of each profession, in

Table 29.   DESCRIPTION OF CURRENT RELATIONSHIP WITH SPOUSE

Description	Percent
Share Work Interests	54
Share Nonwork Interests	40
Intimate	30
Supportive	28
Respectful	24
Influential[a]	24
Incompatible	22
Close	20
Compatible	17
Knowledgeable	17
Enjoyable	15
Share Interests in Children	14
Dependent	13
Independent[b]	12

NOTE: N = 201.

[a] There is an interprofessional difference in the frequency with which male professionals characterize their spouses as being influential. "Influence was mentioned by 8 percent of the male psychoanalysts while the comparable figures for male psychiatrists was 14 percent; for male psychologists, 27 percent; and for male social workers, 35 percent.

[b] There is an interprofessional difference in the frequency with which practitioners characterize their spouses as independent. Specifically, 2 percent of the psychoanalysts characterized their spouses as independent, while the comparable figures for psychiatrists was 14 percent; for clinical psychologists, 9 percent; and for psychiatric social workers, 23 percent.

responding to another question make a generally positive judgment of their current relationship with their husband or wife. The specific figures are: *very satisfying,* 47 percent; *moderately satisfying,* 36 percent; *unsatisfying,* 17 percent. As is documented in Table 29, such satisfaction is derived from a wide range of interactional modes.

In this chapter's introduction we commented on the "tone" of the responses evoked by questioning the respondents on their relationship with their husbands and wives (and children as well). It was cool, at least when compared with their discussion of their parents or patients. The term *cool* points to a lesser level of emotional intensity with which any feeling, positive or negative, is expressed.

The findings presented in Tables 25 to 29 are congruous with this argument. Specifically: first, in Table 28 (description of spouse in Murray's need terminology), the two most salient spousal characteristics were "understanding-intelligent" and "competent"; neither is a denotatively emotional quality. In Table 26 (interest and activities of spouse), the most frequently mentioned area was professional; familial interests and activities ranked second. In Table 27 (interests and activities shared with spouse), socializing with friends is more frequently reported as an area of interaction with spouse than are familial concerns. Reporting in other questions about time spent with spouse, only 26 percent of the sample report spending the greater part of their nonprofessional time with husband or wife; three-quarters of the sample emphasize how "after-hours work" and "independent activities" combine to minimize shared time. In Table 25 (factors effecting marriage), only two-thirds of the sample (68 percent) are unequivocal in identifying some sort of "romantic" feeling as the most important factor in bringing about their marriage. Finally, in Table 29 (description of current relationship with spouse), those characteristics that were first and second rank out of fourteen were the "sharing of work interests" and the "sharing of nonwork interests," neither of which refers primarily to affective states.

From a number of different perspectives, the findings point to a marriage and home life in which, typically, the relationship between husband and wife, while generally satisfying, lacks emotional intensity. The majority of mental health professionals who feel positively about their marriages do so because they are characterized by mutual consideration and respect, and by shared professional, intellectual, social, and cultural interests and activities. For most, the emotional interaction with spouse, while positive, is temperate.

Relationships with Children

As already noted, psychotherapists spoke of their children in the same style as that which characterized their discussion of their spouse—brief, general, and emotionally temperate. However, by comparison, the data on children were limited to two questions: "Tell me about your children and the kind of relationship you have with them." "How much time do you spend with them each week and what sorts of activities do you share with them?"

There is a major interprofessional difference regarding the quantity of interaction with children: 71 percent of social workers report spending a lot of time with their children, in contrast to analysts, psychiatrists, and psychologists, for whom the comparable figures are 38 percent, 49 percent, and 41 percent respectively. The majority of each of these latter three professional groups divide fairly equally between reporting a moderate amount of time spent with their children or note that their children are away (depending on age, either at school or in independent households). This finding might have been anticipated as it fits well with the previously documented greater sharing of familial activities with their wives of male social workers (see Table 27). This connection is strengthened by the fact that this interprofesional difference in time spent with children is *not* due to the larger proportion of women in social work, since the difference stands when men and women are considered separately. Again it appears that male social workers place a greater value on familial interaction than male therapists belonging to other mental health professions.

There are, however, no interprofessional distinctions insofar as what is done in interaction with one's children. The principal activities most frequently described (35 percent) as being shared with children are the informal, unplanned, and naturally recurring events that occur in the course of family routines—sharing meals, watching TV, making small talk. Mutual participation in games and sports was mentioned by almost a quarter of the sample. The remainder were categorized as trips (12 percent), hobbies (11 percent), attendance at clubs or cultural events (11 percent), and other (8 percent).

Again there are no interprofessional differences in terms of how psychotherapists evaluate the relationship they have with their children. Of the total sample, 33 percent characterize their interaction with their children in ways that we have coded as *highly positive;* for example: "I have a son, eight, and a daughter who is five years old. I have a very good relationship with them. We get along very well together. We have a very close family and we do a lot of things together, yet we also try to respect each other's freedoms." Another 45 percent describe their parent-child relationships in terms suggesting the label *positive*. An example of this somewhat less enthusiastic category is "I get along pretty well with my children and they like me too, I think. I always try to be lenient and flexible and let them go their own way." Finally, 22 percent of the sample discuss their relationships with their children in ways that indicate either distance or distress. Two examples are "I am not very involved with the kids. I probably have about average contact for a psychiatrist and a physician, keeping in mind that such professions rarely see their families"; and "There's a continuing mother-daughter rebellion. She's an awfully nice person, but has lots of values that are in conflict with mine. She has rejected the values of the intellect. I don't think she has the capacity for abstract thought that I have or that my husband has and that she compensates for this by getting into things that are not like me."

This distribution of the quality of parent-child relationship—highly positive 33 percent, positive 45 percent, neutral/negative 22 percent—is quite close to that of the quality of husband-wife relationships. There the figures were 47 percent very positive, 36 percent positive, 17 percent negative. Psychotherapists are about equally successful in maintaining each of the basic familial relationships: Whether with spouse or children, about four-fifths of the total sample characterize their relationships as positive.

The richest, most detailed and perhaps most revealing data on children derive from the descriptions of them given casually by the psychotherapists while responding to other questions. These are collated in Table 30. Any given respondent could say several things about each of his several children; hence the percentages presented in Table 30 which categorize both the contact area and quality of child descriptions are based on the number of such descriptions (N = 411) rather than on the number of respondents making them (N = 176).

The area most frequently touched upon by psychotherapists when talking about their children is that of social or interpersonal relations; more than a third of all statements made were directed at such matters. Moreover, it is clear that much of this concentration reflects a concern by the respondents about problems their children are encountering in their social relations. Thirty-eight percent of such statements could be coded as negative in quality; for example: "My oldest son simply doesn't get on well with his teachers. He resents anyone who represents authority. I suppose it starts with me." Although certainly a universal concern of parents, the emphasis here on interpersonal relations may well result from the heightened sensitivity to them indigenous to therapeutic training and practice.

The other areas of importance are intellectual and academic; taken together they account for 30 percent of all comments made about children. This focus on the mind—on intelligence (or its lack) and on academic success (or failure)—recalls the similar primary stress psychotherapists place upon intelligence and competence as desirable characteristics of their spouses and reemphasizes the important role cognitive abilities play in determining the quality of psychotherapists' most intimate relations.

Conclusion

This chapter began by commenting first on the formal characteristics of the data to be presented and second on the interviewers' impressions of the therapists' style of response. The discussions of relationships

Table 30. AREA AND QUALITY OF CHILD DESCRIPTIONS

Nature of Descriptions	Quality of Descriptions					Rank Order Percent of Descriptions Falling in Each Area
	Very Positive	Positive	Neutral	Negative Percent	Total	
Intellectual	59	27	2	12	100	16 ⎫ 30
Educational-academic	33	47	5	15	100	14 ⎭
Vocational	31	60	7	2	100	10
Sports-recreational	34	54	7	5	100	10
Social-interpersonal	24	28	10	38	100	37
General	14	9	77	—	100	8
Physical	15	35	10	40	100	5
						100
Percent of Total Descriptions Falling in Each Category	31	35	13	21	100	(411)

NOTE: N = 411 (statements made by 176 respondents).

with spouse and children were characterized as relatively brief and general and distinguished by a relatively detached delivery. In our judgment, the implications of these stylistic properties have been supported by the analysis of the *content* of these responses. Thus, for the majority of this sample, relationships with spouse and children appear to be calmly positive; that is, generally well worked out, and evenly satisfying, if somewhat dispassionate. As such, these relationships with spouse and children stand in contrast to the more emotionally intense relationships of the psychotherapist's personal past—with parents and siblings—and his professional present—with patients.

6

The Historical Family

In this and the following chapter, the early life experiences of psycho-therapists are explored. Our inquiries into the therapist's relationships with his parents and siblings and into his sexual, social, and intellectual development are based on the underlying hypothesis that such issues would be relevant to an understanding of his distinctive professional choice. A particular logic in the field of the psychology of work suggests that persons seek out occupations that are in harmony with their personalities, that is, they choose to do work that will fulfill their particular psychic needs. These need systems are formed to an important extent through early experience, particularly through interaction with parents.

Undoubtedly, Anne Roe (1953a, 1956) has been the leading exponent of this approach to the study of occupational choice. It has been her working assumption that the emotional quality of parent-child relationships is the decisive factor in determining the eventual occupational area one chooses to enter. But, as Neff (1968) points out, after more than a decade of research on a wide variety of professional groups (artists, physicists, social workers, biologists), "the case for a clear relation between early determiners and later behavior remains unproved." Roe (1964) herself notes: "The choice of occupation is not nearly so direct an indication of childhood experience as had been supposed. . . . [Indeed,] personality is only one broad factor in the decisions made at any occupational choice point; how decisive a factor it is varies from instance to instance.

. . . Any predictions must take external variables—the openness of society, the immediate economic situation, the changing industrial technology —into account. Beyond these are the factors of abilities, education, and experience" (pp. 211–212). Her own work then, has persuaded Roe to retreat from her initial emphasis on the relevance of childhood experience for occupational choice and to advance toward a more pluralistic conception of causality, in which personality—and, by direct implication, the nature of child-family relationships—is but one variable among many.

In an earlier volume (Henry, Sims, and Spray, 1971), we have already examined a number of variables at work in the backgrounds of psychotherapists. That book clearly delineated the role of the family as a transmitter of the values, attitudes, and beliefs associated with ethnicity, class position, and religious and political orientations; and it demonstrated the extraordinary similarity in social origins of those who enter the four mental health professions. It is in this context then, that the emphasis here on the dynamics of early family interaction should be understood.

This chapter focuses on the family as the core context of interpersonal relationships within which the psychotherapist-to-be grew up and documents the similarity of familial dynamics among therapists during their developmental years. Psychoanalysts, psychiatrists, psychologists, and social workers distribute themselves in virtually identical patterns on every facet of both family dynamics and personal development. It should be kept in mind then, that the findings and discussion presented in this and the following chapter, unless otherwise noted, apply to psychotherapists in general, regardless of their professional membership.

Family Structure

Before examining the nature of relationships therapists had with their parents and siblings as they were growing up, there are two aspects of family structure of relevance to those relationships to consider: family size and birth order. Family size is one index of the intensity as well as the density of interpersonal relationships characterizing the childhood environment of the respondent. The data, presented in Table 31, reveal that mental health professionals come from small families. Specifically, the modal parental family of orientation consists of mother, father, the respondent, and one sibling; nearly eight out of every ten professionals had two or fewer sibs and 18 percent were only children. Since there are no interprofessional differences in family size, we are led to conclude that mental health professionals are drawn from families having a small network of interpersonal relationships.

As a general rule, family size is inversely related to socioeconomic level. As a result, we might consider the overrepresentation of small

Table 31. Size of Family of Orientation, by Profession

Number of Children in Family	PROFESSION				
	Psychoanalyst	Psychiatrist	Clinical Psychologist	Psychiatric Social Worker	Total
	Percent and (Base Number)				
One	17.4 (101)	19.0 (129)	19.9 (271)	15.7 (163)	18.2 (664)
Two	36.0 (209)	38.4 (261)	34.7 (472)	36.7 (380)	36.2 (1322)
Three	28.2 (164)	21.6 (147)	24.6 (334)	25.3 (262)	24.8 (907)
Four	12.4 (72)	13.1 (89)	14.1 (192)	13.8 (143)	13.6 (496)
Five or more	6.0 (35)	7.8 (53)	6.6 (90)	8.5 (88)	7.3 (266)
Total	100.0 (581)	99.9 (679)	99.9 (1359)	100.0 (1036)	100.0 (3655)

$\chi^2 = 19.08$ df = 12   p.n.s.
Number of missing units = 337

parental families among mental health professionals to reflect the recruitment of practitioners from the higher social-class strata of society. However, we know the majority of practitioners in each profession come from
middle- and lower-middle-class backgrounds (Henry, Sims and Spray,
1971), although psychoanalysts and psychiatrists are found to come from
the higher levels of this distribution. There are, however, no differences
among the professions in terms of parental family size, suggesting that the
tendency for mental health professionals to be drawn from small families
is not due to their social-class origins. To document this further we examined the relationship between social-class origins and parental family
size *within* each profession.

In two of the professions, psychiatry and clinical psychology, the
various social-class strata do not differ significantly with regard to size of
parental family. The two professions in which social class *is* found to be
significantly related to parental family size, namely, psychoanalysis and
psychiatric social work, differ markedly in the class origins of their practitioners. But these relationships between social-class origins and parental
family size are not uniform; that is, nowhere do we find family size increasing from high- to low-class level. To a very large extent it appears
that mental health professionals come from small families of orientation
irrespective of their social-class origins.

Since the vast majority of the mental health professionals in our
sample have been upwardly mobile, it may be that small family size
facilitates mobility. To a certain extent, of course, the influence of a small
family on entrance into any profession can be viewed in economic terms.
That is, parents with a small number of children are more likely than
parents with many children to have the financial resources available to
enable their offspring to meet the educational requirements for entry into
a profession. However, the influence of the number of children in the
parental family on achievement is not solely an economic one, at least in
the mental health professions. If economic support for education was the
only factor involved, only children would have higher rates of mobility
from the lower social classes than would children having one or more sibs.
Since the proportion of only children coming from the middle, lower-
middle, and lower classes does not differ significantly from the proportions
of respondents in each of the remaining categories of family size having
similar class origins, we are led to conclude that the influence of the
number of children in the family is not confined to economic resources.

It is evident that throughout our examination of family origins
we have used as our measure of family size the number of children in the
family. This, of course, assumes the continued presence of both parents
in the family. Since this family structure is somewhat problematical, we

asked the respondents to indicate whether or not they lived with both parents while they were growing up. The vast majority of practitioners (78 percent) did, and there were no significant interprofessional differences in this regard. Similarly, there were no differences by class level within each profession with regard to the proportion of practitioners living with both parents during childhood. We can conclude then, that mental health professionals come predominantly from stable small families of orientation in which both parents were present during the respondent's childhood.

Research on the relationship between birth order and professional eminence has produced evidence indicating that firstborns are overrepresented in many areas of professional endeavor. Included in these studies have been outstanding scientists; prominent American writers; university professors; the starred listings in *American Men of Science;* the biographies in *Who's Who;* Rhodes scholars; and distinguished researchers in biology, physics, and the social sciences (Schachter, 1963). By themselves, these findings suggest a possible overrepresentation of firstborns in the mental health professions, on the logic that these groups of professionals are eminent, in that they enjoy relatively high occupational status in the United States.

However, some studies show that firstborns are not inevitably more eminent. For example, jet aces and professional baseball players show an overrepresentation of later-borns (Torrance, 1954; Schachter, 1963). Consistent with these findings, Sutton-Smith and colleagues (1964) studied occupational interests and reported that firstborns prefer to achieve success by means of a style of rational strategy, whereas later-borns prefer a style involving physical action. Thus, in positing possible relationships between occupational eminence and birth order, the nature of the field in which eminence is measured must be considered. Certainly, the mental health professions are most appropriately seen as examples of Sutton-Smith's rational strategies.

Other studies provide further qualification of the generally established firstborn–professional eminence relationship. Schachter (1963) reports a series of researches that show that firstborns are overrepresented in samples of college and graduate school students. At the same time, firstborns were not overrepresented in a probability sample of the West German population or in the student body of a Minneapolis public high school.

From an analysis of these and other data, Schachter concludes: "The repeated findings of a surplus of firstborns among eminent scholars appears to have nothing to do with any direct relationship of birth order to eminence, but is simply a reflection of the fact that scholars, eminent

or not, derive from a population in which firstborns are in marked surplus" (p. 768).

Of course, this simply pushes back the search for explanation one
step: Why do more firstborns obtain a higher education? Schachter in-
troduces the idea of economic access to education, but finds it only partially successful:

> In part, of course, the excess of firstborn and only children in col-
> lege is due to purely economic factors. Until recent years birth rate was
> negatively related to socioeconomic status. This should almost inevitably
> result in a large proportion of college students originating in small families,
> from which necessarily would follow the relatively heavy concentration of
> first and only children. This factor alone, however, cannot account for these
> data. By holding family size constant we are to some extent controlling for
> the effects of socioeconomic status. And, as has been noted repeatedly, at
> each family size in both college and graduate school populations, there is
> a marked overrepresentation of firstborns (p. 766).

Granting for the present Schachter's argument that it is educational level rather than eminence per se that is related to birth order, it
again follows that firstborns should be overrepresented in the mental
health professions. All those professions require high amounts of formal
education, either the M.D. or Ph.D. degree or, in social work, graduate
study to the master's level. In sum, the relative high status, the intellectual
nature of the work, and the level of formal education required, which
characterize the four mental health professions—all lead us to expect an
overrepresentation of firstborns in their memberships. The data required
to assess this expectation are presented in Table 32, which compares birth
order and family size for our sample of mental health professionals.

Although they are included in the table, respondents who are only
children will not be considered in our analysis because of the extreme
difficulty in determining whether their number in the sample is dispro-
portionate. To do so would require some estimate of a chance expectancy
figure for the year of each respondent's birth, since the percentage of one-
child families varies over the years. Besides this practical matter, the
evidence is not compelling that the generally established relationship
between professional eminence and firstborns also holds true for only children. While some studies have combined only children with firstborns to
contrast them with later-borns, their equivalence has been assumed rather
than demonstrated.

Table 32 reveals that firstborns are significantly overrepresented
among respondents from families with two or three children. Of the 1316
respondents from families with two children, 57 percent are firstborns.
Similarly, of the 905 respondents from families with three children, 40

Table 32. ORDER OF BIRTH OF MENTAL HEALTH PROFESSIONALS, BY FAMILY SIZE

Birth Order	FAMILY SIZE (Percent)											Total
	1	2	3	4	5	6	7	8	9	10	11+	
1		57.1	39.8	26.3	15.9	18.1	9.6	13.2	15.4	—	6.7	49.4 (1930)
2		42.9	31.5	24.4	15.2	10.1	10.8	7.5	11.5	—	13.3	26.7 (1042)
3			28.7	20.6	15.2	10.9	18.1	11.3	—	27.3	—	11.3 (441)
4				28.7	18.6	10.9	12.0	7.5	11.5	—	—	5.7 (222)
5					35.2	21.0	14.5	9.4	11.5	—	20.0	3.7 (145)
6						29.0	15.7	3.8	15.4	—	13.3	1.6 (61)
7							19.3	17.0	11.5	18.2	6.7	0.8 (31)
8								30.2	15.4	9.1	13.3	0.6 (23)
9									7.7	18.2	6.7	0.1 (5)
10										27.3	—	0.1 (3)
11+											20.0	0.1 (3)
Total	15.4 (602)	33.7 (1316)	23.2 (905)	12.6 (491)	6.8 (264)	3.5 (138)	2.1 (83)	1.4 (53)	0.7 (26)	0.3 (11)	0.4 (15)	100.1 (3906)

percent are firstborn. Both of these overrepresentations are significant at the .01 level. However, the distribution by birth order of respondents from families with four children is very close to the chance expectancy of one-fourth in each cell. Finally, beginning with family size of five, two striking shifts occur: firstborns are no longer overrepresented, and last-borns suddenly become so. Thus, of the 264 respondents from families with five children, 35 percent are lastborn, an overrepresentation signifi-cant at the .01 level. This trend is consistent in family sizes of six, seven, eight, nine, and ten. (For family sizes of six and eight, the chi square statistic was significant at p .01. The relationship was not significant for family size of seven and the case bases were too small to support a statisti-cal test for family sizes of nine and ten.)

Our expectation concerning the overrepresentation of firstborns in the mental health professions is confirmed only for respondents from small families (two or three children). These respondents constitute 67 percent of the sample. Respondents from an intermediate family size (four children) show a near chance distribution regarding birth order and constitute 15 percent of the sample. Respondents from large families (five or more children) show an overrepresentation of lastborns and con-stitute 18 percent of the sample. Thus for a third of the sample, our ex-pectation is not confirmed; and, indeed, for that proportion of the sample coming from large families (18 percent), a result directly opposite to the prediction is found.

Before discussing the implications of this unexpected pattern, it is possible to extend our analysis of the relationship between professional eminence and birth order by taking professional affiliation into account. Specifically, there is a generally recognized status ranking of the four mental health professions of the following order: (1) psychoanalysis, (2) psychiatry, (3) clinical psychology, and (4) psychiatric social work. On the logic that the relative status of a profession is a measure of its relative eminence, we predict that the proportions of firstborns found in the four professions will be similarly ordered; that is, highest in psychoanalysis, followed, in order, by psychiatrists, clinical psychologists, and psychiatric social workers.

Analysis reveals that for males, the percent of each profession who are firstborn follows the predicted order exactly: psychoanalysis, 38.2 per-cent; psychiatry, 34 percent; psychology, 31.5 percent; social work, 29.5 percent. However, for females, the prediction is not confirmed. In fact, the lowest ranking profession in terms of prestige, social work, has the highest percentage of firstborns: psychoanalysis, 31.9 percent; psychiatry, 33 percent; psychology, 31 percent; social work, 34.9 percent. Undoubt-edly social work's traditional availability to women as a career is at work here. Similarly, the fact that females are also more prevalent in clinical psychology than in the two medical professions may explain why the proportion of firstborns does not follow the predicted rank order among females.

In general, the major finding emerging from our examination of the sibling position of mental health professionals is that the majority of respondents in our sample, those from families of two and three children, did show an overrepresentation of firstborns. This result is consistent with the literature on which our initial expectation concerning the prevalence of firstborns in the mental health professions was based: As professions demanding a high level of education, enjoying relatively high status, and performing intellectual work, all four mental health professions meet the definition of work role that traditionally has been found to harbor firstborns.

However, we also found consistent variation by family size: When families of five or more children were examined, firstborns ceased being overrepresented and lastborns became so; for the family size of four children, there was no overrepresentation of any birth-order position.

It was our intent to avoid entering the arena of speculation as to the possible reasons an overrepresentation of firstborns among the professionally eminent has been consistently found. Our data are not substantively relevant to such a discussion. However, we find ourselves necessarily involved with the *logic* of speculated causality in that our findings of an overrepresentation of *last*borns and a *lack* of overrepresentation of *first*borns from *large* size families have implications for all previously offered interpretations.

Such rationales have been extremely varied; they include the suggestion of biological differences such as the greater physical strength or intellectual capacity of the firstborn, but they have most frequently been psychodynamic in nature, arguing that the firstborn experiences some unique pattern of family interaction that leads to outstanding achievement. For example, such psychological hypotheses have cast the firstborn in the role of an overprotected child seeking to compensate by achieving greater independence or have pictured the firstborn as suffering dethronement by his siblings and attempting to regain his position as the exclusive focus of parental love and attention.

All such explanations would have to be drastically revised or supplemented to account for our findings. Such explanations cannot account for the *under*representation of firstborns from large families. It becomes necessary either to speculate on how the biology or early psychological experience of firstborns might differ according to eventual family size, or to posit some intervening variable, which, in the case of large families, inhibits or prevents that unknown something in the firstborn's makeup or experience from manifesting itself in achievement.

In this latter direction one such factor would be Schachter's concept of economic access. Large families are likely to be located in the lower-class strata. With greater demands on lesser resources, their early-born children may be precluded from the education required for a professional career.

This same economic factor contributes in part to an understanding of another of this study's particular findings—the *over*representation of the *last*born from a large family. By the time the question of his advanced education arises, his parents' income is likely to have increased and their expenses are likely to have decreased (as their older children become self-supporting), and hence, they can devote more money to the remaining child. In addition, older siblings may be able to contribute to the lastborn's education.

But if these economic considerations remove for the large family's lastborn what was the stumbling block for the large family's firstborn, economic access is clearly not in itself a sufficient explanation for the over-representation of lastborns from large families. Lastborns from *small* families enjoy such educational opportunity, yet they are *not* overrepresented. Thus, it is necessary to posit some other factor in the lastborn's experience that is peculiar to the *large* family only.

The fact that no previous researches on scholarly eminence report an overrepresentation of lastborns raises a question about the possible uniqueness of the mental health professions. Could the surplus of lastborns found in our data be peculiar to the mental health field? A recent research study suggests not. Using a national sample, Blau and Duncan (1967) report that, in terms of the achievement of occupational status, the oldest children in small families and the youngest children in large families hold the most favored sibling positions.

What may be at work then is the difference between definitions of eminence. Generally, previous studies have defined professional eminence in terms of recognition by colleagues or by society at large for an outstanding contribution to a professional field. We have defined it in terms of simple membership in a high-status profession. It might be argued that our findings of an overrepresentation of lastborns pertains not to professional eminence but rather to the attainment of professional status.

Family Relations

In order to draw the psychotherapist into a general discussion of the kinds of persons he saw his parents being, of how they felt about him, and of the nature of their relationships with him throughout a major part of his life span, we asked our interview respondents the following three questions: "How would you characterize your relationship with your mother (father) when you were a child?" "What about your relationship with your mother (father) when you were an adolescent?" "How would you describe this relationship (mother/father) during your early adult and later adult years?"

These few, very general questions succeeded in eliciting lengthy, elaborately specific answers. With the possible exceptions of what led them to become therapists or the nature of the therapeutic relationship, no subject was talked about with greater ease or fervor. Most respondents clearly thought the subject of parents was relevant, and they had a lot to say about them. It seems fair to suggest that such a response reflects the conviction of the majority of respondents that child-parent relationships had been and were important determinants both of life decisions, such as occupational choice, and of personality. It may also be that the fluency and enthusiasm with which they discussed their relationships with their parents (particularly when contrasted to the relative paucity of response to questions concerning spouses and children) reflects the topic as a primary focus of their own therapeutic experience *as patients.**

Before examining the nature of the relationships which mental health professionals had with their parents as they were growing up, we might first see what kind of persons they remember their fathers and mothers as being. Scattered throughout the discussion of their parents were descriptive phrases or single adjectives that the respondents applied to their mothers and fathers. And occasionally, respondents would paint "word portraits" of their parents, such as the excerpts below illustrate:

> He [father] was an introverted, unworldly, book-dominated, very sensitive but undemonstrative, individual. . . . She [mother] was a good-looking, quiet, unexcitable figure.

> My father was a very masculine man, an artisan by trade. Very intelligent, a thinking person, somewhat uncouth. He had a kind of personal magnetism. . . . He was a good athlete, a hard worker, talented with his hands. And he was a very affectionate person, too.

* If this latter point is persuasive, it raises an interesting possibility. The probability of defensive distortion is a well-known disadvantage of retrospective reporting; but, on the logic that what has been worked through in treatment is closer to the truth (certainly a belief of our respondents), the validity of their memories of parent-child relationships has been increased. Indeed, following this line of argument leads to the conclusion that mental health professionals, about three-quarters of whom have had psychotherapy, constitute a uniquely appropriate group for the use of the retrospective interview technique. They are, supposedly, more familiar with and more understanding of their true pasts.

I remember him [father] as being angry, tough, strict, and then, at times, tender. Not too loving. He was hardworking, honest. . . . I have a clear recollection of her [mother]. As a child, loving, tender, even smotheringly so. I would say openly affectionate, very yielding to me and the other children. Whatever we wanted we could get.

Table 33 presents those categories of descriptive adjectives used by at least 10 percent of the sample to characterize their parents.

Table 33 shows that seven characteristics are attributed to *both* mother and father: loving, extroverted, neurotic, undemonstrative, intelligent, educated, and dedicated (the object of dedication varying by parent: occupation for father, household and familial duties for mother). Each parent has five differentiating qualities: mothers are seen as possessive, dominating, demanding, giving, and physically ill; fathers, as authoritarian, passive, bad-tempered, tender, and moral.

While all the qualities listed undoubtedly had affective consequences for the respondents, it is possible to separate them into two groups —those that focus on the parent's style of emotional interaction with the respondents and those that are far less directly involved in familial interpersonal relations. Thus, within the sphere of familial emotional interaction, fathers are seen to be rigid, warm, strict, passive*, tender, neurotic, and bad-tempered; whereas, more removed from this area of affect, they are characterized as hard-working, educated, intelligent, extroverted, and principled. If the number of mentions of these qualities are grouped this same way and summed, we find a roughly 3:2 ratio of emphasis placed on the two types of characteristics. That is, in discussing their fathers, for every two mentions by the respondents of such nonaffective qualities as his education or dedication to work, three mentions are made of such affective, interpersonal qualities as his affectionate or unaffectionate nature.

The adjectives can also be ordered into positive and negative groups *according to whether the respondent judged a characteristic to be good or bad*. When this is done for fathers, it results in seven "good" qualities (hard-working, educated, warm, bright, tender, outgoing and honest) and five "bad" qualities (rigid, strict, passive, neurotic, bad-tempered). We again derive a ratio and find that for every two mentions of negative qualities, three positive comments are made.

These two ratios of affective to nonaffective and positive to negative differ for mothers. In terms of emotional interaction, mothers are seen to be warm, possessive, dominating, neurotic, rigid, pushy, and giving;

* Nachmann (1960) found that, in comparison with law and dental students, the fathers of social workers were weak, inadequate, or absent. Only 17 percent of this sample so describe their fathers.

Table 33. ADJECTIVES USED TO DESCRIBE PARENTS

MOTHER (N = 275)			FATHER (N = 277)		
Adjective	Percent	Rank	Adjective	Percent	Rank
Loving, affectionate, warm, open	24	1	Dedicated, hard-working, conscientious	25	1.5
Possessive	23	2	*Rigid, undemonstrative, reserved*	25	1.5
Dominating, controlling	22	3	*Educated, intellectual, learned*	24	3
Neurotic, nervous, anxious	16	4.5	*Loving, affectionate, warm, open*	21	4
Intelligent, bright, smart	16	4.5	Strict, stern, authoritarian	19	5
Dedicated, devoted wife and mother	15	6	*Intelligent, bright, smart*	18	6
Rigid, undemonstrative, reserved	14	7	Passive, submissive, weak	17	7
Demanding, pressing, pushing	13	8	Tender, gentle, sweet, kind	14	8
Educated, intellectual, learned	12	9.5	*Neurotic, nervous, anxious*	13	9
Extroverted, outgoing	12	9.5	Bad-tempered, argumentative, difficult	12	10
Giving, supporting, encouraging	11	11	*Extroverted, outgoing*	11	11
Ailing, ill, invalid	10	12	Honest, moral, principled	10	12

NOTE: Italic adjective sets are those that appear for both mother and father.

they are, on the other hand, characterized in nonaffective terms as being intelligent, dedicated, educated, extroverted, and physically ill. When the number of mentions are similarly grouped and summed, they yield a ratio of 2:1; that is, in discussing their mothers, for every mention by the respondents of a nonaffective quality, such as education, there are two mentions of affective qualities, such as loving or dominating. Mothers then, are more likely to be described in affective terms, along dimensions of emotional interaction, than are fathers. This finding fits the roles most students of the family assign to mothers and fathers; for example, Clausen (1964, p. 36) states: "The sheer predominance of the mother in interaction with the child requires that she fill both instrumental and expressive functions but it is nevertheless true that mothers are in general relatively far more expressive and nurturant than are fathers."

A division of mothers' characteristics into positive and negative results in six "good" qualities (warm, intelligent, dedicated, educated, extroverted, and giving) and six "bad" (possessive, dominating, neurotic, rigid, pushy, and ailing). The ratio here is 1:1; for every mention of a positive quality there is a mention of a negative one. Mothers then, are more likely to be seen negatively than fathers.

These two findings may be juxtaposed as follows: That parent (mother) who is more frequently described in affective terms is viewed more negatively; that parent (father) more frequently described in cognitive terms is viewed more positively.

It is not surprising to find that mothers are seen more in terms of emotional interaction than are fathers. Given the most common family balance of provider-father and child-raising mother, it is reasonable to assume more frequent and probably a generally more intense level of emotional interaction between mother and children than between father and children. What does not follow logically is the finding that fathers are seen more positively. Is this a consequence of the lesser amount and/or lesser intensity of interaction? Is it a reflection of the greater number of males in the sample reacting against what becomes, at some point in their development, dangerously close ties with the mother? Data presented subsequently will explore these points.

It was possible to distinguish the respondent's overall evaluation of his relationship with his mother and father separately, for both childhood and adolescence. Each of these four relationships was located on what is essentially a four-point scale: positive, neutral, ambivalent, and negative. The following are examples of interview material on which such coding judgments were based.

My father was a total stranger to me until I was about eleven. He would only see him on Sunday because he would leave for work in the morning before I got up and he would come home after I had already gone to bed. He worked so hard and my mother wanted to give him a day of rest on Sunday so we always got a nickel to go to the show. Actually, I think my mother had to keep everyone only related to her. We did not really have much of a relationship as a family, although we all had excellent relationships with her. She seemed to realize this later, that there was something that she had done that brought this kind of family relationship about. There was much self-awareness in her and a tremendous sense of humor and a great deal of enjoyment of life. Both were immigrants, and fearful that they might not do or say the right thing and this really never quite left them. My relationship with my mother was very close. As a child it was wonderful because I could learn all the parts of the feminine role. In adolescence, because she was so perceptive and so rivalrous and competitive, I could not stand the fact that I had no privacy. I rebelled in some odd ways. For instance, my mother said you should use powder and I wouldn't do it.

I'd say it [the relationship with father during childhood] was somewhat ambivalent. It was a pretty warm, close relationship although I was somewhat rebellious at times. He was somewhat constricted in expressing affection; the affection was there though. He had very high standards, perhaps too high. This was the source of some of the conflict. I know he loved me very much. My feelings as I said, were somewhat ambivalent.

You could call my mother passive-aggressive while my father was more direct in many things. She is never direct, always beating around the bush. This makes it difficult in conflicts. I would get hostile but I wouldn't know what to get hostile at. I wouldn't know what to rebel against. Hers is an insidious way of handling matters. Even now I can only take her in small doses. She always had this tendency to control and manipulate.

Table 34 presents the respondents' evaluations of their relationships with their parents during childhood, adolescence, and early adulthood. It is arranged to facilitate comparisons between mother and father for the same age period and comparisons between age periods for the same parents.

Table 34 reveals two major facts: First, there are virtually no differences between respondents' relations with mother and father for any age period—childhood, adolescence, or adulthood. The largest of the minimal differences is 8 percent and appears in the category "neutral" under childhood. This undoubtedly reflects the more frequent absence of the father and the subsequently greater possibility for a neutral relationship with him.

Second, relations with both parents deteriorate somewhat from childhood to adolescence and improve again in adulthood. The worsening of relationship during adolescence is almost identical for mother and father, approximately a 10 percent decline in positive responses, and a

Table 34. Relations with Parents During Childhood, Adolescence, and Early Adulthood

Nature of Relations with Parent	AGE					
	Childhood		Adolescence		Early Adulthood	
	Mother	Father	Mother	Father	Mother	Father
			Percent			
Positive	61	56	50	46	52	50
Neutral	4	12	2	9	20	25
Ambivalent	18	14	14	9	6	7
Negative	17	18	34	36	22	18
Totals	100 (248)	100 (256)	100 (226)	100 (230)	100 (184)	100 (179)

doubling of negative findings. This finding fits well into the common picture of American adolescence as a period of conflictual family relations.

What runs counter to similarly based expectations is the virtual equality with which relations with mother and father are evaluated. Given the preponderance of the family consisting of a working father and an at-home mother, one might anticipate, especially in childhood, more positive relations with mother. Yet we do not find them, and, indeed, their absence is congruent with the more positive adjective description of fathers already discussed.

This line of reasoning can be checked, at least in part, by data on amount of time spent with parent during childhood and on the closeness of the relationship (over childhood and adolescence combined). The quality of closeness was related to, and yet distinguishable from, the overall evaluation of the respondent-parent relationship. The data show that while we are not likely to find a negative or ambivalent relationship in which there is closeness, it is perfectly possible to have a positive relationship that lacks the special characteristic of being close. Respondents used the word in reference to shared communication. It was something different, somewhat apart from the question of like or dislike, love or hate. We were able to identify three relevant categories of response: the presence of closeness, the absence of closeness due to separation, and the presence of distance or inability to communicate.

If our assumptions about the working father and the at-home, child-raising mother are correct (and they give rise to our surprise at the sameness of their evaluation), we should surely find significantly more time spent with mother and probably a greater amount of communication with mother.

Analysis shows that there are major differences between parents on both time and closeness in the direction anticipated. Forty-six percent of the respondents report spending "a lot of time" with their mothers during childhood; only 17 percent report similarly for their fathers. At the opposite pole, 63 percent say they spent "little or no time" with their fathers, whereas only 29 percent so report for their mothers. With regard to closeness to parents during childhood and adolescence, 69 percent of the sample characterize the relationship with their mothers as close as against 48 percent who so describe the relationship with their fathers. Indeed, an almost equal 42 percent characterize their relationship to their father as distant.

It is clear, then, that the majority of psychotherapists as children spent more time with their mothers and established closer relationships with them. While there is certainly no necessary correlation between amount of time spent together and the positive or negative nature of a relationship, it does seem that the closer the relationship, the more genuine communication between people, the more positively it would be evaluated. We point again, then, to the unexpectedness of the virtual sameness in the respondents' evaluations of relations with their parents. Something appears to be at work in lessening or lowering the positive feelings originally directed toward the mother (as evidenced in the greater closeness experienced with her) and/or in raising the positive feelings toward the father. At this point, the only clues provided by the data presented reside in those adjectives that were attributed exclusively to either mother or father (see Table 33).

The two lists of adjectives have different tones. The negative characteristics attributed to the father appear less threatening. When father is ill-tempered, you can avoid him; if he is strict, you at least know where he stands and can choose to obey or suffer the consequences; if he is passive and weak, you can pity him or, indeed, sympathize with him if his submission is to the same woman who is attempting to dominate you. But it is something else again to handle a possessive, controlling, demanding mother. These characteristics are oppressive, inescapable, and pervasive; they are constant rather than momentary. From this point of view, the greater time spent with mother and the greater closeness of communication could result in an intensification of her threat. Such an interpretation takes a step toward explaining why, in contrast to the relationship with their fathers, the more affective interaction, the larger amount of time spent together, and the greater closeness between respondents and their mothers do not result in greater positive evaluation of that relationship.

Once the conflicts of adolescence have passed, relationships with parents improve, although it should be pointed out that that improvement occurs at the lower end of the scale. That is, comparing adolescence with adulthood, the percentage of positive relationships remains virtually identical, roughly 50 percent; but those relationships characterized as either ambivalent or negative in adolescence have improved to become neutral by early adulthood.

The most relevant comparison is with Bossard and Boll's (1956) figures on family happiness in their study of the large family system. Imperfect as it is, we make this comparison because a hypothesis popular with laymen and occasionally seriously proposed by the professionals identifies an unhappy childhood (that is, negative relationships with mother and/or father) as a major determinant of the choice of a career in the mental health professions.

Asked to characterize the general tone of their family life as they were growing up, Bossard and Boll's subjects reported as follows (p. 81):

50 percent described their familial relationships as happy, 14 percent as unhappy, and the remaining 36 percent fell somewhere between in a nebulous area labeled medium.

Comparing these figures with those shown in Table 34 for either childhood or adulthood, we note their remarkable similarity. To the extent then that family happiness can be equated with the quality of relationships with parents, it seems that subjects from large families and of heterogeneous occupation evaluate the quality of their early family life in almost exactly the same way as do our respondents, two-thirds of whom are from small families and all of whom are psychotherapists.

Douvan and Gold (1964) stress the disparity between the myth and the empirical reality of adolescent independence:

> Traditionally, the autonomy issue at adolescence has been conceived as a struggle . . . the child managing a departure only by means of a rebellion. . . . Let us state at the outset that research findings, by and large, do not support the traditional view. In the large-scale studies of normal populations, we do not find adolescents clamoring for freedom or for release from unjust constraint. We do not find rebellious resistance to authority as a dominant theme. For the most part, the evidence bespeaks a modal pattern considerably more peaceful. . . . The way of most American youngsters is neither to act out nor to suffer the strains and conflicts, the guilts and anxieties of neurosis. It seems, rather, that the normal, the average, the modal youngster, makes his bid for autonomy gradually and appropriately, and that his requests meet reasonable consideration and deference from parents who ally themselves . . . with the child's need to grow (p. 485).

Our data make clear that the mental health professional is closer to the myth than to the "normal, the average, the modal youngster" as to how his autonomy was achieved. In describing how their parents reacted to their moves toward independence, only 37 percent of psychotherapists portray their mothers as approving or encouraging, 63 percent report a strained relationship in which the mother disapproves of or fights her child's attempts at autonomy. The analogous figures for father are 55 percent approving and 45 percent disapproving.

The difference here between parents is striking: almost one-fifth more mothers than fathers are seen as having a negative attitude toward the respondents' moves toward autonomy during adolescence. This finding fits well with adjective descriptions of the mothers as possessive, dominating, and demanding, and in our view supports the discussion of their meaning.

In discussing the issue of autonomy, the respondents frequently mention their "break from home." In the majority of cases, the respondents discuss this in terms of geographical separation from parents. The break is defined in such phrases as "going away to school," "leaving for a job in another city," "left home to go into the army." Both the timing of the break and the way in which the break was accomplished are most often put in such situational-shift terms. The issue of a *psychological* break from parents was rarely discussed explicitly. Nevertheless, it was clear that the move from home had that implication. Thus, for our purposes here, the break from home means psychological independence from parents.

The age at which psychological independence from parent occurs varies but little from mother to father. In terms of both parents, somewhat more than a third of the respondents report making the break before high school graduation, somewhat less than two-thirds delaying the break until young adulthood.

The interview data occasionally provide, in an individual case, information as to just how a particular parental relationship is relevant to the break from home. Thus, one respondent will report it was *because* of conflict with his father that he went away to school rather than living at home and attending a local campus; another reports gratefully greeting the move away from home *necessitated by entering college* because it removed him from conflict with his mother. It was impossible, however, to make such distinctions in the majority of cases. The best we could do was to distinguish those cases in which conflict with parents was involved in the process of breaking away from those cases in which it was not.

For the majority, conflict is present: 15 percent report conflict with both parents, 30 percent with mother only and 15 percent with father only. Thus, only 40 percent of the sample describe their transition to independence as conflict-free. For that 60 percent majority who report strained relationships during the break, it should be noted that the mother is twice as frequently the antagonist as the father. This finding is in line with our continuing argument that characterizes the mother as more of a threat to the respondents' autonomy.

As noted, a situational shift, such as leaving home to go to school, was most often the context within which gaining psychological independence from their parents was discussed. There were four such moves: 55 percent left home for school, 15 percent left to go to work, 13 percent left home to be married, and 9 percent entered the armed services. Only 8 percent describe the psychological break from parents as occurring while still at home.

We cannot argue a clear-cut cause-and-effect relationship between the geographical move from home and psychological independence from parents, but it is clear that these two factors interact. The impingement of age-graded requirements or opportunities may sometimes initiate, sometimes facilitate, sometimes force the needs of the adolescent or young adult for autonomy. Conversely, such needs may sometimes create or take advantage of such external opportunities.

However, it would seem fair to say that for the great majority of mental health professionals (92 percent), geographic separation from parents is a necessary if not sufficient cause of psychological independence. At the very least, it is certainly the standard way of achieving it.

As we have noted, the majority of mental health professionals held the conviction that parents were important if not crucial in influencing their overall development. Hence, it is not surprising to find in Table 35 that the majority of respondents explicitly identify occupational choice as an issue on which such influence was particularly felt. In this respect, psychotherapists are very like other professional groups; Borow (1964) cites several studies in which both male and female subjects name parents most frequently as those persons exercising greatest influence on their vocational plans. Table 35 specifies the ways in which psychotherapists see their parents as having affected their professional choice.

Table 35. PARENTAL INFLUENCE ON PROFESSIONAL CHOICE

Nature of Parental Influence	Mother	Father
	Percent	
Positive		
Served as Role Model for Professional Choice	1	10
Encouraged Particular Professional Choice	17	8
Supported Respondent's Choice	45	40
Neutral		
Exercised No Influence	15	21
Negative		
Displeased with Professional Choice	19	19
Actively Discouraged Professional Choice	3	2
Total	100	100
	(130)	(166)

On the general level of positive, neutral, or negative influence, there are no differences between parents; mothers and fathers are equally likely to be for or against or neutral about their children's career choice. However, *within* the general category of positive influences, there is a difference between parents; fathers are more likely to serve as role models, whereas mothers are more likely to have their influence restricted to encouragement.

Looking at Table 35 as a whole, we see that parents—mother and father alike—are seen as being very active indeed in influencing professional choice. Only about a fifth of parents are reported to have been uninvolved in the decision. Moreover, if we combine the first two categories in the table—"served as a model," and "encouraged choice of a particular profession"—on the logic that they are both determinants of choice, occurring before the respondents' actual decision (whereas the other categories of response are, rather, after-the-fact supports or discouragements), we find that 18 percent of both mothers and fathers are perceived as important, perhaps decisive, influences on professional choice.

In view of the prestige attached to the educational levels necessary for membership in any of the mental health professions (and the even greater prestige attached to the M.D. degree necessary for psychiatry and psychoanalysis), the degree of parental discontent with the respondents' professional choice appears high. Analysis reveals sex differences here: first, both parents are against their *daughters* committing themselves to *any* professional career. Second, there is some parental displeasure at *sons* choosing social work, perhaps because at that time they saw social work as a "feminine" occupation.

The idea is occasionally encountered that the origins of what are the psychotherapist's professional interest and skill—the healing of emotional conflict—can be traced to his having witnessed conflict in his own family. At the conclusion of the discussion concerning the relationship between the respondent and his parents, a single question was directed toward the relationship of the therapists parents as husband and wife: "What was the nature of the relationship between your parents as you were growing up?"

Forty-three percent of the sample judged that relationship to be good, 18 percent described it as mixed, and 39 percent saw the relationship betwen mother and father as poor. The striking point of these figures is the virtually perfect balance between the positive and negative poles of the scale; there is but 4 percent difference between them. For this sample at least, these results clearly contradict any simplistic theory of psychotherapists finding their origins in either happy or unhappy homes.

As noted earlier, 79 percent of mental health professionals come from families in which they had two or fewer siblings.* Given the small

---

* The mental health professional's relations with his siblings were explored in their interview through two questions, one specific and one general: (1) "Do you have any brothers and/or sisters? (Sex and birth order.)" (2) "How would

number of possible sibling relationships, the quality of such relationships assumes strategic importance in the early interpersonal environments from which psychotherapists are drawn. When all 353 relationships with brothers and sisters discussed by 208 respondents are analyzed, 27 percent of the relationships were categorized as very good. These are the relationships characterized by the respondents as loving, close, warm, and manifesting mutual interest, support, and loyalty. A typical statement from the interviews is: "There was a good relationship between all the children; enormous interest in each other. There was no sibling rivalry that I can recall."

Another 33 percent of sibling relationships were classified as good but mixed, a category best defined through illustration: "I played a lot with my sister when we were growing up. We were very close, even though we did a great deal of fighting."

Taken together these two categories sum to 60 percent; thus almost two-thirds of all sibling relationships are characterized by the respondents primarily in positive terms.

We coded a relatively small group of sibling relationships as neutral —again, a classification best described by example: "I was the oldest, then my brother was five years younger and then my sister was eight years younger. I had practically no relationship with them. Very nebulous, tenuous. We had no relationship as children."

The remaining 24 percent of sibling relationships were experienced as poor, characterized at worst by resentment or jealousy and at best by a lack of communication. An example: "I have a brother seven years younger than I am. Our relationship was terrible. I resented him and he resented me. It was impossible for us to talk to each other. He was an excellent athlete and a poor student. Just the reverse of me, you see."

In their study of the large family, Bossard and Boll (1956) approached the question of the quality of sibling relationships somewhat

---

you describe your relationships with them during childhood, adolescence, and young adulthood?"

Concerning the responses to these questions, two methodological points should be made. First, it was found that respondents failed to discuss their sibs according to the time periods specified in the second question; they generally did not differentiate among childhood, adolescence, and young adulthood. They preferred instead the broader, and evidently more relevant, category of "When I was growing up."

A second point concerns the number of siblings discussed. Codes were established for this area of data on the basis of an examination of fifty random cases. Only three of these respondents had more than four sibs, and none of these actually discussed more than four. Consequently, a limit was set so that the data on up to four siblings but no more would be coded.

differently. They had their subjects rate the degree of sibling conflict experienced as they were growing up. Although by no means strictly comparable, it is nevertheless instructive to note that 32 percent of their sample reported virtually no conflict; 24 percent, relatively little conflict; 32 percent, medium conflict; and 12 percent, serious conflict.

All in all, this picture appears quite similar to that presented by our data. Their little or no conflict categories add up to 56 percent, our very good and good but mixed add up to 60 percent. However, it does appear that in our sample of professionals somewhat more sibling relationships were experienced negatively—only 12 percent of Bossard and Boll's sample described sibling rivalry as serious, whereas psychotherapists report 24 percent of their fewer sibling relationships to be poor. But this could easily be a result of classifying differences—poor is almost surely a more inclusive category than serious conflict. In our judgment, the Bossard and Boll data suggest that, in terms of general quality, the sibling relationships experienced by those who became psychotherapists are probably quite similar to those experienced by other members of their generation and class.

Although not questioned along such lines, many respondents, in the context of their discussion of siblings, introduced the issue of which sibling was the dominant one. As used here, the word *dominant* does not necessarily have pejorative connotations. In addition to forcing one's will upon one's sibs, it may also mean a protective stance toward sibs or acting as a substitute parent, in either a physical or emotional way. What is common is the superior position implied. The following excerpts from interviews illustrate these various connotations:

> My sister who is three and a half years older than I, always tried to act about thirty years older. She was a worrier, and always, at least to me, tried to place herself in a maternal role. This relationship has never changed. She still sees me as a bad child, the acting out child and it is her role to straighten me out, to help me see the light. I resist it, but we get along fairly well and keep in fairly close touch.

> As kids, I was very much his protector and defender. He was a handsome, blond, blue-eyed, cuddly person. . . . I paid for his initiation fees to his college fraternity. I also gave him money when he ran out.

> I used to be able to manipulate the two younger sisters. I would have them polish my shoes and my bugle.

Ninety-six respondents (46 percent of the 208 respondents who discussed siblings) voluntarily brought up the subject of sibling dominance—clearly, it was and remains a relevant issue. When their comments are analyzed, we find that 19 percent say that no sibling was dominant,

25 percent name a brother or sister as the dominant one, and 56 percent identify themselves as having played the dominant sibling role. These are striking figures: psychotherapists see themselves as having occupied the superior sibling position twice as frequently as an inferior one and three times as frequently as an egalitarian one.

In light of the fact that dominance as used here includes such nurturant behaviors as protecting and defending, giving support and encouragement, and attempting to "straighten him out," as well as manipulation, it is tempting to connect such findings to the respondents' current occupational endeavors, if not in terms of causation, certainly in terms of noting congruent aspects between the role of dominant sibling and the role of therapist. However, while these data are indeed suggestive of such speculations, caution must certainly limit them. The discussions of sibling dominance were gratuitous, and it seems probable that those respondents who volunteered such information did so because inequality of sibs was an issue for them.

It is on this issue of sibling dominance that one of the rare differences among the various kinds of mental health professionals appears: 82 percent of those psychoanalysts who discuss the issue identify themselves as the dominant sibling; only about 50 percent of psychiatrists, psychologists, and social workers do so. This statistically significant difference holds when the 'data are controlled for sex, age, ethnic origins, and social-class origins—analysts remain the dominant sibling.

Earlier, when discussing the distribution of sibling dominance of the interview sample as a whole, we speculated that the disproportionately high percentage of respondents who described themselves as having occupied the position of dominant sibling appeared congruent with our understanding both of the power relationship and of the nurturance-succor relationship that exists between therapist and patient. In our judgment this makes even more sense in the context of the *psychoanalyst*-patient relationship. Of those theories of emotional healing currently of importance, it seems fair to assess psychoanalysis as the most acknowledging of, or indeed the most professing of, the dominant position of the therapist in the therapeutic relationship (in terms of such things as understanding more about the patient than he does, one-way disclosure, keeping aloof from emotional involvement, and the like). Other theories, such as Rogers' client-centered approach, depart, at least in their avowals, from this emphasis, and so do those professions that may embrace a variety of theoretical orientations in addition to the psychoanalytic one.

Furthermore, quite apart from the therapist-patient relationship, there is the question of psychoanalysts' status and power relative to the other three mental health professions. Among the professionals interviewed there was no question but that psychoanalysts were perceived as the most prestigeful and the most professionally powerful of their colleagues.

In terms of his position in the mental health field as well as his therapeutic belief system, the psychoanalyst is familiar with occupying a position of dominance. The high frequency with which the analyst identifies himself as the dominant sibling suggests he has had appropriate precursory experience with such a role in the context of the family.

Following their discussion of parents and siblings, the respondents were asked about possible relationships with other family members, such as grandparents or aunts and uncles, that had been of significance to them as they were growing up. The specific question was "Were there any other family members whom you feel were of special importance to you during your early years? Who were they, and what was the nature of your relationship with them?"

In answering, the respondents themselves defined what the words "of special importance" meant to them. In essence, two meanings were given: Relatives were important to them because of an emotional bond, such as the love and affection between a grandparent and a grandson, and/or because the relative was perceived as having exerted an influence on the respondent, such as an uncle who was a physician serving as a role model.

Two-thirds of the respondents had one or more relatives with whom they had a significant relationship during their early years. Of the relatives involved, aunts and uncles (equally) account for 48 percent of such relationships and grandmothers and grandfathers account for another 40 percent (here, the 11 percent greater frequency of relationships with grandmother over grandfather is probably due to the shorter life expectancy of males). The remaining 12 percent of these relationships were with cousins. Overall, the great majority of these significant relationships (88 percent) share two characteristics: First, they are with relatives that are but one step removed from the respondent's nuclear family; second, they are with relatives belonging to generations older than that of the respondents. It is clear that relationships with relatives during one's early years are seen to be of importance primarily if they were of a highly positive nature. Eighty percent of such relationships could be categorized as very good and only 4 percent of such significant relationships involved negative feelings. (Only about 20 percent of childhood relationships with parents were categorized as very good and 18 percent were characterized as negative.)

Although not specifically questioned on this point, 20 percent of the sample discussed their relationships with significant relatives in terms of how those relatives influenced them. The influence of relatives was felt in three areas: About a third of this subsample reported being directed toward or encouraged in scholastic-intellectual pursuits; for example: "She helped me chart my college course. She had a tremendous influence on my academic studies." Approximately a fourth of the subsample identified relatives who were influential in determining professional choice, either through encouragement or in serving as a role model; for example: "She went into medicine and I suspect this had something to do with my own choice of medicine." Another 27 percent saw relatives as having had an effect upon them in a variety of personal ways; for example: "Her influence was great in making me look into myself and overcome my inhibitions."

When the category of relative is related to the kind of influence exerted on the respondent, two interesting points are revealed. First, we find that when the importance of relatives is expressed in terms of exerting influence (rather than in terms of positive emotional regard), cousins assume a more important role. Second, as might be expected, aunts and uncles, members of the working generation, exert greater influence in the areas of achievement (scholastic-intellectual and professional) than grandparents, whereas the influence of grandparents is felt more in personal matters.

As with other aspects of early family life, those who become psychotherapists do not appear to be unusual in the extent or nature of their childhood relationships with close family relatives.

Family Disruption

Several questions in the interview were directed toward experiences of family disruption by the illness or death of family members or the separation from parents of the respondent during childhood and adolescence. As was the case when questions about their relationships with parents had been raised, the respondents were clearly convinced of the conceptual relevance of this area of inquiry. Their psychodynamic orientation had already persuaded them that such childhood traumas could be important to consider in understanding an individual's development—both personal and professional.

However, unlike the discussion of their relationships with parents, most psychotherapists had very little to say about family illness, death, and separation. Although many had experienced such events, they were seen as personally relevant to their lives and careers by only a few; most perceived their effects as minor.

Of the 242 therapists who were questioned about serious illnesses to themselves and their families, one-third said that no serious illness had occurred, while two-thirds (162 respondents) mentioned one or more such illnesses. The number of illnesses mentioned by this latter group was 235. The subsequent percentages are based on this number of illnesses, rather than number of respondents.

Of all the illnesses reported, the largest number (28 percent or about 65 illnesses) occurred to the mother, with father (23 percent) and the respondent (23 percent) next in frequency. Siblings (17 percent) and other family members (9 percent) were less frequently mentioned. It is possible that the somewhat greater frequency of illnesses of the mother than of the father is accounted for by the fact that these would more often be remembered, since they would, perhaps, most often affect the child.

However, the chances of illness to siblings in comparison to parents or respondent are increased by the fact that many respondents had more than one sibling and the chances of illness to both siblings and respondent in comparison to parents should be decreased by the lower frequency of serious illness in that younger age group. Yet illness to the respondent was reported as frequently as illness to the father, almost as frequently as illnesses to mother, and more frequently than illnesses to siblings. While this greater frequency of respondent illness is most probably explained by the likelihood that serious illness to oneself is remembered better than that occurring to other family members, the possibility that our group of mental health professionals did indeed suffer from serious illness during childhood and adolescence more frequently than other children cannot be completely dismissed.

What kinds of serious illnesses were experienced by family members? Of the 235 illnesses identified by 162 respondents, 74 percent were classified as physical and 26 percent, or about 61 illnesses, were reported as forms of mental or emotional disturbance. The presence of mental illness was distributed among various family members as follows: 42 percent of the 65 illnesses attributed to mothers (or about 27 illnesses) were so identified; to fathers, 34 percent; to relatives (aunts, uncles, grandparents), 38 percent; to siblings, 12 percent; and to the respondents themselves, 4 percent.

The more frequent occurrence of mental illness in mothers than fathers is consistent with the higher rates generally for women than men in this country and the lower rates for respondent and siblings than parents and other relatives probably reflect the lower incidence among younger age groups. One possible explanation for the more frequent occurrence of emotional disturbance in siblings than respondents may be a reluctance to label one's own illnesses as mental. That such a tendency might exist among our respondents cannot be entirely discounted, but it would run counter to the usual openness they demonstrated in discussing personal matters.

Perhaps the most interesting question these figures raise is the extent to which they might differentiate the early life of those who become psychotherapists. That is, is the incidence of mental illness encountered in the families of our sample high or low, and relative to what norm? We have no comparable data from other studies. However, we can compute one figure that gives us some feeling for how typical or atypical psychotherapists' experience may be. Of the 242 respondents who discussed the question of serious family illness, 27 percent reported the occurrence of emotional disturbance within the family circle. This is only very slightly higher than would be expected on the basis of figures given by virtually all major studies of symptom prevalence in the general population. Thus, the midtown Manhattan study by Srole and others (1962) found 23.4 percent of the population impaired because of psychiatric illness, while in the Stirling County study by Leighton and colleagues (1963), 20 percent of the population was classified as having "psychiatric disorder with significant impairment." In addition to these findings, Plunkett and Gordon's (1960) summary of eleven other studies of the prevalence of mental disorder reported figures generally between 20 and 25 percent. It seems likely, then, that the occurrence of mental illness in the families of those who become psychotherapists is similar to that experienced by members of the general population. We seriously question the idea that the vocational choice of psychotherapists has often been influenced by early personal experience with emotionally disturbed persons.

Of all respondents who were asked about any deaths which had occurred in their families from childhood through early adulthood, 37 percent reported no deaths. A total of 199 deaths were identified by the remaining 146 respondents. These are distributed among family members as follows: mother (6 percent), father (15 percent), sibling (16 percent), grandparent (50 percent), and other, that is, aunts, uncles, cousins (13 percent). Half of all deaths were of grandparents. Chances of such deaths are obviously higher than chances of death of a parent, both because of the greater number of grandparents and their more advanced age. The greater number of deaths of fathers than mothers is in line with higher mortality rates among men and the usually somewhat older age of fathers. The lower mortality rate of siblings due to younger age is offset by the fact that there are more siblings than fathers or mothers. They thus account for about the same percentage of total deaths as do fathers.

The largest proportion of deaths (42 percent) occurred during the respondent's adolescence; 35 percent occurred while respondents were in the six-to-eleven-year age group, and 23 percent during infancy and pre-school years. The increase in likelihood of having a death in the family as one advances in age is a normal expectation.

Whether the respondent judged the effect of a death upon himself to be of major or minor importance depended, of course, upon whose death it was. The percentage of serious effects was greatest for the death of mother (78 percent), and next highest for father (67 percent) and siblings (62 percent). Deaths of aunts, uncles, cousins, and grandparents (17 percent) least frequently had serious effects upon the respondent. These relationships between the effect of death and the family position of the deceased are obvious, except perhaps for that concerning grand-parents, aunts, uncles, and cousins. That the death of a grandparent should be least serious in effect is probably due to the expectation of approaching death that advancing age brings. This constitutes some prep-aration for the death of grandparents, in contrast to the difficulty of accepting the more untimely deaths of members of the parental genera-tion.

Overall, the part played by family deaths in the youth of the psychotherapist appears to be a natural one. The data reveal no surprises. For one-third of the sample no family deaths occurred through their high school years. Although the remaining majority did experience the death of a close relative, it was in almost two-thirds of those cases not a member of the nuclear family, and the effects were described as minor and temporary.

Of the 233 people questioned in regard to separation, just half had been separated for some period of time from one or both parents during childhood and adolescence.

Separations from mother (14 percent) were less frequent than separations from father (50 percent) or from both parents (36 percent). This difference is explained by the reasons given for separation—death of one parent (32 percent), illness (17 percent), boarding school (13 per-cent), divorce or separation (14 percent), and father away in service or on business (24 percent). Clearly more of these reasons result in separa-tion from father than from mother. For example, in divorce or separation the mother is almost invariably given the custody of any children; and, of course, for this generation, it is the father rather than the mother who is called away from home for service in the armed forces or in connection with business.

As would be expected, the longer the separation, the more serious the respondent judged its effect; and serious effects were more frequently associated with separations caused either by the death of a parent or their divorce or separation, than with separations caused by illness or school,

Combining those respondents who experienced separation from a parent either through death or divorce, on the grounds that both result n the severe family disruption defined by an absent parent, reveals that 23 percent of the total sample suffered a broken home at some time up through their high school years.

How does this compare with other groups? Clausen (1964, p. 27) reports that "population surveys in urban centers suggest that by age eighteen between 30 and 40 percent of all children have experienced a broken home." Psychotherapists then, appear to come from relatively stable family situations.

Conclusion

Reflecting upon the findings of this chapter dealing with the early family life of the psychotherapist, the overall impression is one of positive normalcy. Granted, we have no strictly comparable data either on other professional groups or on samples of the general population to test for statistical differences. We must be guarded then, in our conclusions. But two considerations persuade us that on most of those aspects of family life portrayed here, our sample is undistinguished. First, those few comparisons with other groups we were able to make usually demonstrated similarity rather than difference. Second, with minor exceptions, the distributions, from the perspective of face validity, do not strike us as remarkable. Thus, most psychotherapists got along fairly well with their parents as they were growing up, although during adolescence, as would be expected, strain over the issue of independence was widespread. Again, most psychotherapists had good relations with their siblings, although it is in this relationship that a tendency toward assuming a dominant role characterizes therapists. Finally, psychotherapists do not appear to have suffered unusually from the family disruptions of death, separation, or illness. In sum, it is our opinion that in reporting the early family life of those who become psychotherapists we may, perhaps, not be too far from describing the early family life of those who enter a wide spectrum of professions; we find nothing in these early family experiences that would account for their specific choice of mental health work.

7

Origins in Individual Development

A general developmental logic is implicit in this study's inquiries into the childhood life experiences of psychotherapists; that is, a belief that past experiences are major determinants of present behavior. Of course, in line with that assumption, specific judgments were made as to what particular kinds of early experience promised to be most strongly linked to choosing a career as a mental health professional. Foremost among the areas selected was the nature of relationships with parents and siblings, reflecting our evaluation of the family as the single most important formative force in developing those qualities, whether motivations, skills, or values, that would increase the probability of the later assumption of a particular occupational role. These family data were presented and discussed in the preceding chapter.

The present discussion focuses on three other areas of personal development over childhood and adolescence—the sexual, the social, and the intellectual as they are portrayed in the interview data. Although certainly not removed from the sphere of family influence, experiences in these areas involve the youth with institutions and persons in the larger society, notably the school and its teachers and students.

As with our inquiries into early family life, psychotherapists re-

194

sponded with interest and fluency to these investigations. Again, this was surely in part because of their agreement that their early sex experiences, their youthful interaction with peers, and the history of their intellectual development were all relevant to who and what they had become. That is, their own commitment to a developmental logic made them immediately receptive to the idea that perhaps we could identify, winding through their past histories, a path that had led to their becoming psychotherapists.

Early Sex History

Our subjects were asked four general questions about early sexual experiences. These were:

1. What kind of sex education or training were you given? How did you learn the "facts of life?"

2. What can you remember of your earliest sexual experiences? At what age did they occur and what was their nature?

3. How would you characterize your sexual life during adolescence?

4. What were the most significant sexual experiences you had during your early adulthood?

Examples of responses to the first question on sex education follow:

> Well, I would say my sex education took place in the early clubroom days and it was not really education but experience. We would rent a basement and there would be a little room there where everyone could go and sit and neck. That started at about age thirteen.

> Very early, since I had an early puberty—eleven. My mother told me about menstruation around nine years old and also introduced me to knowledge of sexual intercourse. She did it in a way that was depreciating of males, in that I should be aware of the fact that males were often insincere and would soft soap me in order to get something.

> I got my sex education on the street corner. Nothing was discussed at home. My mother was a strict Victorian. She never talked about these things.

Such responses were analyzed along three dimensions: when the facts of life were learned, the main source of this knowledge, and the nature of the parental attitude toward the respondent's growing awareness of sex.

For the majority of the sample (62 percent), learning the facts of life was a gradual process taking place over a fairly extensive time span, beginning in childhood and continuing through late adolescence. However, a little over a third of the respondents did report a specific period, such as "When I was nine years old," or "I found out what it was all about my first year in high school." Such specificity suggests that for these respondents, the learning experience was of an "ahah!" nature, rather than a process of connecting one item of information learned at one time with another learned a year or two later and these subsequently taking on new meaning as new feelings were experienced.

Of those respondents who experienced what might be termed fact-of-life gestalts, the majority reported them as occurring before high school. Thus it appears that if the facts of life are not learned gradually over time but more or less all at once, they are learned *early,* during childhood. (Only 7 percent report such learning during high school and 6 percent post-high school.)

The single greatest source of sex education is *peers:* 51 percent of the respondents fall into this category, more than twice as many as mentioned the next most frequently reported source, which is parents. The remainder of the sample, roughly a fourth, is accounted for primarily by formal sources—adults other than parents (such as family doctors), sex education classes (usually in college, not high school), and respectable sex literature (albeit surreptitiously obtained). Although, as later data will show, many respondents had sexual experiences during childhood, they were only rarely reported as contributing to understanding adult sexual behavior and procreation.

While peers constitute the greatest single source of sex education for the sample as a whole, a rare interprofessional difference appears when the four professions are compared. Specifically, social workers were significantly lower than the other three groups of professionals on peers as the main source of their sex education. Only 34 percent of the social workers learned the facts of life from peers while the corresponding figure for analysts, psychiatrists, and psychologists combined is 63 percent. This interprofessional difference might appear to be a function of the greater percentage of women in social work, on the logic that girls would be less likely than boys to learn the facts of life from their peers. However, analysis showed this not to be the case. Indeed, when sex was controlled for, it was only *male* social workers who remained significantly infrequent in their use of peers as a source of sex education. Their sources for the facts of life are formal—parents, other adults (such as the family doctor), education courses, and scientific literature. On the other hand, analysts, psychiatrists, and psychologists, and particularly males of these professions, share in locating their main source of sex education in peer relations.

When this finding is placed in the context of the significantly lower social-class origins of male social workers as compared with the other professional groups, it takes on added significance for it becomes even more contrary to expectations. It seems necessary to presume the presence of some considerable force to so effectively prevent the peer culture from enlightening part of its own, although we have no data to suggest what that might be.

However, we should make note of two plausible-sounding speculations, which upon consideration must be rejected. First, it might be expected that the part played in the sex education of their children by the parents of social workers would be qualitatively different from that of the parents of the other professionals. However, the analysis of the parental role in sex education revealed no interprofessional differences. Second, it could be argued that those parental attitudes and values associated with the lower social-class status of social workers' parents could indirectly influence the manner in which their children learned about sex; for example, a strong concern with social mobility might restrict the child's friendship choices and peer activities to the "good," the "clean," and the "safe." However, we find that this difference between social workers and the other professionals holds for all levels of social-class origins, the high as well as the low. At this point, then, whatever is at work here remains unclear.

Finally, it is clear that in general the role played by parents in the sex education of mental health professionals was an essentially negative one; 52 percent report that any discussion of sex was avoided, and for another 22 percent it was strictly forbidden. Although a smaller group of parents, 10 percent, were at least willing to answer questions, only a minority of 16 percent felt it their responsibility to initiate discussion of sexual matters.

With regard to the second question, remembrance of early sexual experience, the first three of a respondent's earliest recalled experiences were coded in two ways: (1) *when* they occurred—infancy (through age three), childhood (age four through grammar school), the freshman and sophomore high school years, the junior and senior years, and finally, post-high school—and (2) their nature—exploratory play, masturbation, exposure and viewing, necking and petting, intercourse, and other. Only 4 percent report a sexual experience occurring during their first three years. For almost two-thirds of the sample (64 percent), the earliest sexual experience occurred during childhood, between the ages of four and fourteen. Another 21 percent were well into adolescence, ages fourteen to eighteen, before experiencing either feelings or events that they deemed sexual in nature. For 11 percent such an experience did not occur until after high school. Parenthetically, we note here that the interviewers made it very clear to the respondents that in asking for earliest sex experiences the broadest possible definition was intended. In this light, it is surprising that 11 percent of the sample either did not experience or could not remember experiencing sexual feelings during childhood *or* adolescence.

It is interesting to compare these figures concerning the age of earliest sexual experiences with those reported by Kinsey and others (1948). Only 57 percent of his *total* sample recall some preadolescent sexual experience, whereas 70 percent of his *preadolescent* sample report sexual experiences. Sixty-eight percent of our psychotherapists report preadolescent sexual experience, a figure virtually identical to this latter group. Do Kinsey's figures indicate a historical shift—is it that an indeed greater percentage of the then currently preadolescent sample was having sexual experiences—or do Kinsey's figures merely reflect the disparity between contemporary and retrospective reporting? If the former, then the percentage of psychotherapists reporting preadolescent sexual experiences would be significantly high. If on the other hand, as seems likely, the difference between Kinsey's two groups is a function of distance from the phenomenon being reported, then it would seem rather that mental health professionals are significantly better than laymen at remembering the sexual experiences of their youth. Given both the significance attributed to early sexual experiences in the dominant schools of personality theory and the undoubted attention paid to their early sexual experiences in their own therapies as patients, the latter explanation seems more probable.

There is also strong agreement between Kinsey's preadolescent sample's reporting and psychotherapists' recollection of the *nature* of preadolescent sexual experience. The most frequently reported earliest sexual experience was that of exploratory play involving some physical contact; this involved a third of the sample. The remainder of respondents divided themselves rather evenly, ranging from 11 percent to 16 percent, among masturbation, viewing/exposure, necking/petting, and intercourse.

As one would expect, certain of these experiences are associated with certain ages of occurrence; exploratory play and viewing/exposure are virtually exclusive to childhood; masturbation as a first experience occurs about equally in childhood and adolescence; necking and petting are adolescent experiences; intercourse, with few exceptions, is associated with post-high school years.

With regard to sexual life during adolescence, we were able to make a rough judgment of the amount of sexual activity engaged in (no experience, occasional experience, frequent experience) and to characterize the *nature* of the respondent's various sexual experiences (masturbation, necking/petting, intercourse). In addition, we were able to obtain the respondent's evaluation of his adolescent self in his sex role along two closely related dimensions: feelings of *competence* or *incompetence* in sexual activities and feelings of *ease* or *difficulty* in sexual relationships. The following excerpts from interviews illustrate these points:

> My sex life during high school was pretty much nonexistent. A great deal of fantasying and some actual masturbation. I felt inadequate sexually with girls.

> I think I had a reasonably healthy sex life during my adolescence. I loved many boys and I fell in love many times. I had my fair share of necking. When I was a senior in high school, I went to a law school formal and I was introduced to petting. I was scared to death. Interestingly enough, I never had any premarital sexual relations. This was all part of me and my upbringing. I was raised in a strict household and I would have been a wreck in terms of guilt and fear if my virginity was gone.

> By adolescence I was doing it all over town. And every maid we ever had I screwed.

The important distinction regarding amount of sex experience in adolescence is between those respondents who had none (almost a quarter of the sample) and the majority of the sample who perceived themselves as experiencing either a moderate or heavy sex life.

The most frequently mentioned sexual activity of adolescence was necking and petting (61 percent); a fifth of the sample experienced intercourse during their high school years; and less than a third of the respondents (29 percent) reported adolescent masturbation. In light of the fact that masturbation can be thought of as almost universal during adolescence (Kinsey and others, 1948), this figure appears as a considerable deviation. However, it should be remembered that a respondent was asked only to characterize his adolescent sex life; no questions were directed to any specific sexual activity. This may indirectly account for the low figure for masturbation, an activity seen retrospectively perhaps as irrelevant.

About a fourth of those respondents who were questioned regarding their sex life during adolescence voluntarily brought up the subject of *competence* in sexual activities. As would be expected, this was mostly an issue for those who felt *in*competent in their sexual behavior.

For a larger percentage of the sample (36 percent), the issue of concern was not the adequacy with which one performed sexual activities but the anxiety (or lack of it) that accompanied them. The responding sample is divided almost equally on this point, 46 percent reporting their adolescent sex life to be anxiety-free, uninhibited, and enjoyable; and 54 percent expressing varying degrees of uneasiness.

Respondents were asked to discuss those sexual experiences of early adulthood (post-high school) that they saw as "significant." Their responses define that term in four ways: first intercourse (34 percent), first love (8 percent), sustained affair (28 percent), marriage (26 percent), and other (4 percent). First love, sustained affair, and marriage can all be seen as variations of a relatively enduring intimate relationship. The only other type of sexual experience seen as significant is first intercourse, important for some because it constituted proof that an adult sexual status had been attained and for others because it was the most powerful sexual enjoyment yet experienced.

Roughly half the sample had experienced sexual intercourse by the time of graduation from high school, 16 percent by age sixteen, 45 percent by age 18. The remaining 55 percent divided into two groups—those who experienced first intercourse during college (33 percent) and those for whom such an experience was delayed beyond age twenty-two (22 percent). Thus, for almost a fourth of our sample, sexual intercourse was not experienced until after college graduation and the beginning of professional training.

How do these figures compare with other samples? Kinsey and colleagues (1948) again provide comparable data. Of those males who are destined for college-level education, the incidence of coitus by age sixteen is 16 percent and, by age eighteen, 38 percent. As already noted, the comparable figures for psychotherapists are 16 percent and 45 percent. These figures are in essential agreement and the sex life of those young adults who eventually become psychotherapists appears to be much the same—as measured by this simple but important variable—as that enjoyed by their campus peers.

The age of first experience of sexual intercourse also produced the second of the two interprofessional differences found in the area of sex history. Specifically, psychiatrists and social workers are, on the average, a year later than analysts and psychologists in experiencing sexual intercourse. The mean age at first experience of sexual intercourse is 20.4 for both psychiatrists and social workers while the corresponding figure for psychoanalysts is 19.1 and for psychologists 18.8 years. Why this difference in timing is related differentially to profession is puzzling, especially since there are no correlative interprofessional differences regarding either the timing of other sexual experiences (age of learning the facts of life or age of earliest remembered sex experience) or the timing of beginning dating.

Relationship with Peers

Since interpersonal interaction is both the subject and the *modus operandi* of psychotherapy, considerable attention was devoted in the interview to the development of the psychotherapist's peer relationships.

To initiate the mental health professional's discussion of his development in interpersonal relations the following general question was asked: "How would you characterize your interpersonal relationships with *same* sex and *opposite* sex peers during *childhood, adolescence,* and *early adult-hood?*"

In addition to further questioning appropriate to the particular response, three standard probes were used when necessary to elicit information in these areas: (1) "Would you describe yourself during those years as being 'popular,' or as being a 'loner'?" (2) "What kinds of things did you do with your friends?" (3) "When did you start dating? Was it easy or difficult for you?"

Just as the respondents had impressed their own time dichotomy on the discussion of siblings ("When I was growing up" versus "Now"), they here substituted for our childhood, adolescence, and young adult divisions a two-part breakdown of time into pre-high school versus high school and beyond.

Our analysis enabled us to distinguish five aspects of relationships with both same-sex and opposite-sex peers. These were: (1) the number of close friendships enjoyed by the respondent, (2) the sex ratio among those friends, (3) the nature of the activities engaged in with friends (excluding dating which was separately treated), (4) the respondent's evaluation of the overall emotional quality of his peer relationships, and (5) the respondent's characterization of his "role" in the relationships (for example, as "big man on campus" or a "shy and lonely kid").

Table 36 deals with these five aspects of peer relationships during both the pre-high school and high school periods.

Comparing pre-high school with high school experience on each dimension, one is struck by the overall symmetry. With minimal exceptions, the nature of peer relationships remains virtually unchanged from one age period to the next, at least in terms of these variables. These findings, especially because they include such basic dimensions as number of close friends and degree of satisfaction obtained, strongly suggest that patterns of relating to peers are established early and tend to endure. The shy, shrinking violet of grammar school rarely blossoms in high school, and one who has lots of friends as a kid becomes the popular "big man on campus."*

* To ensure that the remarkable similarity in figures from pre-high school to high school was indeed a result of the same persons remaining unchanged, the data from the two age periods were run against each other. Very little slippage occurred. For example, of those respondents who reported having nothing but same-sex friends prior to high school, 93 percent of them also reported having only same-sex friends during the high school years. Of the five variables in

Table 36. RELATIONSHIPS WITH PEERS (PRE-HIGH SCHOOL AND HIGH SCHOOL): NUMBER, SEX RATIO, ACTIVITIES, EVALUATION, AND ROLE CHARACTERIZATION

Aspects of Peer Relationships	Pre-High School Percent	High School
Number of Close Friends		
None	7.2	2.8
Few	57.7	59.7
Many	35.1	37.5
Total	100.0	100.0
	(208)	(211)
Sex Ratio of Friends		
All Same Sex	43.9	39.4
Mixture	55.3	60.5
All Opposite Sex	0.8	—
Total	100.0	100.0
	(132)	(132)
Activities Engaged in[a]		
Academic/Cultural	3.5	13.5
Socializing	10.4	27.2
Sports	24.4	24.4
"Playing"	18.7	—
Extracurricular	—	20.0
Other	1.3	2.0
Evaluation of Friendships		
Highly Satisfactory	48.7	47.1
Satisfactory	31.7	35.4
Unsatisfactory	16.1	15.0
Highly Unsatisfactory	3.5	2.4
Total	100.0	100.0
	(230)	(240)
Role Characterization		
Normal	9.5	6.9
Hostile-Aggressive	11.1	8.6
Popular, Big-Man-On-Campus	31.7	41.4
Isolated, Shy, Inept	47.7	43.1
Total	100.0	100.0
	(63)	(58)

[a] Percentages based on number of mentions: 230 for pre-high school; 245 for high school.

Of course, as we shall see later, there are dramatic changes over time in the area of heterosexual relations; but, overall, the major point revealed here remains—both the "onslaught" of puberty and the high school experience appear to have little influence on already established paradigms of interaction with peers.

Examining each section of Table 36, we find, first, that slightly more than half of our sample (58 percent pre-high school, 60 percent in high school) possessed a *few* close friends, and roughly a third of them (35 percent in pre-high school, 38 percent in high school) enjoyed many. Isolates are few: 7 percent had no close friends prior to high school, and this figure decreases to 3 percent in high school.

The sex ratio of respondents' peer relations changes surprisingly little (5 percent) between childhood and adolescence; for both age periods slightly more than half of the sample claim friends of both sexes, and slightly less than half possess exclusively same-sex friends. Presumably, puberty has indeed added a sexual character to some of these relationships, but it has not influenced those aspects of peer relations reported above.

Those changes that occur in activities engaged in with peers between pre-high school and high school all appear easily understandable: academic and cultural activities increase, playing stops (or, rather, is no longer called that), and socializing correspondingly increases; finally, extracurricular activities, structured by secondary education, enter the scene.

The great majority of our sample provide evidence of satisfactory peer relationships (80 percent in pre-high school, 83 percent in high school). Indeed, almost half of the sample in both time periods (49 percent and 47 percent respectively) fall in the most positive category. Most mental health professionals have a history of getting along well with their friends.

Only a small percentage of those respondents who discussed peer relations volunteered role characterizations of themselves. Indeed, it seems that virtually only the extreme "successes" and "failures," the popular and the lonely, felt it necessary to do so. We cannot know then, to what extent these two extremes, the "big man on campus" and the shy, socially inept, isolate are representative of the sample as a whole. But what *is* noteworthy here is again the continuity of characterization over time revealed

---

Table 36, the greatest change appeared in evaluation of friendships: of those whose pre-high school relationships were satisfactory, 85 percent had satisfactory relationships in high school; of those whose pre-high school relationships were unsatisfactory; 63 percent continued to have unsatisfactory relationships in high school (30 percent had changed to the satisfactory category and 7 percent to the highly satisfactory).

by the analysis—of those who reported themselves as popular in pre-high school, 88 percent remain so in high school; correspondingly, of those who were isolated and shy, 78 percent remain so.

Thus far, the findings we have presented on peer relationships have applied to the sample as a whole. This reflects the fact that, with two exceptions, the findings reported apply equally well to all four professions. However, the two exceptions are worthy of note. Both of these inter-professional differences distinguish psychoanalysts from psychiatrists, psychologists, and social workers in regard to adolescent peer relations. First, only 14 percent of psychiatrists, psychologists, and social workers report unsatisfactory relations as opposed to 30 percent of psychoanalysts. Second, 71 percent of analysts said they had but few close friends whereas only 60 percent of psychiatrists, psychologists, and social workers so characterize their adolescence.

Although these differences are statistically significant, it should be noted that in neither case are the proportions reversed: thus, while indeed a majority of analysts (71 percent) had only a few close friends in adolescence, so did the majority (60 percent) of the other three professional groups. Similarly, although the percentage of analysts coded as having unsatisfactory peer relationships in adolescence is twice that of the other three professions (30 percent to 14 percent respectively), these percentages constitute minorities of both groups.

The fact remains that analysts differ from psychiatrists, psychologists, and social workers in that more of them experienced difficulties with peers during adolescence—more of them had fewer friends and more of them had unsatisfactory relationships.

Why might this be so? Although we have no further data to elucidate these findings, we can suggest one line of speculation. Of the major psychotherapeutic ideologies, psychoanalysis most clearly stresses the influence of the past upon the present; the acuteness of the childhood and adolescent years in the development of personality is most especially emphasized. Perhaps the appeal of this doctrine, of this approach to understanding oneself as well as others, would be strongest to those persons whose own relatively unhappy experience had early convinced them of its truth. It is natural to see bad experiences as more determining than good ones; the consequences of a lonely adolescence are more visible to the sufferer than are the benefits of popularity apparent to the enjoyer. Thus, those most sensitized to how past developmental difficulties influence the present may be more receptive to the developmental premise basic to psychoanalytic theory.

Returning to the sample as a whole, we find that regarding the respondent's ease of relating to same- and opposite-sex peers during high school, the data demonstrate the expected—only 15 percent experienced any difficulty in their interaction with same-sex peers, whereas 39 percent experienced some discomfort with opposite-sex peers. Thus, even with the opposite sex, the majority managed their high school peer relations with some degree of ease. But we must note that these figures refer only to non-dating relations with the opposite sex; the introduction of sexuality, of the element of romance or passion, changes things.

A third of our sample reports beginning dating just before high school (age fourteen or before), 39 percent say between ages fifteen and sixteen, and another 20 percent between ages seventeen and eighteen. Only 7 percent delayed until age nineteen or older, that is, beyond what are usually the high school years. Thus, by age sixteen, three-quarters of the sample, and by age eighteen, 93 percent of the sample had begun dating. These figures are in substantial agreement with those given as societally typical: "The normal age for beginning dating is fourteen for girls, fifteen for boys. . . . By seventeen, virtually all American girls date" (Douvan and Adelson, 1966, p. 498).

A fourth of the sample accompanied their reporting of age at beginning dating with an assessment of its social timeliness. Of this 25 percent who brought up this subject, 75 percent, or roughly a fifth of the total sample, saw themselves as being late; thus, those who felt themselves to be either early or on time rarely felt it necessary to mention it. It was the "late-bloomers" who felt it important to report; it was they who were troubled by the time dimension: "I was very backward in dating. I was very self-conscious and didn't start dating until college." "I was slow in dating. Everyone else was going steady before I even knew what was going on."

A clue to one possible reason for lateness in dating is contained in the interprofessional difference found regarding "on-timeness" of dating. Of those same respondents who commented on the timing of their beginning dating, 90 percent of psychoanalysts and 92 percent of psychiatrists considered themselves to be late, while the corresponding figures for psychologists and social workers are 67 percent and 65 percent, respectively. In short, a much higher proportion of the medical professions reported starting late. Perhaps such a delay is associated with the early serious devotion to studies necessitated in anticipating medical school. Undergraduate premed programs are notoriously preoccupying, and the medical school entrance requirements are probably effective even further back, influencing high school performance.

While a fifth of the sample as a whole report being late in beginning to date, an even larger proportion, 30 percent, report the absence of any dating during high school.* Further, half the sample report the absence of any "romantic" element in their relationships with members of the opposite sex during high school. What dating these respondents engaged in was determined by motives other than heterosexual desire. In this respect, the dating motives of those who become psychotherapists are similar to those of general population samples. As Douvan and Gold (1964, p. 498) state: "The function of the American dating system is to reintroduce the child to the forms of heterosexual social life . . . [and has] much less to do with sex. . . . Both high school and college students see dating primarily as a social relationship."

Finally, half the sample report feelings of discomfort associated with high school dating. We may ask whether this discomfort accompanies or prevents the first steps in establishing that kind of heterosexual relationship characterized by sexuality. Comparing feelings of ease or anxiety about dating with the nature of the dating experience, we find that of those reporting no romantic element, 100 percent also reported feelings of acute discomfort. For that half of the sample whose dating was of a romantic nature, only 40 percent reported such feelings of discomfort. It would appear that the anxiety accompanying dating is more often a hindrance to heterosexual intimacy than a result of it.

A comparison of these high school peer relationships with those of young adulthood reveals no surprises: The amount of dating increases markedly, there is a growing ease in such relationships (although about a third of our sample still expresses a sense of discomfort in heterosexual relations during the college years), and, finally, the majority of the sample (71 percent) reports experiencing an intense heterosexual relationship of a clearly sexual nature sometime in young adulthood.

As seemed to be the case with their early sexual experiences, the pattern of psychotherapists' relationships with both same- and opposite-sex peers during childhood and adolescence is not visibly distinctive. At those few points at which our sample could be compared directly with other groups, the findings proved to be in general agreement. Conviction that mental health professionals have experienced a developmental history of peer relationships more or less the same as that of the general population would, of course, require many such empirical comparisons. But we note that no variable examined here appears to hold much promise as a characteristic differentiating those who become psychotherapists.

---

* The seeming discrepancy between this figure and the 7 percent figure for beginning dating beyond age eighteen reported in the discussion of age of dating is accounted for by the large number of respondents who graduated from high school before age eighteen.

Intellectual Development

The extensive education and continuing interest in learning that characterize mental health professionals earn them a place among the "intellectual" professions. Certainly, an intense engagement in intellectual activities was essential to their achieving professional status. How do they describe their intellectual development? What was their early intellectual environment as shown in the intellectual interests of their parents? What other people figured in their intellectual growth?

Our discussion of these issues will rely primarily on the responses given to three interview questions: (1) "What were the main sources of intellectual stimulation for you as you were growing up?" (2) "What about any artistic or literary interests?" (3) "Were there any people outside of your family or peers whom you think exerted significant influence on your intellectual development during childhood, adolescence, early adulthood? (If so) Who were they and in what ways?" In addition to these questions, which focused specifically on the respondents' intellectual development, we found that in their descriptions of parents and of their relationships with them during childhood, adolescence, and young adulthood, the respondents provided much information about their parents' intellectual interests and activities, their intellectual aspirations for the respondent, and the respondent's reaction to them.

It is here, in the area of intellectual development that we at last encounter occasional significant differences in the early backgrounds of psychotherapists belonging to different professions. It is here, too, that the sex of the therapist sometimes assumes paramount importance. These interprofessional and between-sex differences will constitute a major part of our description of the intellectual development of those who become psychotherapists.

Figures of Intellectual Influence. Of our total interview sample of 283 respondents, 252 discussed their intellectual development. A third of these identify their fathers as the figure exerting most influence. Only 12 percent see their mothers as having played that role. However, 20 percent report that both parents, together, were equally influential. Thus, the father was an important intellectual influence (either alone or along with mother) for half of the total sample, and similarly, the mother for a third. Three other figures are occasionally identified as major influences: 11 percent mention a particular teacher, 10 percent a relative, and 8 percent a peer or older friend. Finally, 7 percent report the absence of any single, outstanding influential figure.

Obviously, it is the parents who dominate the intellectual environment of the psychotherapist's youth, and certainly the influence of the father is much greater than that of the mother. Her impact is mainly felt *in conjunction with* the father; as a lone figure, her influence drops to the level of the nonfamily figures of teacher, peer, and relative.

This is true for both men and women, so it is not simply a matter of a father having a more profound influence on his son. It is, rather, a reflection of the father's dominant intellectual role in the households of the parent generation here concerned.

Although this general picture of parental influence holds true for the sample as a whole, there is an important variation that contrasts the two medical professions of analysis and psychiatry with the professions of clinical psychology and social work. On the one hand, the figure of the father, acting alone, is identified as the most influential figure with significantly greater frequency by analysts and psychiatrists. On the other hand, the parents, as a team, are more frequently so identified by psychologists and social workers. Consequently, although the father remains the single most influential figure for all four professions, his influence is more pervasive among those who enter the two mental health professions requiring the M.D. degree. And further, although the influence of the mother, acting alone, is the same for all professions, her influence, exerted as part of a parental pair, is more frequently felt by psychologists and social workers.

Modes of Intellectual Influence. In what ways did these major figures exert their influence over the psychotherapists' early intellectual development? The respondents delineated two modes of influence, which cast the figures of father, mother, teacher, relative, and peer into two conceptually distinct roles: first and more important was the role of *model*. That is, a given figure exercised his influence over the respondent by simply being a desirable example, by serving as an ideal for identification. An extract from an interview illustrates this role:

> Actually, I would say that my grandfather, who was in his seventies at the time, was my male ego ideal. He was a professor of psychiatry at the university. I had daily contact with him. I felt toward my grandfather with great admiration. He was an imposing, powerful figure. The professor in Germany is one of the most revered figures. I can recall accompanying him to lectures occasionally or visiting patients in the hospital. It was a most impressive kind of thing, the respect and deference paid him as we went up the steps of the hospital and the entire staff would bow from the hip down.

A second role identified by the respondents was that of *stimulator*. In this role, the figure influenced the respondent by active and deliberate arousal of his intellectual aspirations. An example of this mode of influence:

> My parents encouraged intellectual activities, but it was my older sister who emphasized education very strongly, sensing that I would not be able to go to college if I didn't win an academic scholarship.

Fathers were more frequently models or model-stimulators than mothers. The figures for fathers are: as model, 21 percent, as model-stimulator, 55 percent; for mothers, the corresponding figures are 5 percent and 39 percent. Correlatively, mothers were more frequently stimulators, 56 percent as compared to fathers' 24 percent. This is a reflection of the lesser intellectual and professional involvement of women in this parent generation. These differences between parental modes of influence were true for both male and female psychotherapists, so it is not simply a matter of fathers more frequently being models to their sons. They also tended to be models for their daughters.

As would be anticipated, the role of stimulator alone (that is, of actively assuming responsibility for the intellectual aspirations of the respondent) is rarely played by the figures of relative, teacher, or peer. These figures serve almost exclusively as models or model-stimulators.

Intellectual Interests. Given the importance of the role of model as a means of influencing the intellectual development of those who become psychotherapists, the intellectual interests of those who served as models assume considerable importance. Table 37 presents the area of major intellectual interest of father, mother, relative, teacher, and peer, and for the respondent himself, as he was growing up (childhood through adolescence).

Only the first-mentioned or most important interest is used in the calculations; therefore, a low frequency does not mean that such interests do not exist for the majority of people coded, but only that they are rarely mentioned as the primary or major interest.

The first observation to be made from Table 37 is that a number of interprofessional and sex differences occur in these data. These will be discussed later. Because of these differences, the sample as a whole cannot be characterized in terms of the major intellectual interests of father or mother. However, some statements can be made about the differences between father and mother that obtain for each profession when considered separately and that also hold true for both male and female respondents. Mothers, more frequently than fathers, are described as having *no* intellectual interests. They are also more frequently described as interested in the humanities. Fathers, on the other hand, are rated consistently higher than mothers in social science and a variety of specific "other" intellectual areas. In general intellectual interests there is no significant difference between fathers and mothers.

Table 37. MAJOR INTELLECTUAL INTEREST OF INFLUENTIAL FIGURES AND RESPONDENT

	Father	Mother	Relative	Teacher	Peer	Respondent as Youth
				Percent		
None	12[a]	28[a]	—	—	—	—
Humanities	19[a,b]	35[a]	44	56	54	48[a]
Social Sciences	25[a]	11[a]	15	19	17	15[a]
General	18[a]	17[a]	24	10	21	12
Other Specific Areas (e.g., Religion, Physical Science, Medicine)	26	9	17	15	8	25
Total	100 (217)	100 (155)	100 (80)	100 (59)	100 (24)	100 (247)

[a] Sex difference exists.
[b] Interprofessional difference exists.

The higher percentage of mothers who are perceived as lacking intellectual interests is, of course, not surprising. Their roles, particularly in the generations of which we are speaking, seldom allowed for the development of such interests. The one exception would be the humanities. Cultural-artistic-literary activities were regarded as properly feminine.

Other relatives, teachers, and peers can be characterized as being mainly interested in the humanities (44 percent, 56 percent, and 54 percent of each of these groups, respectively).

The respondent's youthful intellectual interests were most frequently in the humanities (48 percent), with social science, physical science, and general interests mentioned with much less frequency. Significant differences between the mental health professions appear on one of these areas and between men and women on most areas, but humanities, nevertheless, is the most frequently mentioned area for each profession and for both men and women.

Comparing the interests of respondents with those of their fathers and mothers, there appear to be many significant differences as well as areas of relative similarity. Because of the number and magnitude of the sex and interprofessional differences, however, only a few of these can be said to characterize our total sample in any general way. First, we note that *all* respondents had some intellectual interests in contrast to 12 percent of the fathers and 28 percent of the mothers whom the respondents, even as adults, perceived as devoid of intellectual interests. Second, interest in the humanities occurred much more frequently among the respondents-as-youths than among their fathers. This is an intriguing finding. It is not simply an artifact of the respondents' more frequent intellectualism, for, despite their fathers "disadvantage" (12 percent had *no* intellectual interests), more fathers than respondents were mentioned as having both "social science" and "general" as categories of major interest. The respondents' greater interest in the humanities, then, is truly a distinctive characteristic. We can suggest two possible factors at work: first, mothers may have had more of an intellectual influence on their children at an early age than did fathers (and almost twice as many mothers as fathers manifested interest in humanities); second, the respondents themselves may have simply preferred learning in that area most directly and obviously concerned with people rather than objects or abstractions.

With regard to the professional difference noted above, analysis reveals that the fathers of psychiatrists differ from the fathers of other mental health professionals in the relative infrequency of their interest in the humanities. Specifically, only 4 percent of the fathers of psychiatrists show an interest in this area, compared to 20 percent of the fathers of psychoanalysts, 22 percent of the fathers of clinical psychologists, and 27 percent of the fathers of social workers. Put another way to explicate this finding, of the 41 fathers with a primary humanities interest, only two were fathers of psychiatrists, although psychiatrists represented almost one-fourth of the sample. On the other hand, psychiatrists' fathers show a corresponding greater interest in the sciences—physical, biological, and social. While not significant, there is a tendency for mothers of psychiatrists likewise to be less frequently interested in humanities and more frequently interested in other areas. Of the four mental health professions, certainly psychiatry can be fairly seen as placing most emphasis on the medical-physical-chemical treatment of emotional problems. This perspective appears to have some logical relationship to the intellectual climate of psychiatrists' early intellectual environment.

As indicated, male and female respondents differed significantly regarding both their own early intellectual interests and those of their parents. Men saw both father and mother as more frequently *not* having intellectual interests. To the extent that this constitutes a handicap to the development of achievement motivations, men would be more able than women to surmount it because of the more favorable climate in our culture for intellectual achievement by men. Such a handicap for women would tend to be reinforced by the discrimination against women in our culture and further depress the likelihood of their achieving the status of a mental health professional.

Humanities as an interest area was much more frequently characteristic of the parents of women than of men, while the areas of social science, physical science, and general intellectual interest were more frequently found in the parents of men. These same differences mark the respondents' early intellectual interests. Women indicated much more frequently early interest in the humanities (80 percent for women compared to 35 percent for men), and almost no interest in physical or social science (1 percent in each compared with 19 and 22 percent for men).

Assuming that cultural constraints make it more difficult for a woman to become a mental health professional, the finding that women respondents come from families in which the humanities interest of both parents is more frequently predominant, might argue that such a family background constitutes another aspect of the climate necessary to enable them to attain professional status eventually. The humanities is that area of intellectual endeavor in which early achievement by females is socially approved.

Intellectual Aspirations. The figures that psychotherapists saw as influencing their intellectual development not only served in the essentially passive role of model but also frequently played the active role of stimulator. That is, they held aspirations for the respondent and acted to effect them. However, these ambitions for intellectual development were not necessarily intended to lead to the achievement of a particular professional status but included expectations or hopes for a respondent's enduring interest and participation in intellectual activity per se. Indeed, a slim majority of both fathers (56 percent) and mothers (61 percent) were reported as having aspirations for their children's intellectual achievement of only a general and open-ended nature.

On the other hand, a substantial minority of parents pushed for intellectual progress toward a wide variety of specific professional roles—artist, writer, rabbi, lawyer, engineer, teacher. Of these, only one, that of physician, was mentioned with any significant frequency; 20 percent of fathers for the sample as a whole and 17 percent of mothers wanted their children to become doctors. Of course, as one would expect, there is an interprofessional difference here; medically trained mental health personnel, psychoanalysts and psychiatrists, more often had mothers and fathers who wanted them to become physicians than was the case with clinical psychologists and social workers.

Area of parental aspiration also varied by sex of the respondent. Both fathers and mothers of male respondents more frequently had aspirations for them in medicine than did the fathers and mothers of female respondents. This reflects the general sex difference in our culture with regard to expectations of professional achievement in general, and particularly in the field of medicine. Discrimination against women in medicine still prevails to some degree and expectations for women in this field are still very low. It is often regarded as a profession hard to reconcile with the marriage and family roles of women. It is not surprising, then, that this generation of parents did not aspire to medical careers for their daughters.

The figures of relative and teacher differed in regard to the nature of their aspirations for the respondents. Somewhat more than two-thirds of those relatives who were remembered for their intellectual influence directed the respondents' development toward some specific area; indeed, 25 percent focused on medicine. By contrast, teachers tended to promote intellectual development in general.

Reactions to Aspirations. How did the respondent react to the particular aspirations that his parents and other significant figures held for him? Analysis shows that the response was positive in about half of the cases with regard to parents (no difference between father and mother) and virtually universally positive in regard to other figures. To look at the other side of it, about half of the respondents reacted either with indifference, rebellion, or mixed feelings to the particular area of aspiration that their parents held for them. For this half of our group of mental health professionals, then, parental urging elicited a negative reaction. That this negative reaction is virtually absent in regard to relatives, teachers, and peers is a result of the fact that such figures were only rarely mentioned unless they were a positive influence.

Considering parental influence only, what kinds of aspirations were most likely to get a positive response from the respondents? The answer is that general, open-ended aspirations on the part of the father and mother receive the highest percentage of positive responses (80 percent for father, 65 percent for mother). Next come aspirations in the area of medicine (63 percent positive responses to father's aspirations in this area, 50 percent to mother), then aspirations in a variety of other specific areas (35 percent positive to father and 35 percent to mother).

In general, then, respondents reacted more positively to general aspirations than to specific ones. Parents in a generally supportive role would allow for more autonomy on the part of the respondent and would be expected to elicit a more positive reaction than specific aspirations that would more often be destined to conflict with the respondent's own aspirations for himself. On the other hand, if aspirations *are* specific, those for achievement in the area of medicine get a more positive reaction than those in any other specific area. This is probably due to the prestige and power generally attached to medicine (and early recognized), which make achievement in that area seem more attractive and thereby more frequently elicit a positive response to influence directed toward it. Certainly the one interprofessional difference found here is consistent with this interpretation. In brief, psychiatrists and analysts are significantly more positive in their reaction to the pressures emanating from their fathers than are psychologists and social workers. Specifically, 67 percent of psychiatrists and 68 percent of analysts had a positive reaction to the father's area of aspiration while the comparable figures of psychologists was 47 percent and for social workers 55 percent. Fathers of these two medically trained professional groups more frequently held aspirations in the area of medicine for their children than did fathers of psychologists and social workers. Hence, the suggestion that this more favorable reaction might stem from the early awareness of the great prestige of medicine seems plausible.

Intellectual Mutuality. In an attempt to further our understanding of the process of intellectual development, we examined whether or not respondents felt a mutuality of intellectual interests and concerns with their parents. The following interview quotation illustrates what is meant by mutuality: "During my childhood I was very close to my father. We shared a deep interest in literature and writing. He was very involved in intellectual things and so was I."

Mutuality with the father was present in over half of the cases while mutuality with the mother was present in only about one-third of the cases. This is not unexpected in view of cultural sex differences, particularly in the parent generation, which makes it likely that the father would be the intellectually dominant parent. Also, our data show that mothers more frequently than fathers had no intellectual interests.

However, examination of the differences in intellectual mutuality by sex of respondent reveals that women respondents much more frequently show intellectual mutuality with their fathers than do male respondents. They also more frequently show mutuality with their mothers. This sex difference occurs not only for the sample as a whole, but also when each professional group is examined separately.

In interpreting this finding, we must remember that the coding of mutuality was based on indications that the respondent had *experienced* this rather than merely that parent and respondent shared interests in the same area. It would be thus possible to experience mutuality even though interests were not the same and, on the other hand, possible to fail to experience mutuality even though interests were held in common. We find no differences between male and female respondents in the extent to which there is an identity of interest for father-son, father-daughter, mother-son, or mother-daughter. (Of course, here it must be remembered that we can do this only on the basis of primary interests, since our analysis does not take into account additional secondary interests that might have been present.) But the point remains: Although matching of primary interest areas between parents and respondents reveals no difference between men and women, female respondents indicate more frequent sharing of intellectual interests with both father and mother than do male respondents. One explanation of this finding rests upon the logic that to overcome the social discrimination against women becoming professionals, extra supports for intellectual achievement are necessary. For men then, intellectual mutuality with parents is less important in providing backing for a career than for women, who require such reinforcements in order to withstand the greater social counterpressures that they experience. This is in effect an extension of the interpretation we made earlier about parents with no intellectual interests being found more frequently among men than women respondents.

Intellectual Activity. What type of intellectual activity did these various influences produce? Although a wide variety of specific activities were identified, they were, with one exception, mentioned infrequently. That exception was *reading;* four-fifths of the sample reported it as their primary early intellectual activity. The following interview excerpt demonstrates the importance of reading as an early intellectual habit: "Books were definitely the main source of my stimulation. I read everything I could read. There was no selection in what I read. I would go from one extreme to the other. One week I would read *Tom Swift* and the next *The Decline and Fall of the Roman Empire.*"

Not only did the majority engage in the same intellectual activity but they also exhibited considerable uniformity in the age when their intellectual interests first emerged. Specifically, three-fourths of our respondents reported that their intellectual interests began during their grammar school years, indicating a somewhat early commitment to intellectual activities. For most of the remainder of the group intellectual interests of one sort or another began during their high school years. Only 3 percent delayed interest in intellectual activities until after high school.

Given their commitment to intellectual activities, it comes as no surprise to find that the majority (65 percent) of our group did superior work in elementary and secondary school. An example of a typical reporting of school experience is: "I was always good in school. I had a very good high school record; I graduated high school when I was sixteen and entered college then. My formal education was always a couple of years ahead of my age." Of the remainder of the sample, 21 percent described their performance as good, while only 14 percent said they did average or poor work. Together with the early emergence of intellectual interests mentioned above, this factor of early success and thus of early reward becomes in all probability a significant factor in the continuing intellectual concerns of our mental health professionals. When the professions are compared on school performance, analysts distinguish themselves by a greater frequency of superior grades than the other professional groups. Only 5 percent of analysts did poor or average work, and only 17 percent did work described as good, whereas 78 percent of analysts reported superior achievement. The pattern of intense intellectual activity on the part of psychoanalysts began for the vast majority of them in their early school years.

Although we must again lament the lack of comparable data on professionals from a different occupational field, our findings do suggest that this area of intellectual development holds more promise for distinguishing the backgrounds of those who become psychotherapists than does either early sexual history or social development.

8

Being a Psychotherapist

To be a psychotherapist is to live in a unidimensional world defined in terms of psychodynamic language. For psychotherapists, psychodynamic language is more than simply a way of describing psychological states and processes; it also provides a concrete system for identifying and classifying individuals. On the basis of previous training and experience psychotherapists have learned not to rely on common, everyday criteria for categorizing individuals but, instead, to view persons as concrete manifestations of a general theoretical framework. For most of the psychotherapists practicing in Los Angeles, New York City, and Chicago this theoretical framework is composed of psychodynamic concepts, particularly psychoanalytic concepts derived from the Freudian and neo-Freudian schools of thought. To the extent that these psychodynamic concepts provide the psychotherapist with a set of rules for interpreting human behavior, as well as a set of guidelines for imputing meaning to individual thoughts and actions, they serve to delimit the therapist's world. The specialized world of the psychotherapist is one in which the terminology of everyday conversation is avoided and psychodynamic language becomes the basic mode of communication. Psychodynamic language is, therefore, a highly specialized and individualized form of communication designed to enable the practitioner to interpret, translate, and recognize the meaning of experiences. To a certain extent, therefore, the psychodynamic paradigm serves to

217

redefine the social behavior of individuals so that they come to be viewed as functions of specific personal dynamics.

Although psychodynamic language takes a highly personalized form, it is generally applicable to all individuals with whom the psychotherapist has close, intimate relations. Perhaps this is why the psychotherapists in our sample tend to describe their own early development, as well as their past family life in an ahistorical format composed of psychodynamic processes that could not possibly have been part of their experiential world when they were growing up. In view of the fact that psychotherapists were not asked for psychodynamic descriptions of their relationships with family members and peers when they were growing up, it is significant that they chose to describe their early development in these terms. It is also significant that these descriptions were given as *facts* about, rather than interpretations of, early biographical experiences. The pervasiveness of the psychodynamic paradigm is also manifest in the manner in which psychotherapists described their relationships with spouse and children. Typically, psychotherapists characterized these close personal relationships as being emotionally temperate, mutually satisfying but clearly controlled. When contrasted with the way relationships with patients were described, relations with spouse and children appeared to be theoretically less exciting and emotionally less charged. It is clear, therefore, that psychotherapists do distinguish between therapeutic relationships and familial relationships. Thus, our findings do not support the "spillover hypothesis," which states that the psychotherapist relates to his spouse and children in the same way that he relates to his patients. Our sample of psychotherapists did not confound familial and therapeutic relationships and they did not confuse spouses and children with patients.

The unique nature of the psychotherapeutic relationship undoubtedly contributed to the therapist's ability to distinguish between intimate personal and intimate professional relationships. Unlike close personal relations, the therapeutic relationship is affect-laden but asymmetrical. That is, only the patient is supposed to reveal the intimate details of his life. The psychotherapist is not only free to determine what he will reveal and conceal about himself, but also to choose how to react to what the patient is saying, if indeed he decides to respond at all. The relationship is also asymmetrical in that only the therapist is supposed to interpret and impute meaning to what the patient is saying and only the therapist can evaluate the degree to which therapeutic objectives are being achieved in the relationship. In sum, the therapeutic relationship is a highly circumscribed, personal relationship conducted in accordance with the ground rules laid down by the therapist. These rules result in a relationship in which the therapist comes to know all about the patient as a person while the patient never comes to know the therapist as anything but a therapist. Thus, from the therapist's standpoint, the therapeutic transaction provides intimacy and close personal familiarity without, at the same time, involving the risks entailed in revealing one's inner thoughts and feelings to another. Some schools of therapy recently have espoused a more symmetrical relationship between therapist and patient, with specific claims for the value of therapist self-disclosure as well. We can only note that no significant number of our sample appear to represent this view in their therapeutic behavior.

The situational supports implicated in the development of a psychotherapeutic relationship in the practitioner's office are, of course, not found in his home. Even though psychotherapists tend to use psychodynamic language to describe their spouses and children, it is clear that the personal relationships the therapist has with members of his family are qualitatively different from the intimate relationships established with patients. The relationships between the therapist and his spouse and children are undoubtedly much more symmetrical than the typical psychotherapist-patient relationship. The therapist has less control in familial relations, in part because family members know him as a person and not as a therapist; consequently, they are not likely to respond to him as a patient, even if he approaches them as a psychotherapist. The personal closeness of the family also means that the therapist has much less control over what private feelings and actions can be concealed and what comes to be revealed in intimate personal relationships with spouse and children. In comparison with therapeutic relationships, familial relationships contain both high emotional rewards and high psychological risks. Of course, the psychic risks entailed in familial relationships can be reduced by reducing the degree of intimacy invested in the relationships. The emotionally temperate language used by psychotherapists to describe their relationships with spouses and children suggests that therapists do, in fact, make this adjustment in these family personal relationships.

The emotional gratification derived from therapeutic relationships with patients can be used by psychotherapists to offset the emotional deprivation incurred in lowering the degree of intimacy in familial relationships. Since the degree of control exercised by the therapist in psychotherapeutic relationships reduces the psychic risks involved in intimate relationships, it is possible that the therapeutic encounter becomes the primary focus of concern for practitioners. Relationships with spouses and children tend to focus on shared intellectual perspectives and common recreational activities rather than primarily on affective communication. Since the psychodynamic language is designed to facilitate description of emotional states and intrapsychic processes, it is understandable that when psychotherapists use this language to describe familial relationships, the characterizations that emerge are rather neutral in tone.

The distinctive character of the therapeutic encounter provides some basis for understanding aspects of the therapist's personal life. And it also provides some understanding of the particular kind of patient with whom the therapist does and does not interact. By agreeing to enter into a psychotherapeutic relationship, the therapist assumes responsibility for helping to reorient the patient to his everyday world. Since the patient's problems can be transmitted only through language, the psychotherapist must be able to understand what the patient is saying in order to help him. The level of understanding desired by the therapist is not that of ordinary, everyday communication about mundane behavior but, rather, at the level of personal motives and desires. Psychodynamic language, of course, provides the inventory of human motives and is, therefore, an indispensable tool for the psychotherapist to use in his attempt to understand the patient.

Reliance on the psychodynamic paradigm requires that the psychotherapist be cognizant of his own inner life and that he view his own personal dynamics as crucial equipment for understanding others. Thus, in order for the psychotherapist to be able to meet the patient's need for assistance in various aspects of his personal life, the therapist must be able to identify, understand, and accept both his own and the patient's perspective on life. Consequently, the decision to accept a person into psychotherapy rests, in part, on the therapist's judgment as to whether or not the potential patient's perspective is compatible with the therapist's. Insofar as the capacity to understand and identify with the patient's personal motives is based on the therapist's backlog of experience, the practitioner can alleviate the problems associated with different motives by selectively recruiting patients he can relate to and who can easily relate to him. But this is not something that can always be determined on initial contact with potential patients. In consequence, therapists tend to rely on social attributes as salient initial clues to the psychodynamic qualities of potential patients. We find that private-practicing therapists selectively use level of educational attainment to screen potential patients. Since insight, verbal ability, and psychological-mindedness are related to educational level, therapists probably use amount of education as one clue to the ability to the patient to learn to communicate his motives and feelings in such a way that the psychotherapists can conceptualize them in psychodynamic terms. This is consistent with our findings concerning the contribution of patient-therapist educational congruence to the relationship between the social-class origins of psychotherapists and their patients. In addition, we found religiocultural congruence to be a powerful mechanism for allocating particular types of patients to various types of private-practicing psychotherapists. This suggests that religiocultural characteristics are used by therapists as salient indicators of the psychodynamic suitability of potential patients. Specifically, the findings showed that psychotherapeutic religiocultural congruence involves an affinity between the patient's current commitments and the therapist's religiocultural origins.

In the everyday social world, "birds of a feather flock together," presumably in part because they talk the same language and, hence, feel comfortable not only with the terminology used but also with the trend and flow of the conversation and with the cognitive and intellectual processes used in deriving conclusions. Since psychotherapists specialize in the performance of verbal therapy, it is not surprising that they actively prefer patients who can speak their own language. However, the psychotherapeutic relationship, particularly when the therapist focuses on psychodynamic processes, differs radically from everyday social relationships. In particular, the psychotherapeutic encounter is set apart from other social encounters by its reliance on affective issues. Because the therapeutic relationship is not like other social encounters, it is understandable that mutual attraction takes a unique form in psychotherapy. Since affect constitutes the bond that connects therapist and patient together in psychotherapy, such interpersonal factors as similar intellectual abilities and cognitive styles are necessary but not sufficient conditions for the endurance of the relationship. What is needed in addition is a communality of feeling states. To the extent that social-class standing accurately reflects personal motives and interpersonal skills, the therapist can use patients' class position as an index of his social suitability for psychotherapy. However, the private practitioners in our sample apparently find the degree of fit between their own religiocultural background and the patients' current religiocultural affinity to be the single best screening device. Support for this view comes from the fact that it is primarily the relationship between the therapist's religiocultural origins, rather than his current position, and the patient's current religiocultural affiliation that constitutes the primary basis of congruence in psychotherapy (Marx and Spray, 1972). To the extent that this is true, it appears likely that as long as psychotherapists rely primarily on the psychodynamic paradigm to treat mental and emotional disorders, private psychotherapy will continue to be restricted to a small segment of the population composed of persons reared in one or two cultural groups.

Given these considerations, it should be clear that the heavy reliance on the psychodynamic paradigm by psychotherapists has implications not only for the quantity but also for the quality of therapeutic relationships. Specifically, in terms of the number of patients receiving treatment, our findings clearly document the fact that private practice remains the primary context for the provision of intensive psychotherapy. Private practice is, of course, the ideal setting in which to structure a therapeutic relationship in accordance with psychodynamic principles. Since our sample of psychodynamically oriented psychotherapists clearly prefer private therapeutic relationships, one might well ask what this fact implies for the nature of institutionally based treatment relationships. We earlier noted that psychotherapists exercise much less control over the kinds of persons they treat in institutions, when compared with individuals treated privately. That is, in private practice the therapist commonly conducts the initial interview and decides, on the basis of information gained personally, whether or not to accept the patient. In institutions, the intake interview is frequently conducted by someone other than the psychotherapist who eventually treats the patient. The initial institutional screening process, designed to assess the compatibility between the patient's needs and abilities and the resources and goals of the institution, clearly affects the types of patients seen by organizationally based psychotherapists. Furthermore, institutional screening mechanisms influence the criteria used by organizational therapists to select patients. The various evaluative and diagnostic tools that are available to institutional therapists enable them to rely heavily on standardized assessments of patients' insight and verbal ability, while private practitioners necessarily rely more on their own judgment as to whether or not patients should be accepted for psychotherapy. Thus, with regard to the selection of patients, the disparity in the extent of professional responsibility of therapists affiliated with institutions and therapists working in private practice is marked. In private practice, the therapist has sole responsibility for determining whether or not the candidate will become *his* patient. For institutional therapists, the issue of personal responsibility for therapy is mitigated by previous decisions involving the initial screening as well as by the possibility of easily referring a patient to other therapists working in the institution. In sum, the institutional setting tends to undermine the basic factors, such as personal responsibility, individual judgment, and freedom of choice, that private therapists use in establishing a therapeutic relationship. Undoubtedly this is why we found that psychotherapists were much less likely to know the social characteristics of their institutional patients than they did the characteristics of those seen in private practice. The implication, of course, is that the grounds for establishing a psychodynamically oriented, emotionally based psychotherapeutic relationship are frequently absent in mental health institutions. Since the overwhelming majority of our sample of institutional psychotherapists are adherents to a psychodynamic therapeutic orientation, this deficiency is of critical importance. Since the vast majority of patients seen in institutions by members of all professional groups, except psychiatrists, were not considered by the therapists to be extremely disturbed (that is, psychotic), the degree of personal distance between therapists and their institutionalized patients cannot be solely attributed to communication difficulties associated with extreme disorientation on the part of the patient. In any case, institutional therapists are frequently more remote from their patients than is true for their private-practicing colleagues. This probably explains why fewer intensive psychotherapeutic relationships are found in institutions than in private practice. It also suggests that the emotional qualities of many institutional therapeutic relationships are inferior to those characteristically found in private practice. To the extent that an effective psychodynamically oriented relationship rests on a firm foundation of affect, the quality of institutional psychotherapy would appear to be problematic.

The Community of Psychotherapists

To a greater extent than is true of most other professions, psychotherapists manifest a tendency to adopt a unidimensional view of both personal and professional relationships. Since psychotherapists tend to discuss personal relationships in the same way that they discuss professional relationships, it is clear that the psychotherapist's therapeutic perspective becomes a world view, a way of viewing all personal relationships, and not only an orientation toward work. Given the unique nature of psychotherapeutic work, it is, perhaps, inevitable that therapists would succumb to the tendency to reify their theoretical orientation toward human behavior. That is, in order to engage in dynamically oriented psychotherapy, the therapist has to be able to relate to others in a singularly specialized fashion. The therapeutic situation is one in which everyday social expectations are frequently upset, in which certain behavior is either avoided or controlled, and in which the therapist must frequently refrain from responding to the patient's talk and actions in a "typical" way. For psychoanalytically oriented practitioners, the therapist is obliged to adopt what Blum and Rosenberg (1968) have termed a "psychotherapeutic face," by which they mean a neutral, nonreactive stance toward the therapeutic encounter. Thus, to perform psychotherapy the practitioner must set aside normal social considerations and relate to the patient in terms of an explicit theoretical formula, whether it be psychoanalysis or some other approach. In short, the psychotherapist's world becomes delimited by the psychodynamic paradigm he has adopted, and social experience becomes interpretable primarily in its context.

We found psychotherapists to be generally uninterested in professional societies and rather detached from the everyday affairs of home and community. In short, the therapist has his own rules for interpreting events and endowing social experiences with meaning; and, for him, they are reality. Interpretation and meaning endowment occur, the psychotherapist has learned, primarily in the context of close personal relations; and, therefore, it is the irrationality of the affective relationships that guides his actions in social encounters. Such an orientation stands in marked contrast to usual social situations in which more direct processes are utilized to describe the meaning of social action. Adherence to the psychodynamic paradigm thus serves to set the psychotherapist apart from other persons. This separation, and the special interpretive system upon which it is based, is part of the mystique that tends to surround psychotherapists. As such, this distancing aura is an excellent example of the way in which the therapist sees social interaction in highly specialized terms—terms that tend to create tensions in nontherapeutic contacts and to provide a sense of personal comfort primarily in therapeutic contacts.

Since psychotherapists rely on psychodynamic language to describe human motives and desires, their own as well as those of others, we might expect therapists to feel closer to their colleagues than to others who do not speak their special language. To ask this question is to raise the issue of the relationships between the therapist and the social world. Specifically, is the psychodynamic perspective completely personal or does it provide the basis for a therapeutic community? There is, in therapeutic encounters, very limited opportunity for the sharing of direct work experiences with a colleague. Except in some training situations, only the patient and the therapist are present, and even in group or family treatment, most commonly only one professional is present. The sense of community that might develop among therapists, therefore, must be based far more upon sharing the psychodynamic language about patients than upon any sharing of the actual experience with the patient.

Scott and Lyman (1968) suggest how a language might produce a sense of community: "Speech communities define for their members the appropriate lingual forms to be used amongst themselves. Such communities are located in the social structure of any society. They mark off segments of society from one another, and also distinguish different kinds of activities. . . . The types of accounts appropriate to each speech community differ in form and content. The usage of particular speech norms in giving an account has consequences for the speaker depending upon the relationship between the form used and the speech community into which it is introduced" (p. 61).

To the extent that a sense of community derives from the utilization of a common, shared vocabulary for accounting for one's actions, our findings clearly document the existence of a community of psychotherapists. That is, not only do psychotherapists reveal a common tendency to talk about members of their family in terms similar to those used to describe patients, that is, psychodynamic terminology, they also tend to describe fellow practitioners with the same language. In fact, the reason why so many negative terms were used by therapists to describe members of mental health professions other than their own may well be related to the fact that psychodynamic language itself is heavily negative in tone.

Not only is membership in the psychotherapist community maintained by describing current relationships with a common language, but psychotherapists also share a tendency to describe their past biographical experiences in a way that is consistent with the psychodynamic paradigm (Henry, Sims and Spray, 1971). Thus, for example, most psychotherapists claimed that the decision to undertake a career in the mental health field was more strongly influenced by personal experiences than by professional role models. Similarly, the motives that therapists associated with original choice of a therapeutic speciality, as well as its continued practice, were considered to be largely personal and idiosyncratic. Finally, graduates of each of the four training programs evaluated clinical experiences as being much more important than academic experiences in transforming them into therapists. Much more importance was attached to supervised practice, contact with patients, work experience, and personal psychotherapy by certified practitioners, than was true for course work, formal training, and similar intellectual activities. Similarly, in all four professions, the clinical work that was considered to be the most important in transforming recruits into professionals was that which occurred near the end of training and, consequently, was the most practical in its content. While these clinical experiences were felt to be important sites for the acquisition of professional skills they also contributed importantly to the learning of psychodynamic language. Perhaps of equal importance in this regard was personal psychotherapy—an experience not formally incorporated into the training program of any of the professions except psychoanalysis.

Since psychotherapists view their professional training experiences as being only loosely organized and highly variable, the training can provide only a minimal basis for the development of a common language and the concomitant sense of community. However, we have noted before that there is a remarkable homogeneity in the sociocultural origins of members of the four mental health professions. Moreover, the model experiential background of members of each professional group consists of experiences highly relevant to the eventual learning of the psychodynamic paradigm. Specifically, there is a pronounced tendency for practitioners to claim a Jewish cultural affinity; to have Eastern European ethnic ties and foreign-born fathers; to have rejected, in adolescence, the religious beliefs and political views of their parents; to have experienced, during their own lifetimes, upward social mobility. These biographical characteristics have been found to be associated with those personal qualities that experts believe applicants to therapeutic training programs should have; namely, an introspective orientation, an intellectual predisposition, and a relativistic perspective. Placed in the context of the patterns of professional selection and recruitment, the development of a commitment to a psychodynamic paradigm can be viewed as the product of the individual practitioner's total biography. Commitment to the psychodynamic paradigm is the end product of a continuous dialogue between the individual and his social environment, which leads him ultimately to seek membership in the community of psychotherapists. Careers terminating in the performance of psychotherapy are populated, to a very great extent, by persons with similar personal and professional biographies. These biographical forces not only activate the individual's interest in a therapeutic career but also sharpen and narrow the focus of concern down to psychodynamic therapy. The present preoccupation with individual psychotherapy in the mental health professions can, therefore, be traced to the kinds of persons who seek and are permitted entry into professional training programs.

We have argued that entrance into the therapeutic community is currently restricted to those who can speak the psychodynamic language. This line of reasoning leads to the conclusion that, in order to change the nature of professional practice in the mental health field, it is not adequate to simply change the nature of professional training recruits are required to undergo in order to become certified practitioners. At a more basic level, what is required to produce meaningful, enduring change in the nature of therapeutic services offered in the mental health field is a fundamental change in the types of persons entering the professions. Specifically, if mental health services are going to be extended to all segments of the population and if the nature of the services offered are going to be broadened to include the identification of the needs of people, along with the development of procedures for anticipating and meeting those needs, then practitioners who speak a different language, a social rather than a psychodynamic language, are going to have to be permitted and encouraged to enter the mental health field.

More specifically, in terms of therapeutic ideology, the vast majority of the membership of each profession are adherents to a psychoanalytic orientation. Psychoanalysis can fairly be viewed as the ideological school that most emphasizes the intrapsychic determinism of emotional and mental illness and concomitantly most emphasizes the intrapsychic forces leading to improvement. On the other hand, that orientation seemingly most congruous with the ethos of a community mental health center, namely, sociocommunity, represents a definite minority in each of the professions. Similarly, in all four professions the preferred method of treatment is one-to-one therapy, with only a small proportion of professionals engaged in group or family therapy. And, further, of those professionals who have had personal therapy, virtually all have had this crucial experience in a one-to-one format, further illustration of the absence of any social or community experience related to treatment. In terms, then, of ideology and experience, it is clear that mental health professionals approach problems with an individualistic orientation. This orientation, while seemingly appropriate to individual psychotherapy, can be questioned as to its relevance to the most notable recent innovation in the mental health field, the concept of community mental health.

Might this orientation make therapists less attuned to situational determinants, less appreciative of the influence of social forces? Or might such an orientation lessen their ability to develop programs for the treatment of groups rather than individuals? Finally, would it operate to preclude their acceptance of a career in an institution that emphasized the impact of societal forces and that was organized around group programs, employing orientations far removed from those with which the therapist feels competent?

Community-Oriented Training

Our data show that dominant modes of training continue to be organized along the lines of professional specialization. Furthermore, within each profession, training continues to focus primarily upon the individual client. Thus, we may ask, first, to what extent does such training constitute an obstacle to the new models of interprofessional coordination in community mental health centers? Second, to what extent has the training of any of the four groups of professionals prepared them for participating in community affairs, for developing programs of social action, for sensitizing them to political issues encountered in instituting preventive programs? While the training programs designed to meet these needs are currently being developed, they have little or no impact on those already trained; and, since they are essentially supplemental to traditional procedures, their influence on current trainees is open to question.

Our data show that in terms of patients treated, our professionals are highly specialized. Not unexpectedly, a disproportionately large percentage of patients are Caucasian. Further, few children (8 percent of all patients) and few older people (one-fourth of all patients are over 40) are seen; the majority of patients are either adolescents or young adults. The majority of patients are also drawn from fairly well educated groups —the majority of all patients have had at least some college; for those seen in institutions, 60 percent of them are high school graduates and more than one-third of all institutional patients have had some college. Finally, in terms of diagnostic categories, fully 63 percent of the patients treated in organizations are accounted for by two diagnostic categories— psychoneurosis and character disorder. Only 27 percent of the patients treated in organizations are psychotic (functional or organic), and addicts and alcoholics make up only 5 percent of the patient population in institutions.

Given the community mental health centers' purpose of inclusive service to all in the community, these comments on patient characteristics document rather extensive experiential limitations currently existing among the majority of psychotherapists. Most have little experience with blacks, low-income groups, children, the aged, psychotics, alcoholics, and addicts. Thus, for most mental health professionals, the decision to pursue a career in the community mental health area requires a willingness to adopt an orientation to the future that is not guided by past experience.

In making these suggestions, we are aware that we imply an inability to make major changes in orientation to these experienced adult therapists. It would hardly be surprising if, like most competent well-trained adults in special fields, they found such shifts extremely difficult. For some, either the young, or the most notably flexible older, this may not be true. There are undoubtedly instances of both kinds of persons who have made significant changes in view and hence been able to contribute in major ways to the community mental health movement. Certainly among those who have shifted into this context, in administrative not treatment roles, many have done so.

But, of course, we are not proposing to do away with psychotherapists, nor to change them all into community mental health workers. We are only raising the question of what role, in the new mental health context, can such individualistically oriented therapists have; and, correlatively, if that is a limited role, how do we best train other personnel for the roles not enacted by psychotherapists? For some therapists, reports on mental health centers suggest, no change is needed. They merely continue being psychotherapists, only their context is the institution, the sign over the door says "community," though perhaps they lose some autonomy in the selection of their patients. The continuation of the therapeutic one-to-one model seems inevitable for a significant period, even in new quarters. There are, after all, therapists who wish to exercise the skills involved in either one-to-one therapy or in psychodynamically oriented small-group treatment; and there is clearly need for these particular skills and there are patients ready to receive this care. In any case, there seems little question that the services now being rendered by such therapists are meaningful and socially useful, whether in institutions or in private practice.

What is more at issue is the question of whether it would not be more economical and potentially of broader social usefulness to provide for a single training program for those persons who now end up in psychotherapy careers out of the present four different routes we have described. Even continuing the present therapeutic model involved in present training, some effort to condense and interrelate these separate programs to the single end of psychotherapist production would seem highly profitable.

If one were not satisfied with merely a more economical production of psychotherapists, would it not also be more possible in a somewhat new setting, less bound to the traditions of medicine, psychology, or social work, to provide for these therapists both new and broader training experiences? This latter suggestion is one that attempts to broaden therapeutic ideologies and techniques, though still within the essentially psychodynamic model.

We did indeed claim earlier that we need new recruits, recruits of a different social stamp who will be able to orient themselves more readily to new views, more community-oriented ideologies and tasks. We still think that is the case. However, even such an effort would necessitate altered training experiences and additional role models in these training settings. No raw recruit from a "different" social background can long resist the socialization pressures of the traditional training setting. Perhaps this would be easiest if a new training program—either for a single profession of psychotherapy or for the broader, more community-oriented roles— were located in a social work context. Here there is already an image not only of patients of broader social backgrounds and cultural orientations, but even of instructors and supervisors themselves of more variegated backgrounds. It would be harder for academic psychology to serve as the principal setting of such an effort. The research ideology is too strong, and the range of role models is restricted. Medicine would seem the least likely, having in general the tightest ideology, the most fixed curriculum, and the most prestige to maintain.

Special institutes, having only loose affiliations with formal training centers, might also be appropriate. The aim, for any particular setting, would be that of developing a training program that would permit the entry of recruits from a broader range of social, educational, and experiential backgrounds than is now the case. It should devise a curriculum that would perhaps be variegated enough to allow some to follow a fairly traditional—but more socially varied—route to psychotherapy competence, and others to follow a route concerned with prevention, with community organization, with milieu treatment, with specialized problems of addiction and alcohol. Hopefully, these would not be entirely separate tracks but would encourage an overlapping of social contact, training experiences, and emotional involvements, so that in time one might have a group of people with sufficiently common understandings to focus upon overlapping approaches to the problems of people in living communities rather than merely upon the exercise of their specialty.

But whether one tries for a one-therapy model in a new setting, or attempts to modify present programs, three factors are still relevant and necessary. One is that since the learning of skills in these areas seems to be so related to past personal experience, recruits of broader, or more mixed, experiential backgrounds should actively be sought. Whatever the training program, selective learning will occur, and hence much more attention should be given to the selection of entrants. Second, given entrants of any particular background, the training experiences themselves must reflect more of the complexity of the final setting of mental health work than they tend to now. This includes both formal course work and direct experiences related to the mental health problems of a wider variety of people and to the nature of group life and community structures. Third, but perhaps most importantly, one needs a more variegated set of role models in instructional and supervisory positions.

The psychotherapist is clearly a person of deep conviction and whole-hearted devotion to his patients and to psychodynamic explanations of behavior. And he is well trained, both personally and conceptually, for techniques and settings of therapeutic care which rely upon this individual or small-group model of psychodynamic explanation. The current disjunctiveness between paradigms of community mental health and the established belief system of the psychotherapist is in part an educational and conceptual one. Insofar as community mental health rests upon explanations of a social, community, and group nature, mental health professionals are not trained for it. Insofar as the activities of caretaking personnel relate to community residents, to nonprofessionals, to educational and welfare personnel, the mental health professional is inexperienced and, further, is specifically trained in a manner that leads him to believe that these persons are not accessible to curing. Some of these issues are educational and curricular, and efforts can be made to modify training programs in the direction of a broad set of assumptions and range of issues and techniques thought germane to mental health and to mental distress and its treatment.

But some of this disjunctiveness seems to stem from the broad personal and social background of the therapist, from whatever training systems he might emerge, and is not principally a matter of formal education and training. It is rather a life-style issue, a belief issue, a result of a particular set of life experiences clearly not coterminous with professional training, but including and in fact influencing that training. Originating in a systematic disjunction from parents in systems of social, religious, and political belief, the future therapist finds himself in need of an ideology. The separation from parents appears indeed to be only in these social and belief system areas and not in areas of affect and interpersonal relations. The therapists were not estranged psychologically from their parents, their siblings, their early friends. They remain as positively related to these early experiences as educated adults generally, but perhaps they are more in need of a secular belief system to replace the one earlier abandoned and perhaps more in need of explanatory systems that do not recreate the earlier social and political categories but that rely upon the individual personal and affective relations they have retained.

We do not know how such individual belief preferences may have been accentuated during early school years or why some people with similar social backgrounds do not find the psychodynamic paradigm a satisfactory belief. But those from such backgrounds who are eventually psychotherapists begin to select experiences from their early professional education which emphasize the individual explanation and the individual context. And they continue to develop this emphasis through their experiences in specific mental health training and accentuate it as a life style in their subsequent practice.

The close relationship between the professional and the personal gains of these training and practice experiences implies considerable conviction and involvement. This same intensity of relationship between the intellective and professional on the one hand and the purely personal on the other raises questions about the degree of flexibility possible in considering different views and techniques. In a significant sense a substantial degree of personal identity is integrally tied to professional acts among these therapists, as indeed it is to some degree in any profession. As we see the psychotherapist in periods of social and value change, however, the intensity of belief in the psychodynamic paradigm may well be a block to the adoption of altered belief systems and of more socially related contexts and modes of treatment.

We have already said that psychotherapists seem significantly similar in many aspects of belief and professional activities, regardless of their different routes in training and their different professional labels. And we find it hard to believe that the several training systems we now support for these various professions are optimally devised to produce economically the therapists we get—whether we examine the four routes individually or whether we ask why we need four routes at all, considering the similarity of the resulting therapists. But the broad question, and the one with which we are faced in changing times, is whether, with these systems of providing therapeutic or preventive personnel, we can indeed meet the challenge of a broadened concept of mental health and illness. As the awareness of broadened social and community involvement in both the development and alteration of mental distress spreads among citizens and professionals alike, the need for altered systems of prevention and care will become obvious, as will the need for personnel both more broadly located in the social system and more flexible in their beliefs, convictions, and professional skills.

Research Methods
and Samples

In our efforts to study the origins and practices of members of the four core mental health professions, we used two distinct but related approaches involving different samples and different instruments. The first, intensive, approach consisted of approximately 300 interviews with mental health professionals, 100 each from Chicago, Los Angeles, and New York City. The second, extensive, approach consisted of a survey by mailed questionnaire, with the target sample of the total population of mental health professionals in the metropolitan communities of Chicago, Los Angeles, and New York City. This Appendix describes in detail the objectives and methods of both the interview and the survey.

Interview Design

The interview was designed to probe with some depth the personal histories, careers, and personalities of mental health professionals. Each interview lasted for four hours (in most cases executed in two equal sessions), during which time three instruments were administered. The first involved questioning the respondent following a fifteen-page guide that

233

covered, in an open-ended manner, the areas of vocational choice, education, and professional training; work history; experience as a therapist;
view of the mental health professions; family background and personal
development; experience as a patient; and current personal life (spouse,
children, friends, and leisure activities). This procedure usually took about
three and a half hours; the final half hour was devoted to the administration of an especially designed five-card Thematic Apperception Test
(TAT) and an Identity Scale (a semantic differential in format). (Analyses of the TAT and Identity Scale data will be presented in later
publications.)

Because of the nature of these interviews, in terms of both the
substantial time demand and the intimacy of the material requested, it
was thought that the necessary cooperation could not be obtained by
means of a random sampling approach. On the other hand, a carefully
assessed stratified sampling was impossible because reliable information on
the makeup of the population was, at that time, nonexistent. These
practical issues would have made it very difficult for us to achieve a
sample that was statistically representative of the population. However, we
were prompted by choice as well as by necessity to obtain a biased sample.
First, we wanted a sample whose composition would enable us to make
certain comparisons we thought vital. For example, we wanted to be sure
to include enough male social workers so that we could contrast them with
their female colleagues. Second, we wanted to ensure that our net would
be wide enough to capture at least a few examples of all of the many
species of therapeutic orientation. For example, we wanted to be certain
we had some Adlerians and Jungians as well as Freudians. Given the
limit of 300 interviews, the sample had to be deliberately biased to achieve
these ends.

The interview target sample was selected as follows. A number of
highly visible, respected professionals in the fields of psychoanalysis, psychiatry, clinical psychology, and psychiatric social work in Los Angeles,
Chicago, and New York City were contacted, informed of the study's purpose and nature, and asked for their assistance. These informants made
up lists of potential respondents and provided us with information on
them with regard to age, sex, work setting, and therapeutic orientation.
In an attempt to guarantee heterogeneity regarding these variables, we
devised a design to guide our selections. This quota sample is shown in
Table 38.

In addition to therapeutic orientation and work setting (indeed,
very roughly categorized), two other considerations determined our selections: age and sex. Thus, as far as possible we attempted to fill each of
the cells in Table 38 with representatives of three age groups: the "early

Table 38. Target Interview Sample

Chicago (100)
Los Angeles (100)
New York City (100)
Total (300)

PSYCHOANALYST (45)	PSYCHIATRIST (105)	CLINICAL PSYCHOLOGIST (75)	PSYCHIATRIC SOCIAL WORKER (75)
Freudian (27) pp: N = 14 org: N = 13	Freudian and other Psychotherapeutic (45) pp: N = 23 org: N = 22	Freudian (39) pp: N = 19 org: N = 20	Freudian (39) pp: N = 19 org: N = 20
Other-than-Freudian (18) pp: N = 9 org: N = 9	Somatic-organic (45) pp: N = 23 org: N = 22	Other-than-Freudian (36) pp: N = 18 org: N = 18	Other-than-Freudian (36) pp: N = 18 org: N = 18
	Social-community (15) pp: N = 7 org: N = 8		

NOTE: pp means exclusively or primarily in private practice; org means exclusively or primarily in organizational practice.

careerists" (respondents in their thirties), the "well-established" (respondents in their forties and fifties), and the "old pros" (respondents over sixty). Furthermore, we wanted at least fifteen of the social workers to be male and fifteen of each of the other three professional groups to be female.

Not surprisingly, we encountered a number of difficulties in realizing the sampling desideratum shown in Table 38. First, the information we had used for initially classifying a prospective respondent was not always correct. For example, a professional described to us as working exclusively in an institution would often be found, after the fact, to be engaged in private practice as well. Second, we occasionally found it impossible, despite the hundreds of names submitted to us, to find sufficient numbers to fill, *even potentially,* some cells—for example, those involving somatic-organic psychiatrists. Third, the exigencies inherent in the field trips, limited in time and personnel, often prevented us from adhering strictly to the design. For example, all of the four of five respondents fitting a certain cell in a particular city might respectively be on vacation, attending a convention, unavailable except when the interviewer already had another appointment, or, indeed, unwilling to participate.

Such are the realities of research. We met them as best we could, lessening or strengthening our efforts to obtain respondents of given categories according to how many or how few we already had. What degree of success we attained can be seen below in Tables 39 and 40, in which the achieved interview sample is described regarding profession, therapeutic orientation, work setting, age, and sex.

What is more important than how near or far we came to realizing the target sample design is the question of how close the sample we actually obtained came to achieving our larger purpose—to ensure coverage of the full range of roles and players in the mental health field. In our view this aim was generally accomplished, with one major exception: the somatic-organic psychiatrist. We wanted forty-five but got only six. Two determining factors can be identified here: first, psychiatrists professing a somatic-organic therapeutic orientation are scarce; there simply are far fewer than we thought, at least in the three urban communities studied. (We have some indication that they would be found practicing with greater frequency in areas geographically beyond our sampling purview, such as in out-of-city state mental hospitals.) One index of their rarity is the unique difficulty our informants, all highly knowledgeable of their respective mental health scenes, had in suggesting prospective interviewees who would fit this category. As a consequence, we entered the field with fewer candidates than the target cell size dictated.

Table 39. Achieved Interview Sample: Therapeutic Orientation and Work Setting

Chicago (92)
Los Angeles (95)
New York City (96)
Total (283)

PSYCHOANALYST (57)	PSYCHIATRIST (65)	CLINICAL PSYCHOLOGIST (80)	PSYCHIATRIC SOCIAL WORKER (81)
Freudian (45) pp: N = 26 org: N = 19	Freudian and other psychotherapeutic (39) pp: N = 22 org: N = 17	Freudian (34) pp: N = 16 org: N = 18	Freudian (51) pp: N = 9 org: N = 42
Other-than-Freudian (12) pp: N = 5 org: N = 7	Somatic-organic (6) pp: N = 3 org: N = 3	Other-than-Freudian (46) pp: N = 21 org: N = 25	Other-than-Freudian (30) pp: N = 9 org: N = 21
	Social-community (11) pp: N = 3 org: N = 8		
	Eclectic and Unclassifiable[a] (9) pp: N = 2 org: N = 7		

NOTE: pp means exclusively or primarily in private practice; org means exclusively or primarily in organizational practice.

[a] For these nine cases, either their therapeutic orientation was virtually equally balanced between psychotherapeutic, somatic-organic, and social-community (eclectic), or the components of their avowed eclecticism were unspecified (unclassifiable).

Table 40. ACHIEVED INTERVIEW SAMPLE: SEX AND AGE

	Psychoanalysts		Psychiatrists		Clinical Psychologists		Psychiatric Social Workers		Total	
	N	Per cent	N	Per cent	N	Per cent	N	Per cent	N	Per cent
Sex										
Male	45	79	58	89	61	76	35	43	199	70
Female	12	21	7	11	19	24	46	57	84	30
Total	57	100	65	100	80	100	81	100	283	100
Age										
Under 30	—	—	—	—	1	1	1	1	2	0.5
30–39	12	21	22	34	25	31	19	24	78	28
40–49	17	30	23	35	28	35	36	44	104	37
50–59	19	33	12	19	20	25	23	28	74	26
60–69	7	12	8	12	6	8	2	3	23	8
70 and over	2	4	—	—	—	—	—	—	2	0.5
Total	57	100	65	100	80	100	81	100	283	100

The second factor accounting for the dearth of somatic-organic psychiatrists was our failure to win the cooperation of many of those we had located. In this single category of respondents we encountered an identifiable resistance. Why this was so is unknown; what is clear is that, as a group, they were unsympathetic to our purpose.

With this one exception, we are satisfied that the interview sample successfully captures the main components of the diversity that characterizes the mental health professions under study.

Once the lists constituting the target samples in the three cities were prepared, the potential respondents were contacted as follows. Each received one letter inviting his participation and describing the purpose of the research, the nature of the interview, the length of time required, and the period scheduled for data collection. The letter explained that a staff member would phone to set up the pair of two-hour sessions. It also explained how they had been selected, telling them the name of the informant who had proposed them as an interview candidate. This was done for two reasons: first, to answer the natural question "Why me?" and, second, to allow the respondent to check with the informant to learn more about us from a first-hand, known source. We were, after all, asking a great deal, both in time and substance, and we wanted to facilitate the respondent's evaluation of us.

The logistics involved in gathering approximately 300 four-hour interviews in three months (100 in each city per month) with a staff of seven interviewers were formidable. A week before the month of interviewing, two staff members set up the appointments so that when the interviewers arrived, each had his entire month's interview timetable arranged. The scheduling of 200 two-hour sessions was a frenzied process. First of all, mental health professionals are difficult to reach at work. The fifty-minute therapeutic hour cannot be interrupted; hence, after fifty minutes of "unavailability," we would be deluged with returning calls for a ten-minute period. Secondly, our letter requesting their participation had naturally promised to schedule the sessions at their convenience to the extent of making ourselves available "at any time of the day or night and at any place." This often necessitated elaborate arrangements concerning time and place, not infrequently including lengthy directions as to how to get on and off the appropriate freeway. Third, with a limited staff, we could accommodate only a given number of preferences for the same time spot; this inability to oblige the respondent's first choice led to a further proliferation of telephoning and an ever more complicated interviewing calendar. Finally, the overall schedule, once set, did not of course remain so; changes had to be made constantly.

Let us say immediately that our respondents showed patient understanding of our scheduling difficulties. They met us more than halfway, often greatly inconveniencing themselves to fit appointments into the time slots we still had open. And this initial consideration accurately presaged the cooperation extended by the respondents with regard to the interview itself. It is not easy to give up four hours, it is more difficult still to give four hours of personal revelation. But, with rare exceptions, the respondents made a total and committed effort to make a rich and genuine contribution. When difficulties were encountered (the recollection of a painful memory, embarrassment, or even fear), the consequent unwillingness to continue was involuntary in nature and immediately overcome by a conscious effort not to withhold. About three-quarters of the interviews took place in the respondents' offices during work hours. The others were held in a variety of locales, mostly homes but ranging from bars to hospital bedsides to sailboats.

From the interviewers' point of view, the interviews were fascinating experiences; from the study's perspective, they yielded a rich harvest. Did the respondents get anything from them other than the rather abstract satisfaction of having made a contribution to research? Many of them expressed gratitude to us for structuring a process through which, unanticipated, they gained a sense of perspective on their lives and work. They recognized patterns, made connections, reevaluated experiences—in a word, made a further discovery of self that they deemed valuable. We were often in the astonished position of being thanked for having interviewed them.

The question arises as to who would not participate as an interviewee. This question is difficult to answer because, although overt refusals were rare, it is impossible to distinguish between false and genuine regrets due to lack of time, conflicting schedules, illness, and so on. However, it is our *impression* that most of those professionals who could not see us could not, in fact, for legitimate (from our point of view) reasons.

In addition to a willing and able subject, a good interview is the result of a talented and skilled interviewer. This study has been fortunate in the quality of its staff. The core group of interviewers, for all three cities, consisted of a psychologist, a sociologist, and three doctoral candidates from The Committee on Human Development of The University of Chicago. All five of this group had had extensive interviewing experience. This permanent staff was augmented in the several cities by three or four part-time people (social workers, graduate students, professional interviewers) who again came to us experienced.

Naturally, any research involving the interview as a method of data collection benefits from highly skilled and knowledgeable interviewers. However, for three reasons they were crucial to this study. First, the psychological sophistication of our respondents demanded that the interviewer himself be sufficiently sophisticated to assure the respondent that he was being understood. Like anyone else, mental health professionals want an understanding as well as a sympathetic listener; but to be such with *this* sample required considerable psychological knowledge on the part of the interviewer. Every profession has its unique vernacular, but that of the mental health professions happens to overlap with that of psychological research; thus our subjects, more than other groups, expected the interviewers to understand them literally on their terms.

The particular method used to record interviews constituted the second major demand on our interviewers' skill. In the planning of the study we had been advised by our contacts in the mental health field *not* to tape the interview sessions; such a procedure was thought to act as an inhibiting force. Consequently, the interviews were recorded as follows: extensive notes were taken (in fact, much of what was said was taken down verbatim); immediately following the session, the interviewer dictated onto tape his reconstruction of the interview. It is difficult to estimate how much is lost in this process. Certainly something of what is said is missed (as is, of course, *how* it is said). This anticipated but unknown quantity had to be balanced against the equally anticipated and unknown loss that taping would produce. At any rate, it is clear that the feasibility of such a method of recording depends on confidence in the skill of the interviewers.

A third demand on the ability of our interviewers came from our particular use of the interview schedule. This fifteen-page guide contained 132 questions covering a dozen major areas of the respondent's personal life and work. Even with four hours available, we knew from our trial interviews that it would not always be possible to cover the entire guide with the desired depth. At the same time we were reluctant to further cut the guide, which was already greatly reduced in scope from what we had originally wanted to encompass. As an alternative, we decided to let the interviewers determine how much of the guide would be covered. They were to decide when an area had been sufficiently explored and hence when to go on; and, if the pressure of time required that only several of many remaining areas be covered, the interviewers, on the basis of what had already taken place in the session, were to choose which of them should be discussed. Such decisions required of the interviewer both a continuous evaluation of the material he was getting and a continuous assessment of the respondent himself.

This method of interviewing reflected our choice of "accounting"; we thought it more desirable to cover fewer areas deeply than more areas superficially. This choice was difficult to make, for it meant that for many questions covered by the interview our sample was reduced. We think our choice here was congruent with the aim that dictated the selection of the interview sample—namely, a desire for heterogeneity and coverage—but here in terms of what was meaningful to the respondents. For, although the interviewers directed the discussions, they in turn were guided to a considerable degree by what the respondent offered. What the interviews covered, then, was in part dictated by what we, the investigators, thought important. But it was also, in part, a fishing expedition, wherein the respondents placed into our gathering nets what they thought important.

In keeping with this emphasis on the respondent's freedom to offer what he thought relevant (within the broad limits set by the guide), the interview data were coded inductively. We wanted to be sure that we knew what the *respondents* said *before* we began to speculate as to the meaning of what they said. We were careful, therefore, to avoid early imposition on the data of any preconceived schemas of interpretation. Each staff member was assigned certain areas of questioning and, using a minimum of fifty random cases, established inductive codes. Of course, any process of categorizing data involves by definition some degree of interpretation; some decision as to the data's meaning is necessitated by putting two different responses, however subtle that difference may be, into the same box. The point here is that we made every effort to keep the interpretation involved in the initial coding to a minimum, anticipating that we could always later collapse coding categories and move to higher levels of abstraction when it was necessary for analysis.

Once the codes for an area of questioning had been drafted, copies were distributed to the entire staff and conferences were held during which everyone could suggest modifications of or additions to the codes based on their own study of the interviews. Most important, this process allowed the codes to be evaluated and changed by the interviewers in the light of their first-hand experience. This procedure, then, was a further effort at keeping the analysis close to the data.

In most cases the major part of the actual coding of any given area of the interview data was done by the person who had established those particular codes. Checking the reliability of his coding was a standard procedure. The completion of such coding constituted the basic step in the preparation of the interview data for analysis. The extent to which the data were further manipulated depended on the problems confronted in any particular area of analysis. These manipulations are specified in the context of the particular issue being discussed.

In analyzing the interview data for differences between the four mental health professions, a probability level of .10 was used. This less-than-usual stringency seems to us more appropriate to the size of the interview sample, the nature of the interview data, and the intent of the study's analysis, which is heuristic rather than demonstrative, involving the building of hypotheses rather than the testing of them.

Of course, in determining interprofessional differences, other factors had to be controlled. For example, what appeared to be a professional difference between social workers as opposed to analysts, psychiatrists, and psychologists might in fact be a sex difference determined by the significantly higher proportion of women in social work. Thus we conducted our examination of professional differences holding constant such variables as sex, age, and social-class origins.

Unfortunately, the small sample size permitted us to control for only *one factor at a time*—sex, or age *or* social-class origins. Thus we are unable to consider the interactional effect of these variables as they might relate to professional differences.

Our procedure, then, for arriving at interprofessional differences was as follows. First, the data were broken simply by the four professions and those differences that were statistically significant at the .10 level were noted. Second, a series of interprofessional runs was made, holding constant, separately, such factors as sex and age.

In deciding whether a professional difference "held up," our liberal policy was guided by the desire to avoid throwing out the baby with the bath water or—to put it positively—the desire to include those data that would point out *probable* differences between the professions. Accordingly, we decided that if the majority of comparisons were in the same direction as the original professional difference *and* if no one of them was significantly in the opposite direction, we would report and discuss the difference as a *professional* one, although noting the exceptions. In our judgment this position is reasonable in the context of the interview sample size.

Survey Design and Sample

The questionnaire survey was designed to investigate the full range and diversity of roles, interests, and settings characterizing the professional component of the mental health field in three metropolitan communities. In addition to the fact that mental health practitioners are concentrated in and around metropolitan areas, there is a further rationale involved in deciding to select from geographic clusters rather than attempting to sample the national professional population. This rationale is based on the assumption that the metropolitan community forms the "basic" or "natural" population unit in modern society (Gras, 1922; McKenzie, 1933; Bogue, 1950). For our purposes it is possible to consider this unit as an autonomously functioning "service area" covering the variety of personnel and facilities utilized in treating mental illness. The characteristics of this basic unit thus provide the investigator with the diversity of activities that occur within the professions as a whole. Moreover, the metropolitan community provides a microcosmic representation of the mental health field, which allows us to examine the relations between, as well as within, the professions. The sample unit in each case was therefore defined as the central city and its immediate suburbs, and this unit was designated the metropolitan community. To ensure that the widest range of professional activities would be represented, the three largest communities in the nation, New York City, Los Angeles, and Chicago, were selected for study. To further ensure comprehensive coverage, questionnaires were sent to the total population of professional therapists working in the three metropolitan communities.

For purposes of the survey, the Chicago metropolitan community was defined as the area referred to as the Chicago Standard Metropolitan Statistical Area and the Gary–Hammond–East Chicago Standard Metropolitan Statistical Area in the 1960 U.S. Census. The Los Angeles metropolitan community consists of Los Angeles County, which contains within it the Los Angeles–Long Beach Standard Metropolitan Statistical Area. Finally, the New York metropolitan community consists of Manhattan and the four adjoining boroughs.

The target population receiving questionnaires in each of the metropolitan communities consisted of all psychoanalysts, psychiatrists, clinical psychologists, and psychiatric social workers involved in treating mental illness. (It is important to note that the focus of the study is exclusively on the four core mental health professions and not on mental health practitioners in general. Excluded from consideration are those practitioners who do not belong to the four major professions but do engage in therapeutic activities or actually treat the mentally ill. Examples of personnel excluded from consideration include general medical practitioners, ministers, psychiatric nurses, psychiatric aides, and nonprofessionally trained "therapists" and "counselors.") Enumeration of these practitioners was accomplished through the use of professional directories. Specifically, for psychiatrists the 1963 edition of the *Biographical Directory of Fellows and Members of the American Psychiatric Association* was used. This directory also provided information on those psychiatrists who had graduated from or were currently attending a psychoanalytic institute recognized by the American Psychoanalytic Association. (Throughout the study the term *psychoanalyst* will refer only to those psychiatrists who have attended or are currently attending a psychoanalytic institute recognized by the American Psychoanalytic Association. Professionals who had received or were receiving psychoanalytic training in organizations not recognized by the American Psychoanalytic Association [William Alanson White Institute of Psychiatry, Psychoanalysis and Psychology; The Alfred Adler Institute; National Psychological Association for Psychoanalysis] were classified according to their general professional affiliation and not as psychoanalysts.) Since both previous research and official professional statements indicate that psychoanalysts constitute a separate subspecialty in the mental health field, they were treated as a separate professional group (Strauss and others, 1964).* The 1964 edition of the *American Psychological Association Directory* was used to obtain the population of psychologists. Those who listed as "interests" in their autobiographical sketches in the *Directory* any of the areas concerned with mental health were included in the sample of clinical psychologists. (The specific interests defined as being concerned with mental health included psychotherapy, counseling and guidance, evaluation psychotherapy, play therapy, psychodrama, hypnodrama, family therapy, psychotherapeutic technique, family and marriage therapy, psychological counseling, nondirective counseling, and clinical psychology.) As a supplement to this directory the most recent directories of organizations composed of clinical psychologists interested in and/or practicing psychotherapy were checked. (These organizations were Psychologists Interested in the Advancement of Psychotherapy, Psychologists in Private Practice, and The American Academy of Psychotherapists. In general these directories provided very few names of psychologists not already selected from the *Directory of the American Psychological Association*. This check provided limited reassurance that the primary criterion used for selecting clinical psychologists involved in treatment—mentioning any of the above interests in the APA *Directory*— possessed validity.)

For psychiatric social workers the sources used to define the population varied by city. For Chicago and Los Angeles the *Directory of Professional Social Workers* existing at the time of the surveys (1964–1965) could not be used because it was outdated. However, it was possible to obtain lists of persons classified as "qualified, experienced" psychiatric social workers from the local chapters of the National Association of Social Workers in the geographic areas comprising the two metropolitan communities. A few additional names were secured from the 1964 *Directory of Professional Social Workers in Private Practice*. In New York City it

---

* Representative of official pronouncements on the differences between the two groups is the following statement by a former president of the American Psychiatric Association: "The only true specialty inside the general field of psychiatry is psychoanalysis. It has a body of knowledge, criteria for selection and training of its candidates, institutes to carry out training and a method of certification" (quoted in Blain, 1953).

was impossible to secure lists of psychiatric social workers from the local chapter. This made it necessary to use the 1966 *Directory of Professional Social Workers,* which was published immediately before the survey in New York City. The actual selection of psychiatric social workers from the directory listing of all social workers in New York City was conducted in two stages. First, all social workers in the New York metropolitan community who indicated in the directory that they had received a degree in psychiatric social work were included in the list. Second, all social workers who were listed as being in private practice or as working in settings classified as mental health agencies in the *Directory of Social and Health Agencies of New York City 1965–66* were included in the population of psychiatric social workers. (This *Directory* lists facilities classified according to function. Under the general category of "mental health" the directory lists the following types of facilities: agency services; clinics for the general public; aftercare clinics of the State Department of Mental Hygiene; hospitals for mental disorders, retarded children, and adults; alcoholism; and narcotic addiction.)

Using type of work setting as one of the criteria for defining the population of psychiatric social workers in New York City was necessitated by the fact that in 1955 the various specialized organizations, including the American Association of Psychiatric Social Workers, merged to form the National Association of Social Workers (NASW). The formation of one professional association resulted in the abolition of specialty degrees, including that of psychiatric social work. Hence all graduates of schools of social work after that date are simply listed in the professional directory as having an M.S.W. The standardization of the degree awarded reflects the fact that all students take the same core courses in schools of social work. However, students can still specialize in psychiatric social work by electing to take their fieldwork placement in a psychiatric setting and by taking methodology courses in psychotherapy, group therapy, and related topics. Thus psychiatric social work is still a specialty in social work training, even though it is no longer a field in which a degree may be obtained. Given this fact, it was necessary to take into account both type of degree and work setting of social workers in New York City in order to most closely approximate the lists of "qualified, experienced" psychiatric social workers provided by the local chapters of the NASW in the other two metropolitan communities. The procedure used in New York City did, however, result in our contacting a number of social workers who were neither qualified nor working as psychiatric social workers. When evidence to this effect was obtained from respondents, either through correspondence or from the returned questionnaire, they were dropped from the population. As a result of this process it seems safe to conclude that the samples of psychiatric social workers in the three metropolitan communities were roughly equivalent.

Considered from the perspective of metropolitan mental health communities, Chicago, Los Angeles, and New York City generally resemble one another in certain respects. For example, nonmedical professional practitioners in all three metropolitan communities have only recently come under the control of state licensing standards. Similarly, the relatively recent growth of the professional mental health field has meant that the patterns of professional training and accreditation have only recently become formalized in training centers in each of the cities. The emergence over the past three decades of dynamic, intensive psychotherapy as the dominant therapeutic orientation has also had a strong impact on all three communities. Finally, all three cities have been affected by the increasing emphasis on community mental health and related programs.

More important than the general similarities among the three metropolitan communities are the marked differences among them. These differences range from general characteristics such as size and religious composition of the population to specific differences between training programs and adherence to various therapeutic orientations. Thus New York City is unique among the cities in the size of its Jewish population, whereas Chicago holds a similar position in terms of the proportion of Catholics in the metropolitan population. Similarly, the states of New York and California both have much larger budgets for mental health programs than is true for Illinois; hence we would expect New York City and Los Angeles to have many more professionals involved in community mental health and related programs than does Chicago.

With regard to professional training and treatment orientations, several factors make Chicago unique among the three metropolitan communities. One such factor is that Chicago possesses only one Institute for Psychoanalysis; Los Angeles has two and New York City three recognized institutes. That institute is the sole repository of authorized psychoanalytic training and certification in the Chicago metropolitan community. This undoubtedly contributes to a far more homogeneous ideological environment in Chicago compared with the other two cities. The existence of only one recognized institute also means that fewer psychoanalysts are being trained in Chicago than is true of the other two communities. Moreover, since psychoanalysts tend to remain in the city where they received their analytic training, this means that the psychoanalyst-population ratio is smaller in Chicago than in either Los Angeles or New York City.

Another unique feature of the professional mental health training

situation in Chicago that affects the distribution of therapeutic orientations held by practitioners is the prominent position of the Counseling
and Psychotherapy Research Center of the University of Chicago.
Founded in 1945 by Carl Rogers, the Counseling Center has since been
devoted to the application of the Rogerian approach to the problem of
emotional disturbance. A large number of clinical psychologists practicing
in Chicago have received at least part of their training at the Counseling
Center. Thus the porportion of mental health professionals committed to
a Rogerian approach is much greater in Chicago than in Los Angeles and
New York City. These factors also indicate that the Rogerian orientation
is primarily restricted to one professional group, clinical psychologists.

Although Chicago is unique by virtue of its homogeneity in training
and ideological climate, New York City is set apart from the other communities by its unmatched diversity. Specifically, New York City not only
has three psychoanalytic institutes recognized by the American Psychoanalytic Association but it also has a larger number of other postgraduate
institutes, each specializing in one or another of the various therapeutic
schools in the mental health field. Thus, for example, the following are
some of the institutes located in New York City: The Training Institute of
the National Association for Psychoanalysis (Reikian in orientation); The
Alfred Adler Institute; The William Alanson White Institute of Psychiatry, Psychoanalysis and Psychology (Sullivanian orientation); and the
American Institute for Psychoanalysis (Horney approach). While the
other two cities have representatives of the various approaches, New York
City is unique in having a large number of divergent camps strongly
supported through formally organized centers. Moreover, if, as Strauss and
others (1964) found in their study of Chicago, major cleavages in the
professional mental health field follow ideological lines, then the competition and conflict characterizing the field should be most clearly revealed
in New York City.

Perhaps even more important than the variety of therapeutic
ideologies represented in the training centers in New York City is the fact
that many of the postgraduate institutes accept candidates who do not
have medical degrees. This means that clinical psychologists and psychiatric social workers in New York City have a much greater opportunity
to obtain postgraduate training in psychotherapy than is true in Chicago
and Los Angeles. As a result of the greater training opportunities, New
York City should have a larger proportion of clinical psychologists and
psychiatric social workers in private practice, either on a part-time basis
or full time as lay analysts.

Most of the factors that differentiate Los Angeles from the other
two metropolitan communities seem to revolve around its frontier char-

acter. Los Angeles was the last of the three cities to establish a psycho-analytic institute, and this founding occurred only after the psychoanalytic movement was well established in this country. The rapid growth in population and the subsequent demand for mental health practitioners have resulted in Los Angeles having a larger proportion of psychothera-pists trained in other areas of the country than is true for either Chicago or New York City. These factors have resulted in Los Angeles' practi-tioners being less influenced by established training centers than are practitioners in other cities. This fact, combined with the sprawling nature of the urban area, partially accounts for the high incidence of inno-vative and experimental mental health practices in Los Angeles.

On the basis of this brief outline of the mental health field in three cities, it seems clear that there is no typical mental health community. Certainly none of the three metropolitan communities studied can be used as a basis for making generalizations about the distribution of professional therapeutic activities in the other two. However, it is also clear that the differences among the three mental health communities follow a general pattern and are not simply random. Specifically, in terms of the variability of professional training and practices, the three metropolitan commu-nities can be broadly thought of as forming two different but related con-tinua. The first continuum refers to the distribution of professional personnel and training facilities. Chicago, being the most homogeneous of the three communities in terms of training and professional composition, would be at one end of the continuum; the heterogeneity of New York City places it at the other end. The second continuum refers to the amount of innovation or traditionalism represented in professional practices. Using this criterion, Chicago is clearly the most traditional and Los Angeles is the most innovative. Here New York City would be between the other two cities but probably closer to Los Angeles than to Chicago. In any case, the three cities, taken together, contain a wide range of mental health characteristics. Since the objective of the study was to investigate the full range of professional activities in the mental health field, these three men-tal health communities seem ideally suited for that purpose.

The focus of the questionnaire was on five general areas of profes-sional characteristics and behavior. The first area concentrated on the personal and sociocultural characteristics, past and present, of the practi-tioners. A second area dealt with formal and informal professional edu-cation and training as well as organizational affiliations and professional activities of the practitioners. The third area focused on the social struc-tural matrix of professional behavior in the mental health field; question-naire items in this section were designed to obtain information on career lines, role structures, work history, and settings in which therapists practice. The fourth area was designed to assess the therapeutic ideologies of mental health practitioners from a variety of perspectives. The fifth and final area was composed of a series of questions about the various characteristics of therapists' patients.

The questionnaire made many demands on the practitioners. It was comprehensive in its coverage of the professional field and hence required a long period of time to complete. It was also unusual in that the density of information requested in the various areas approximated the kind of data gathered in interviews rather than questionnaires. Specifically, many sensitive areas, such as marital history, respondents' own experiences in therapy, characteristics of patients, and professional fees and income, were explored intensively. Normally, questions of this type are thought appropriate only for semistructured interviews. Thus, in completing the questionnaire, the respondent not only gave us at least an hour of his time but also answered questions requiring considerable thought about issues normally considered private, either in the professional or personal sense. In sum, the questionnaire contained the basis for many different types of refusals by the mental health professionals contacted. However, it also contained many interesting questions on topics considered to be important to practitioners in the field.

The questionnaire was sent to all psychiatrists, clinical psychologists, and psychiatric social workers identified by the sampling procedures. Four attempts were made to obtain questionnaires from members of the target population in each community. These attempts included two mailings with accompanying cover letters, a telephone contact with those who had not returned the questionnaire after the second mailing, and, finally, a postal reminder to those who, when contacted by telephone, had agreed to return the questionnaire but had failed to do so after three weeks.

The return rates for each profession in each of the metropolitan communities are presented in Table 41. Response to the survey was much better in Chicago and Los Angeles than in New York City. There are undoubtedly many reasons for the lower return rates in New York City, but the major factors appear to be related to the field work itself rather than to characteristics of the practitioners. Thus the large size of the professional population in New York City made it impossible for us to spend as much time as we did in the other two cities in trying to contact each respondent. As a result, a larger proportion of New York City psychotherapists were not contacted by telephone than was true in either Los Angeles or Chicago. The difficulty in locating respondents in New York City means that we probably incorrectly left more practitioners in the population than was true in the other cities. Also, during the course of the field work we discovered that there were four other studies also send-

Table 41. QUESTIONNAIRE SURVEY: RETURN RATES

Profession	CITY			Total
	Chicago	Los Angeles	New York City	
	Percent and (Base Number)			
Psychoanalysts	63.1 (103)	68.9 (166)	48.5 (369)	54.5 (638)
	(168)	(241)	(761)	(1170)
Psychiatrists	57.2 (151)	50.8 (214)	40.9 (368)	46.3 (733)
	(264)	(421)	(899)	(1584)
Clinical Psychologists	77.2 (268)	71.9 (417)	62.1 (780)	67.1 (1465)
	(347)	(580)	(1256)	(2183)
Psychiatric Social Workers	78.0 (213)	75.1 (217)	64.1 (724)	68.2 (1154)
	(273)	(289)	(1130)	(1692)
Total	69.9 (735)	66.2 (1014)	55.4 (2241)	60.2 (3990)
	(1052)	(1531)	(4046)	(6629)

NOTE: The percentages in the table represent the proportion of all questionnaires sent to a given profession in a given city that were returned. For example, in Chicago 168 questionnaires were sent to psychoanalysts; 103 or 63.1 percent of them were completed and returned.

ing questionnaires to New York City psychiatrists and psychoanalysts. Finally, during the field work it became apparent that respondents in New York City were less familiar with the personnel of the staff and with the University of Chicago than was true in Los Angeles. This was particularly true of the large number of medically trained psychotherapists in private practice in New York City who were unable to check the legitimacy of the study with knowledgeable colleagues.

Although New York City differs in aggregate return rate it should be noted that the order of return from the four professional groups is similar in each of the cities. In each case the two nonmedical professions returned the questionnaire at a higher rate than did the medical professionals. A combination of factors seem to account for this difference between the return rates of the two groups. First, the medical groups have a larger proportion of members in private practice than is true for either clinical psychology or psychiatric social work. If we assume that private practitioners are generally less familiar with and less interested in research than their institutionally affiliated colleagues, then we would expect them to feel less compelled to participate in the study. Also, being high-status professionals and the elite of the mental health field probably results in the medical practitioners' having less available time as well as less inclination to participate in research conducted by academicians. Finally, it is possible that both psychiatrists and psychoanalysts are, in general, more strongly committed to intensive case studies than the other professionals and hence less willing to participate in a survey study.

A second uniform pattern revealed in Table 41 is that in each metropolitan community the lowest response was obtained from psychiatrists, with psychoanalysts being much more likely to return the questionnaire than their medical colleagues. If we consider the difference in the training received by psychiatrists and psychoanalysts, it becomes possible to offer a tentative explanation of the differential participation of these two groups in the research. Briefly, the additional psychological training received by psychoanalysts results in their having closer ties with the academic community and hence being more receptive to research on social and psychological issues. If this is true, then their additional psychoanalytic training would lead them to respond to the questionnaire differently from psychiatrists and in the direction of being similar to the nonmedical professions. This, of course, is precisely what they do. As a result, the greatest weakness in the study, as revealed in Table 41, is the extent to which psychiatrists are underrepresented, both in the aggregate return and in the response from each city.

The telephone contact not only increased the questionnaire returns but also provided information on reasons for not participating in the study. Although the reasons individuals gave for not returning the questionnaire were not analyzed systematically for the three metropolitan communities, an attempt was made to isolate the dominant refusal themes.

One main category of refusals was composed of individuals who, when contacted by telephone, promised to return the completed questionnaire but never did. This category of unfulfilled promises to return accounted for about one-third of the population of nonreturns. Within this category psychiatrists were by far the largest professional group. Another one-third of the nonreturns consisted of practitioners who either could not be contacted or who were contacted but gave no specific reason for not participating. Psychoanalysts made up the largest proportion of this latter group who did not feel compelled to complete the questionnaire and could not be persuaded to explain the reasons for not participating in the study. The two nonmedical professions contributed heavily to the category of those who could not be contacted. For the remaining one-third of the nonreturns the specific reasons for refusing to participate in the study fall into four categories. The most frequent reason for not returning the questionnaire involved pressures of time (which were undoubtedly felt by all practitioners contacted). Psychiatrists in particular claimed that they were just too busy, that the questionnaire was too long, that there were so many other demands made on their schedule, and that they received too many questionnaires. The next most frequent specific reason for refusing to complete the questionnaire involved the feeling that it was too personal in the information it sought. Very frequently this reason was linked to distrust of the confidentiality with which the information would be treated. Finally, some individuals in this category (which was dominated by psychiatrists) felt that the questionnaire represented a direct invasion of professional privacy and were, furthermore, indignant over the additional attempt to persuade them to fill out the questionnaire.

Although psychiatrists represented the majority of respondents in both of the first two categories of specific refusals, with psychoanalysts intermediate between them and the nonmedical professions, a higher proportion of psychoanalysts than psychiatrists refused to participate on the ground that they were opposed to the research. This was most often explained as opposition to research using this method on this particular subject matter and undoubtedly reflects their preference for intensive case studies.

The other category containing individuals who gave specific reasons for refusing to participate in the study includes a range of idiosyncratic rationales not dominated by any single theme. Moreover, this category was small and the four professional groups were fairly equally represented in it.

Since the survey was conducted on the total population of mental health practitioners in Chicago, Los Angeles, and New York City, it is important to assess the extent to which the sample of returns is representative of the population in each of the communities. In an attempt to achieve this objective, we compared the sample of returns with the target population using data drawn from the professional directories used to enumerate the professional population. Unfortunately, data on the entire target population are of variable quality; the information on psychiatrists, psychoanalysts, and clinical psychologists is the most reliable and recent and the information on psychiatric social workers is the least complete. Bearing in mind the limitations of the data, it still seems useful to compare the survey sample and the target population on the few available basic characteristics.

The first basic consideration is simply the extent to which the professional composition of the sample reflects the composition of the population in each metropolitan community. Table 42 provides the evidence relevant to this issue.

As Table 42 indicates, the greatest discrepancy appears for psychiatrists with the proportion of practitioners in the population being significantly greater than the proportion in the sample in each of the communities. The discrepancy in the proportion of psychiatrists in the sample and in the population is greatest in New York City; Los Angeles has the second greatest difference and Chicago the least difference. This, of course, is the same as the order of overall return from the three cities. Although the difference in aggregate return rates among the cities was not determined solely by the differential return from psychiatrists, it is true that the lower the city rate of return, the greater the difficulty in getting psychiatrists to return. Since there is very little difference between the proportion of psychoanalysts in the sample and in the population in each of the communities, we are led to conclude that the discrepancy noted for psychiatrists is due to their unique characteristics rather than a factor common to all medically trained psychotherapists. As indicated earlier, the general factor that sets psychiatrists apart from the other groups is their greater emphasis on a medical approach to mental illness. Using this reasoning, we are led to conclude that the relatively large discrepancy in the proportion of psychiatrists in the sample and in the population in New York City can be accounted for, in part, by the fact that it is the community with the largest concentration of medically oriented psychiatrists. Similarly, the difference between Los Angeles and Chicago could be accounted for by the same proposition.

Table 42 also provides a description of the professional composition of the three mental health communities. Looking at the population distributions, we find that New York City has the most uniform distribution of the four professional groups, which is understandable in terms of the variety of training centers in that city. Similarly, the composition of the Los Angeles professional population is consistent with its tendency to recruit personnel from other regions and its high rate of experimentation

Table 42. COMPARISON OF PROFESSIONAL COMPOSITION OF SAMPLE AND POPULATION

Practitioners	Chicago		Los Angeles		New York City		Total	
	Sample	Population	Sample	Population	Sample	Population	Sample	Population
	Percent							
Psychoanalysts	14.0 (103)	16.0 (168)	16.4 (166)	15.7 (241)	16.5 (369)	18.8 (761)	16.0 (638)	17.7 (1170)
Psychiatrists	20.5 (151)[a]	25.1 (264)	21.1 (214)[a]	27.5 (421)	16.4 (368)[a]	22.2 (899)	18.4 (733)[a]	23.9 (1584)
Clinical Psychologists	36.5 (268)	33.0 (347)	41.1 (417)	37.9 (580)	34.8 (780)	31.0 (1256)	36.7 (1465)	32.9 (2183)
Psychiatric Social Workers	29.0 (213)	25.9 (273)	21.4 (217)	18.9 (289)	32.3 (724)	27.9 (1130)	28.9 (1154)	25.5 (1692)
Total	100.0 (735)	100.0 (1052)	100.0 (1014)	100.0 (1531)	100.0 (2241)	99.9 (4046)	100.0 (3990)[b]	100.0 (6629)

[a] Significant at the .05 level. The t ratio was used to test the difference between percentages. (For a discussion of the t ratio see Deming, 1950, p. 314.)

[b] Two respondents refused to designate their professional affiliation.

in psychotherapeutic practices. Specifically, Los Angeles has the largest proportion of clinical psychologists and psychiatrists and the smallest proportion of psychiatric social workers and psychoanalysts. The latter two groups probably tend to be somewhat more traditional in their professional practices, whereas clinical psychologists tend to be the most mobile group and, together with psychiatrists, are probably more likely to be involved in innovative programs.

A more refined assessment of the representativeness of the sample in each metropolitan community was made by comparing the returns and nonreturns by sex, age, major job title, and type of work setting. (Tables showing the distributions of returns and nonreturns by these dimensions are available upon request from William E. Henry, Committee on Human Development, The University of Chicago.) In general, the returns accurately reflected the sex composition of the population in each of the communities. However, the proportion of female clinical psychologists and psychiatric social workers in the return group is smaller than the proportion in the nonreturn group, by 4.5 percent and 8 percent, respectively. Since females in these two groups were more difficult to locate and are, perhaps, less research-oriented than males, these differences were expected. Similarly, with regard to city totals, the proportion of males in the nonreturn group exceeds the proportion in the return group by 4.2 percent, which reflects the tendency of the male-dominated groups, psychiatry and psychoanalysis, to return at a lower rate than the two groups having more female members. But it seems safe to conclude that the differential sex composition of the population of mental health practitioners in the three metropolitan communities is adequately reflected in the survey returns.

The second factor on which we compared the returns and nonreturns was age. Unfortunately, the comparisons had to be limited to psychoanalysts, psychiatrists, and clinical psychologists, since information on age, job title, and work setting was not available for psychiatric social workers. The findings on age are similar to those on sex in the extent to which the returns and nonreturns have comparable distributions. The only groups with a significantly larger proportion of nonreturns than returns are middle-aged psychiatrists and psychoanalysts—in both cases by about 8 percent. Thus, in terms of totals, we had less success in getting returns from practitioners over fifty years of age than from younger professionals. However, in none of the comparisons does the distribution of returns grossly underrepresent the population distribution.

In addition to comparisons on the general characteristics of age and sex, it was also possible to make more specific comparisons of returns and nonreturns by examining the job titles that members of the total population listed in their autobiographical sketches in the professional directories. (Both the American Psychiatric Association and the American Psychological Association directories indicate all professional positions currently held by their members.) The representativeness of the survey returns was clearly revealed when the three professions were examined. These job titles were classified into the same nine categories for each of the three professions. Of these thirty-six comparisons, there were only six in which the proportion of nonreturns exceeded the proportion of returns by 1 percent. The most notable difference was found in the distribution of *total* returns and nonreturns for private practitioners. A larger proportion (by 3.3 percent) of professionals in the nonreturn category listed private practice as a job title than was true for professionals in the return category. The striking element about this pattern is that there is no significant difference between return and nonreturn private practitioners within any of the professions in any of the metropolitan communities. In fact, the difference between returns and nonreturns is about the same for all three professions, with the proportion of returns always slightly smaller than nonreturns. The differences in total returns and nonreturns apparently reflect the distinction between solo and institutionally affiliated practitioners rather than medical/nonmedical professional differences. The explanation for the lower return rate of private practitioners would therefore seem to revolve around their lack of interest in research, particularly survey research.

The final basis for comparing the returns with the nonreturns is according to the types of work settings the practitioners listed in the professional directories. Of all the population characteristics discussed, type of work setting is undoubtedly more strongly related to the behavior of these professionals than any of the others (Spray, 1968). It is for this reason that the strong similarity we found in the distribution of returns and nonreturns among the categories of work setting provides strong assurance that the sample is generally representative of the population. However, the importance of work setting also dictates that the specific differences that were found between returns and refusals should be carefully noted.

As expected, the most notable difference in return rates by setting is in the category of private practice. Here, as in the case of job title, the significant difference is confined to the total sample (returns = 30.8 percent, nonreturns = 33 percent). Similarly, the tendency for the nonreturn category to be larger than the return category holds for two of the three professions. The plausibility of the explanation offered to account for the reluctance of professionals listing private practice as a job title to return the questionnaire is strengthened by this additional evidence on work setting. Specifically, these two sets of findings indicate that solo

practitioners are unique in their unwillingness to participate in the research. To a certain extent this unwillingness may stem from their limited
professional contacts and lack of interest in research of this type. It may
also stem from the fact that they work longer hours and have more patients than other professionals.

The second setting having a larger proportion of nonreturns than
returns is that of general hospitals (returns = 13.2 percent, nonreturns =
17.8 percent). Since these differences are largely confined to medical professionals, it seems likely that the refusals are either hospital psychiatrists or
psychoanalysts in administrative positions. The former group undoubtedly
contains many practitioners who adhere to a medical or organic approach
to mental illness, which would result in their being antagonistic to the type
of research represented by the questionnaire. For psychoanalysts, it seems
likely that refusals were based less on ideological grounds and more on the
basis of situational determinants, such as lack of time or inability of the
research staff to contact them. The fact that the difficulty in getting professionals in general hospitals to return the questionnaire was largely confined
to New York City tends to support both these contentions.

In assessing the quality of data gathered by the questionnaire survey, we have emphasized the statistical characteristics of the sample of
returns. However, there are several unusual characteristics of the study
that should also be considered in any assessment of the quality of the data.
First, the survey was conducted on the total population, rather than a
sample, of mental health professionals in three metropolitan communities.
Inferences from the relatively high returns can therefore be made to the
total population of practitioners with a high degree of confidence. Second,
the return rates from each of the professions in the three communities
included in the study compares favorably with the rates achieved by other
surveys of comparable populations in the mental health field (Kissinger
and Tolor, 1964; Strauss and others, 1964; Sundland and Barker, 1962).
This is true in spite of the fact that the study included all four high-
prestige professions in the mental health field and used an intensive
questionnaire requiring more than one hour to complete. Given these
considerations, we are led to conclude that the overall quality of the data
is high and that generalizations to the professional population in each of
the cities can safely be made from findings drawn from the sample of
returns. However, there is no basis for drawing conclusions either about
all metropolitan communities or about all mental health practitioners. All
generalizations about the mental health professions are intended to pertain
only to Chicago, Los Angeles, and New York City and should be evaluated
from this perspective.

References

AMERICAN MEDICAL ASSOCIATION, AMERICAN PSYCHIATRIC ASSOCIATION, AND AMERICAN PSYCHOANALYTIC ASSOCIATION. "Joint Statement." *American Journal of Psychiatry,* 1954, *3.*

BECKER, H. S. "Notes on the Concept of Commitment." *American Journal of Sociology,* 1960, *66.*

BECKER, H. S., AND CARPER, J. W. "The Development of Identification with an Occupation." *American Journal of Sociology,* 1956, *61.*

BLAIN, D. "Private Practice of Psychiatry." *The Annals of the American Academy of Political and Social Sciences,* 1953, *286.*

BLAU, P. M., AND DUNCAN, O. D. *The American Occupational Structure.* New York: Wiley, 1967.

BLUM, A. F., AND ROSENBERG, L. "Some Problems Involved in Professionalizing Social Interaction: The Case of Psychotherapy Training." *Journal of Health and Social Behavior,* 1968, *9* (1).

BOGUE, D. J. *The Structure of the Metropolitan Community.* Ann Arbor: University of Michigan Press, 1950.

BOROW, H. "Development of Occupational Motives and Roles." In M. Hoffman and L. Hoffman (Eds.), *Review of Child Development Research,* Vol. 2. New York: Russell Sage Foundation, 1964.

259

BOSSARD, J., AND BOLL, E. *The Large Family System.* Philadelphia: University of Pennsylvania Press, 1956.

BUCHER, R., AND STRAUSS, A. "Professions in Process." *American Journal of Sociology,* 1961, *66.*

CLAUSEN, J. "Family Structure, Socialization, and Personality." In M. Hoffman and L. Hoffman (Eds.), *Review of Child Development Research,* Vol. 2. New York: Russell Sage Foundation, 1964.

DEMING, W. E. *Some Theory of Sampling.* New York: Wiley, 1950.

DOUVAN, E., AND ADELSON, J. *The Adolescent Experience.* New York: Wiley, 1966.

DOUVAN, E., AND GOLD, M. "Modal Patterns in American Adolescence." In M. Hoffman and L. Hoffman (Eds.), *Review of Child Development Research,* Vol. 2. New York: Russell Sage Foundation, 1964.

EHRLICH, D., AND SABSHIN, M. "Psychiatric Ideologies: Their Popularity and the Meaningfulness of Their Self-designation." *American Psychologist,* 1963, *18* (6).

EHRLICH, D., AND SABSHIN, M. "A Study of Sociotherapeutically Oriented Psychiatrists." *American Journal of Orthopsychiatry,* 1964, *33* (3).

EISENDORFER, A. "The Selection of Candidates Applying for Psychoanalytic Training." *Psychoanalytic Quarterly,* 1959, *28.*

ERIKSON, E. *Insight and Responsibility.* New York: Horton, 1965.

ERIKSON, K. T. "Patient Role and Social Uncertainty—A Dilemma of the Mentally Ill." *Psychiatry,* 1957, *20.*

FIEDLER, F. A. "A Comparison of Therapeutic Relationships in Psychoanalytic, Nondirective and Adlerian Therapy." *Journal of Consulting Psychology,* 1950, *14.*

FROMM-REICHMANN, F. *Principles of Intensive Psychotherapy.* Chicago: University of Chicago Press, 1960.

GILBERT, D., AND LEVINSON, D. J. "Ideology, Personality and Institutional Policy in the Mental Hospital." *Journal of Abnormal and Social Psychology,* 1956, *53* (3).

GOFFMAN, E. *Encounters: Two Studies in the Sociology of Interaction.* Indianapolis: Bobbs-Merrill, 1961.

GRAS, N. S. B. *An Introduction to Economic History.* New York: Harper & Row, 1922.

GREENBLATT, M., LEVINSON, D. J., AND WILLIAMS, R. H. (Eds.) *The Patient and the Mental Hospital.* New York: Free Press, 1957.

GREENSON, R. "The Selection of Candidates for Psychoanalytic Training." *Journal of American Psychoanalytic Association,* 1961, *9* (1).

HENRY, W. E., SIMS, J. H., AND SPRAY, S. L. *The Fifth Profession: Becoming a Psychotherapist.* San Francisco: Jossey-Bass, 1971.

HOLLINGSHEAD, A. B., AND REDLICH, F. C. *Social Class and Mental Illness: A Community Study.* New York: Wiley, 1958.

HOLT, R., AND LUBORSKY, L. *Personality Patterns of Psychiatrists.* New York: Basic Books, 1958.

JANOWITZ, M. "Some Observations on the Ideology of Professional Psychologists." *The American Psychologist,* 1954, *20* (9).

KADUSHIN, C. *Why People Go to Psychiatrists.* New York: Atherton Press, 1969.

KARTUS, I., AND SCHLESINGER, H. J. "The Psychiatric Hospital Physician and His Patient." In M. Greenblatt, D. J. Levinson, and R. H. Williams (Eds.), *The Patient and the Mental Hospital.* New York: Free Press, 1957.

KENNARD, E. A. "Psychiatry, Administrative Psychiatry, Administration: A Study of a Veterans Hospital." In M. Greenblatt, D. J. Levinson, and R. H. Williams (Eds.), *The Patient and the Mental Hospital.* New York: Free Press, 1957.

KINSEY, A., POMEROY, W., AND MARTIN, C. *Sexual Behavior in the Human Male.* Philadelphia: Saunders, 1948.

KISSINGER, R. D., AND TOLER, A. "The Attitudes of Psychotherapists Toward Psychotherapeutic Knowledge: A Study of Differences Among the Professions." *Journal of Nervous and Mental Disorder,* 1964, *140.*

LEIGHTON, D., AND OTHERS. *The Character of Danger.* New York: Basic Books, 1963.

LEVINSON, D. J. "Medical Education and the Theory of Adult Socialization." *Journal of Health and Social Behavior,* 1967, *8.*

MC KENZIE, R. D. *The Metropolitan Community.* New York: McGraw-Hill, 1933.

MAHER, B. (Ed.) *Progress in Experimental Personality Research,* Vol. II. New York: Academic Press, 1965.

MARX, J., AND SPRAY, S. L. "Psychotherapeutic 'Birds of a Feather': Social Homophily in Psychotherapy." *Journal of Health and Social Behavior,* 1972.

MUNCIE, W., AND BILLINGS, E. G. "A Survey of the Conditions of Private Practice Throughout the United States and Canada." *American Journal of Psychiatry,* 1951, *8.*

MURRAY, H., AND OTHERS. *Explorations in Personality.* New York, London: Oxford University Press, 1938.

MYERS, J. K., AND SCHAFER, L. "Social Stratification and Psychiatric Practice: A Study of an Out-patient Clinic." *American Sociological Review,* 1954, *19.*

NACHMANN, B. "Childhood Experience and Vocational Choice in Law, Dentistry and Social Work." *Journal of Counseling Psychology,* 1960, *7.*

NEFF, W. S. *Work and Human Behavior.* New York: Atherton Press, 1968.

PARSONS, T. *The Social System.* New York: Free Press, 1951.

PLUNKETT, R. J., AND GORDON, J. E. *Epidemiology and Mental Illness.* New York: Basic Books, 1960.

ROE, A. *The Making of a Scientist.* New York: Dodd, Mead, 1953a.

ROE, A. "A Psychological Study of Eminent Psychologists and Anthropologists and a Comparison with Biological and Physical Scientists." *Psychological Monographs,* 1953b, *67* (2).

ROE, A. *The Psychology of Occupations.* New York: Wiley, 1956.

ROE, A. "Early Determinates of Vocational Choice." *Journal of Counseling Psychology,* 1957, *4.*

ROE, A. "Personality Structure and Occupational Behavior." In H. Borow (Ed.), *Man in a World at Work.* Boston: Houghton Mifflin, 1964.

ROE, A., AND SIEGELMAN, M. *The Origins of Interests.* Washington, D.C.: American Personnel and Guidance Association, 1964.

ROSENTHAL, D., AND FRANK, J. D. "The Fate of Psychiatric Clinic Outpatients Assigned to Psychotherapy." *Journal of Nervous and Mental Disease,* 1958, *127.*

ROWDEN, D. W., AND OTHERS. "Judgments About Candidates for Psychotherapy: The Influence of Social Class and Insight-verbal Ability." *Journal of Health and Social Behavior,* 1970, *11.*

RUSHING, W. A. *The Psychiatric Professions: Power, Conflict, and Adaptation in a Psychiatric Hospital Staff.* Chapel Hill: University of North Carolina Press, 1964.

SCHACHTER, S. "Birth Order, Eminence, and Higher Education." *American Sociological Review,* 1963, *28.*

SCOTT, M. B., AND LYMAN, S. "Accounts." *American Sociological Review,* 1968, *33.*

SHARAF, M., AND LEVINSON, D. J. "Patterns of Ideology and Role Definitions Among Psychiatric Residents." In M. Greenblatt, D. Levinson, and R. Williams (Eds.), *The Patient and the Mental Hospital.* New York: Free Press, 1957.

SPRAY, S. L. "Mental Health Professions and the Division of Labor in a Metropolitan Community." *Psychiatry: Journal for the Study of Interpersonal Processes,* 1968, *31* (1).

SROLE, L., AND OTHERS. *Mental Health in the Metropolis: The Midtown Manhattan Study.* New York: McGraw-Hill, 1962.

STRAUSS, A., AND OTHERS. *Psychiatric Ideologies and Institutions.* New York: Free Press, 1964.

SUNDLAND, D. M., AND BARKER, E. "The Orientations of Psychotherapists." *Journal of Consulting Psychology*, 1962, 26.

SUTTON-SMITH, B., AND OTHERS. "Sibling Associations and Role Involvement." *Merrill-Palmer Quarterly*, 1964, 10.

TORRANCE, E. "A Psychological Study of American Jet Aces." Paper read at Western Psychological Association, Long Beach, Calif., 1954.

TRYON, R. C. *Cluster Analysis*. Ann Arbor, Mich.: Edwards Brothers, 1939.

WHEELIS, A. *The Quest for Identity*. New York: W. W. Norton, 1956.

WILENSKY, H., AND LEBEAUX, C. N. *Industrial Society and Social Welfare*. New York: Russell Sage Foundation, 1958.

WOOTTON, B. *Social Science and Social Pathology*. London: George Allen & Unwin, 1963.

ZANDER, A., COHEN, A., AND STOTLAND, E. *Role Relations in the Mental Health Professions*. Ann Arbor: University of Michigan Research Center for Group Dynamics, Institute for Social Relations, 1957.

Index